Here's what profe

The ⅃.

"The MECE Muse is something not just for those thinking about or trying to get into consulting, but also for those in the middle of it or reflecting on their time in the space who seek to understand more about their experience. Having spent six years as a management consultant, I found myself repeatedly smiling by the clarity of the insights Christie shares, and wishing I had a mentor like her during my career to help it all make sense. As she says, "The journey to greatness is infinite," so I can use this book now to continue on the path I started on as a consultant."

—*Bryan Falchuk*, *ex-McKinsey consultant, Inc. Magazine contributor, and author of "Do a Day: How to Live a Better Life Everyday"*

"This book should be required reading for all new-hire consultants. Christie neatly packages and delivers lessons that normally are learned through years of high-pressure client meetings, late-night deliverables, and early-morning sprints through airports. Consulting is a journey, and the MECE Muse provides a practical roadmap for anticipating obstacles and maximizing the experience."

—*Destin Whitehurst*, *ex-Deloitte consultant and Founder, ConsultingInterviewCoach.com*

"The MECE Muse is what the consulting industry has been waiting for! Christie Lindor masterfully ties together the untold significance of soft-skills, political nuance comprehension, technical skills and relationship management that set great consultants apart from the rest. The consulting leader interviews are powerful and answer all the questions that I wanted to know as an MBA student and former consultant. This book offers critical tools and stories that have never been covered before in all the books I've read on consulting and fills a gap of knowledge on the industry."

—*Natalie Gill-Mensah*, *ex-PwC consultant and non-profit senior manager*

"Compelling, engaging, and ripe with useful insights, The MECE Muse serves as a quintessential guide to the world of consulting that is ideal for young professionals pursuing a future career in the industry. By leveraging her vast array of experiences, Ms. Lindor's collection of anecdotes and advice equips the reader with valuable knowledge that is crucial in order to succeed in consulting, doing so in a manner that is informative yet highly immersive."

—*Matt Boyle*, *College Student & Aspiring Consultant*

"Christie Lindor provides a critical resource for all types aspiring and seasoned consultants. The vivid examples of life as a consultant and overview of the industry's landscape offer realistic previews for those interested in such a career and a reality check for those of us who have lived in that world. The learned lessons from Lindor and those interviewed for the book apply to all in fast-paced, high-stakes professions."

—*Susan M. Adams*, *PHD—Professor & Chair, Management Department, Bentley University*

The
MECE
Muse

100+ *Selected* **Practices,
Unwritten Rules, and
Habits of Great Consultants**

CHRISTIE LINDOR

The MECE Muse: 100+ Selected Practices, Unwritten Rules, and Habits of Great Consultants, Published February, 2018

Editorial and proofreading services: Kathleen Tracy, Karen Grennan
Interior layout and cover design: Howard Johnson

Credits:

Sidebar design: Avatar Icons courtesy of Deposit Photos; https://depositphotos.com/13789946/stock-illustration-avatar-icons.html

Image in Figure 8: Iceberg Floating in Arctic Sea, courtesy of istockphoto.com; http://www.istockphoto.com/photo/iceberg-floating-in-arctic-sea

Front cover image: Torn paper textures, Free Vector "Designed by Freepik"

All interviews published with permission by the interviewees.

 **SDP Publishing**

Published by SDP Publishing, an imprint of SDP Publishing Solutions, LLC.

SDP Publishing
Permissions Department
PO Box 26, East Bridgewater, MA 02333
or email your request to info@SDPPublishing.com.

ISBN-13 (print): 978-0-9986730-8-0
ISBN-13 (e-book): 978-0-9986730-9-7

Library of Congress Control Number: 2017960258

Printed in the United States of America

MECE MUSE MANIFESTO C

CONSULTANTS

Ma
cho

s always personal in business.
reate good consulting karma every day
et out of your own way.   a fu
s not about being right   rewa
ut about being effective.   sus

ake ownership Step up to a   co

and higher standard. C

accountability

of your
career

De

an

ind a like tribe

bas

ou love
and stay

remark

put; the grass is not alw

Be empathically inclusive   E

nd compassionate to others.   autl
a compet

DEDICATION

This book is dedicated in loving memory of my ancestors: Chrysotome Jean-Baptiste, Alice Tingue, Gregoire Montasse Jean-Baptiste, Berenice Nicolas, Marie Therese Cadelien, Blythe Anderson, and most of all my mother, Itesse Jean-Baptiste. Because of your unconditional love, dedication, and sacrifices I have been given opportunities of a lifetime. I wake up every day with your ambition in my eyes; your generosity in my heart; and your fortitude, strength, and courage running through my veins. You are in my heart now and forever. If I become at least a quarter of the person you were, I will have lived a successful, impactful life. In the meantime I hope I make you proud.

TABLE OF CONTENTS

PREFACE
· · · · · · · · · · · · ·

When I Decided to Write This Book, a Teachable Moment

I remember the exact moment I said I was going to write this book. I was underneath a conference room table picking up scattered papers thrown at my team lead from an irate client the first week of my first consulting engagement. It was Thursday morning, September 13, 2001, just days after events that changed the course of the United States' history and also my career.

My first day on the project I walked in on the client yelling at my team lead, Jeremy—not once, but twice in the same hour. The second time she started yelling at Jeremy, she flung copies of a status report right in his face. I immediately knelt on the floor to help Jeremy pick the papers up. In that moment, I thought: *I have got to write a book about consulting so people know what they are getting themselves into.*

Had I been better prepared prior to arriving at the client site, I would have connected with Jeremy beforehand to understand the current state of the project. While that incident may have still happened on the first day, it might not have been as shocking or impacted me as much as it did. The client's reactions were based on high tensions resulting from having been recently acquired.

Let me take a step back and retrospectively share the

top five insights about the consulting profession I learned in the first year of my consulting career. While the ride would have been less bumpy and certain mistakes were avoidable had I known this information earlier, I would not have had enough experience to write this book nor the motivational drive to help others succeed in consulting years later.

Consultants Must Live in a Constant State of Adaptive Execution in Order to Survive and Thrive in the Profession.

I learned this lesson before I even graduated college. Within six months of being offered an IT strategy analyst role at a large firm, I went from being elated to my entire consulting future being in jeopardy due to sudden market shifts. It was 2000–2001, the height of the dotcom bust era. The company gave me a choice: either defer my offer or join the firm as an IT implementation analyst where there was plenty of work. I decided to join the implementation side of the consulting practice, which changed my career trajectory—it took close to a decade to course correct toward my desired consulting area. (See Chapter Six to understand how to position yourself in consulting.)

Downtime in Between Projects Is Just as Critical as Project Time

What you do during that time can either be a setup for success or failure of your next engagement and over time, your career.

I spent the first six months of my career on the unstaffed, learning how to do java code programming, testing, and a slew of other core technical skills. The first project I finally landed was a post-acquisition IT systems integration of a regional bank. Since my training was not targeted for a particular project, none of the training prepared me for my first consulting project role. Six months of wasted time. (See Chapter Seven to learn how to maximize downtime in between consulting engagements.)

Consultants Have to Understand the Dynamics of Organizational Politics of Their Environments to Determine How to Best Add Value

There were a lot of politics played after that first incident with Jeremy and the client. Word got back to engagement leadership about our client's rage. By the time I returned to the client site the following week, Jeremy had been rolled off the project to my surprise. Another team leader arrived in full damage control mode. We ended up successfully delivering on the work, and there were no other hiccups with the client. (See Chapter Eleven on managing relationships and navigating organizational politics.)

In the Midst of Chaos, Understand How to Best Proceed to Take Accountability for Your Career

Consultants must have the fortitude to take a step back and reflect on lessons learned with mentors or leadership.

Jeremy taught me the power of being a professional under immense pressure in the short time we worked together. When the client screamed and wagged her fingers in his face and then threw papers at him, not once did he raise his voice, show emotion, or say anything smug, even after she left the room.

Reflecting back on that experience, I didn't know what I didn't know to set my career in the right direction. In consulting ignorance is not bliss; it's quite expensive. I showed up to work without knowing any details about the client's environment, their industry, or key challenges. I just showed up and let life happen to me. (See Chapter Seventeen to learn how to own your career experience.)

Consultants Must Learn to Embrace the Journey

Granted, I was a newly-minted college graduate, and it was my first job out of college. Just like coal under pressure creates diamonds, irritated oysters create pearls, and the earth's crust creates gems and crystals, my experience as a consultant has been a cumulative journey. Over time, experiencing constant pressure under certain conditions allowed me to professionally grow into a competent, successful consultant. (See Section III, *Reflections of a Consulting Career.*)

In this book, *The MECE Muse: 100+ Selected Practices, Unwritten Rules, and Habits of Great Consultants*, I discuss defining career successes and failures. Not as humblebrags or regrets but as illustrations of the knowledge, experiences, and wisdom gained over my fifteen-plus years of consulting experience to give you an informed perspective. I focus on helping you maximize your opportunities as a consultant before you begin your career or walk onto your next client site toward a journey of consulting greatness.

Introduction: Setting the Context
on Consulting Basics

In consulting context is everything. One of the initial steps toward being a great consultant is to first understand the definition of the role, history of the profession, and to have an impartial mental map of what excellence looks like in consulting. Having an understanding of how the expertise you possess fits the broader consulting ecosystem and your chosen industry is important grounding, particularly as you become a seasoned consultant. This context helps you better prioritize how to compete in the marketplace, acquire clients, build relationships, and create impact earlier on in your career. Since there are a lot of misconceptions out there, I will begin this conversation with a high-level primer on the profession. Having been in consulting my entire professional life, this book is about creating the building blocks of the profession in the most MECE (ME-see) way possible. But what does MECE mean?

MECE: Mutually Exclusive and Collectively Exhaustive

The MECE rule is consulting lingo and for many management consultants a way of being. MECE describes a technique on how business problems are visualized and understood in order to solve the root cause. When applying the MECE rule, information is grouped logically into distinct categories without any overlap (mutually exclusive). All categories added together cover all possible options (collectively exhaustive) then explored through the process of elimination based on data collected and insights gathered.

I was inspired to write the book as an adaptation of the MECE rule to pass along selected practices of great consulting in three distinct categories: the mindset of great consultants, how great consultants are conditioned for success, and ways to create a sustainable consulting career. I say inspired because this book is not truly MECE; however, it is about the humanity of consulting (i.e., the emotional intelligence side of the profession that sometimes gets lost in translation). It is about the stuff that is hard to quantify and compartmentalize into neatly packaged, black-and-white categories without overlapping concepts. Great consultants are able to operate well in the complex and ambiguous gray of life. I share resources in the appendix to provide exhaustive details of many concepts outlined in the book that deep dive into strategies and tactics on topics covered in this book.

Definition of a Consultant

Kris Pederson, a strategy consulting partner sums up the definition nicely.

"I usually use the analogy of a business doctor when people ask me what I do. It's kind of daunting to describe our work. Strategy consultant, what does that mean? I help diagnose problems just like a doctor would. I start out with a full examination and help provide a path forward to remedy the problem. Things like preventive maintenance to have that patient not land in the hospital again."

The term consultant is also synonymous with advisor, confidante, or coach. Consultants provide advice, knowledge, support, and experience that a client deems valuable. Clients tap into consultants based on the perceived intellectual value of an individual's or firm's expertise to speed up the learning process in a competitive marketplace.

In this book I focus on selected practices, unwritten rules, and habits of business consultants that solve problems for organizations. The goal of a business consultant is to do three key things:

1. Become a trusted advisor who is to be called upon at any time to help leaders shape strategic decisions to address complex business problems within their organizations.

2. Create value-added impact to a client's career, team, department, division, or company through influencing, advising, designing, implementing, or supporting business recommendations in a way that empowers clients to stand on their own.

3. Constantly create relationships, make decisions, build experiences, sustain networks, develop skills, leverage tools, reinforce habits, and share knowledge to do steps 1 and 2 phenomenally well.

Ecosystem of the Consulting Profession

There is a wide variety of consultants across industries that fall into two big categories: internal consultants and external (or market-facing) consultants. Internal consultants partner with various business units, leaders, and key stakeholders within an organization. External consultants are hired to provide expertise to clients on a temporary basis to help solve complex business problems. Internal and external consultants have a wide variety of career paths to consider, which are discussed in Section III of this book.

> Consulting is a cyclical business that mirrors trends in the marketplace. Staying one step ahead of their client's market is a critical component of a consultant's role.

Consulting is a cyclical business that mirrors trends in the marketplace. Staying one step ahead of their client's market is a critical component of a consultant's role.

Internal or external business consultants specialize in a variety of industries, domains, and sectors including:

- ◆ strategy consultants
- ◆ advisory consultants
- ◆ functional consultants (marketing, IT, finance)
- ◆ industry consultants (consumer, energy, healthcare, government)
- ◆ domain consultants (supply chain, customer, and transformation)

There are two ways you could gain experience as a business consultant: as a generalist or a specialist.

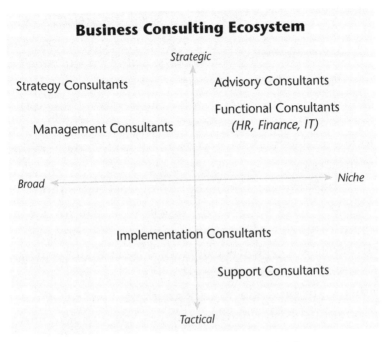

FIGURE 1. An Illustrative View of the Consulting Ecosystem

Generalists are focused on different types of business problems with breadth, typically under a broad knowledge area. Specialists are focused on one type of business problem with depth. Figure 1 provides a visual of the consulting ecosystem from a generalist (broad) to specialist (niche) view by types of consulting (from pure strategy to implementation to tactical support).

The type of consulting one does dictates the types of clients one will most likely gain exposure to. For example, strategy consultants tend to have the company's board of directors—chief executive officer (CEO) and other C-suite executives—and venture capitalists as clients.

The clients of advisory, functional, and industry consultants range from C-suite executives other than

CEOs to the executive layers such as executive vice president (EVP), senior vice president (SVP), and vice president (VP). For example, clients of IT consultants are usually a chief technology officer; for HR consultants it is a chief people officer or VP of human resources (HR). For domain and operations consultants, VP to directors to middle management such as product owners and managers are also potential clients.

Consultants have the option to work as an independent contractor, freelancer, consulting firm owner, or as an employee of a consulting firm. Consulting organizations are typically categorized by size and prestige. Size wise, consulting firms are grouped as boutique, midsize, or large global organizations. Gartner defines a boutique firm as having fewer than one hundred employees and earning less than $50 million in annual revenue. Midsize firms employ 100–1000 employees earning $50 million to $1 billion in annual revenue. Large global firms have more than a thousand employees with $1 billion-plus in annual revenue.

Consulting and Prestige as a Differentiator

Prestige provides a general way to differentiate amongst the competitive landscape of consulting firms. Prestige is collectively assessed by factors such as the level of expertise provided, firm culture, and selectivity in recruitment practices. The degree of innovative disruption in thought leadership has become an important vantage point for all firms in today's business environment. Prestige is a polarizing topic, constantly debated in the consulting community. For the purposes of this book, I codify the profession based on four types of organizations and will use these definitions when referencing certain types of consulting firms.

- ◆ Top strategy firms are historically known for their expertise in strategy and ability to solve general management problems. One can sensibly argue that there are no longer any pure strategy firms anymore given the heightened convergence and consolidation activities that have taken place in the market. Examples of top strategy firms include McKinsey & Company and Boston Consulting Group.
- ◆ Big Four+ firms are a network of professional services firms that offer consulting, audit, and tax offerings. What started as the Big Eight firms through most of the twentieth century are now dubbed Big Four after years of market impacts, mergers, and consolidation activity. For simplicity purposes I've collectively called this group of firms Big Four+ since there are time periods discussed in the book when they were called Big Six or Big Five. Examples of Big Four+ firms include Deloitte & Touche LLP and Pricewater-houseCoopers (PwC).
- ◆ Hybrid firms are both midsize and global organizations that focus on a broad category of consulting advisory and implementation services in core business functions such as finance, HR, and technology. Examples of hybrid firms include Navigant Consulting and IBM Global Services.
- ◆ Boutique firms are smaller consulting firms with

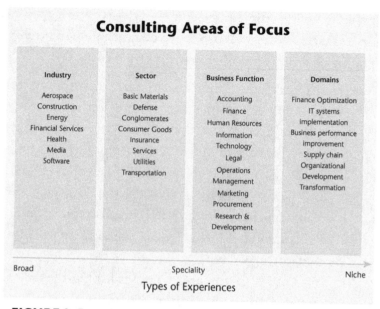

FIGURE 2. Examples of the Different Areas of Focus Within Consulting

either a broad or narrow focus of professional services. Examples of boutique firms include Acquis Consulting and Putnam Associates.

Within consulting firms, divisions (or subdivisions) are called practices, which are grouped by a combination of industry, function, solutions, or domains.

Disruptive Convergence: State of the Consulting Industry

According to Consultancy.UK, the global management consulting market is worth an estimated $250 billion. While the top ten firms currently account for 56 percent of the global management consulting market share, accelerated convergence is the key theme for the consulting industry as we continue to progress into the twenty-first century. Three key disruptive trends are driving convergence activities: (1) the pending boom of artificial intelligence that will rapidly impact every single industry and sector at scale, (2) the paradigm shift toward micro-entrepreneurship where individuals will inevitably drive their careers through projects instead of full-time jobs, and (3) the rise of niche boutique firms positioning themselves to gain a stronghold in the consulting market share. Regardless of the pendulum swings that will continue to take place in the operating models of the consulting organizations of today, I believe great consultants will always be in demand. (In Chapter Twenty-One I discuss how to prepare for consulting of the future.)

Closing the Journey to Greatness Gap

The ever-evolving art of consulting. As with any profession there is pomp and circumstance that give it a uniqueness and appeal. Watch great servers at a fine-dining restaurant as an example of pomp and circumstance. These servers are usually well-groomed and walk upright with their heads held high. They come into work early to prepare and memorize the day's specials. The language used to describe the dishes leaves you salivating in anticipation of the pending experience. Great servers exude confidence, credibility, and ultimately provide a memorable dining experience. Great servers are better compensated and highly sought after. While consulting is a different profession from hospitality, the guiding principles of exceptional client service are the same.

Demonstrated mastery of basic habits and decision-making skills is what makes a great consultant.

DEMONSTRATED MASTERY OF BASIC HABITS AND DECISION-MAKING SKILLS IS WHAT MAKES A GREAT CONSULTANT.

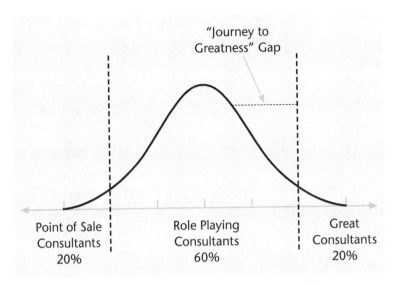

FIGURE 3. Different Types of Consultants on Bell Curve

From this moment on you have to decide if you are going to be a point-of-sale (POS) consultant, a role-player, or a great consultant. And you have to wake up and make this decision every single day of your consulting career. If you compare résumés, there is not much difference between the three types of consultants until you experience them in action, like a great server at a fine restaurant. Using a bell curve, let's discuss illustrative examples of what a POS, role-player, or great consultant looks like in action on a journey to greatness continuum.

POS Consultants

POS consultants comprise the bottom 20 percent of consultants. They show up to work unprepared, without a plan, or having done any previous research or due diligence. POS consultants complete work as outlined in the contracts without regard to the client's long-term strategy or needs. As long as the work is good enough to satisfy the contract, it's good enough for them. Anything over and above meeting contractual obligations is not their job.

POS consultants don't put a lot of time and energy into creating a personal brand. POS consultants are often reactionary, letting life happen without taking any accountability for the outcome. It's never their fault why something happened nor is it their problem to fix it. POS consultants become immediately threatened by high-performing consultants who in their minds appear to be trying too hard. POS consultants will constantly focus on ways to create division on a team to make up for their insecurities. They sit back and criticize the ideas or work of others but do not offer any alternative value in return. They do not want others to think they are not working, but they are not willing to try harder either. POS consultants are energy vampires; being around them is draining and uninspiring. They present themselves as average and do average work.

Role-players

Role-player consultants comprise 60 percent of consultants. Most role-players focus on playing their position to maintain status quo to obtain project extensions rather than focusing on long-term impact. Role-players remain indifferent on many topics in order not to ruffle any feathers. Some role-players struggle with imposter syndrome; the fear of embarrassment or being wrong keeps them paralyzed with inaction to innovate. This fear of not being good enough forces role-players to follow the beaten, tried-and-true path of their environment.

Role-players secretly wish to be great but (1) do not want to put in the work to go from good to great performance; (2) have not found the right methods, processes, or tools; (3) lack the proper support system of peer groups, mentors, and sponsors; (4) do not know what the mechanics of consulting greatness actually looks like in action; and (5) are in a cultural environment infused with emotional contagion of mediocrity. Deep down role-players know there are better ways to do things, but the mentality is: *If no one asks for it or is expecting it, then why kill myself? What I am doing is good enough to get by.* Role-players are smart, and their work is good but not great. Or memorable.

Great Consultants

Great consultants comprise the top 20 percent. You know a great consultant when you see one; you actually never forget them. Similar to a great server at a fine-dining restaurant, great consultants carry themselves with confidence, charisma, and authentic purpose. Great consultants take life by the reins and nothing seems to faze them no matter how large of an issue. It's not that great consultants don't sometimes suffer from imposter syndrome from time to time, but they don't allow those fears and insecurities to drive their career.

Great consultants make everyone around them step up their game. Clients thank role-players; clients are wowed by great consultants. Their actions appear

Great consultants make everyone around them step up their game. Clients thank role-players; clients are wowed by great consultants.

effortless given the amount of preparation they undertake. Great consultants empathetically keep their client's needs at the forefront throughout a project. Great consultants provide insights from the moment they walk on site.

Great consultants are natural leaders who take care of their people. They are confident enough to admit fault and not having the answer. Great consultants give credit to their teams and have authentic interactions. They seek to understand others instead of focusing on being understood. Great consultants usually say what others think but don't have the courage to say out loud. They understand how to harness the power of community and know that in order to succeed they cannot operate on an island alone. They create an environment of supportive mentors/advisors, sponsors, and a tribe of like-minded colleagues.

Great consultants purposefully manage their brand. They show up looking put together and ready to work. There is a certain energy and *je ne sais quoi* about them. They have the ability to walk into a room and shift the energy or pace of the conversation just with their presence. Great consultants take the clients and teams through an engagement experience. Great consultants are made by the decisions they make and daily habits they create.

POS consultants wake up every day and let life happen to them. POS consultants work at the firms that allow them in. They secure projects that need their skills.

POS vs ROLE-PLAYER vs. GREAT CONSULTANTS

POS	Role-players	Great Consultants
Shows up unprepared to work	Shows up asking a lot of questions that could have been answered through research	Shows up asking questions based on well prepared research and provides insights in every client interaction
Delivers meh work per contract	Delivers quality work	Delivers an experience
Connects only with the people needed to do the work in front of them	Connects with people they think are worthy of knowing	Connects and treats all people with the same level of respect and honor irregardless of rank, status, and title
Transactional interactions	Manage relationships within proximity and access	Constantly seek and cultivate a tribe of colleagues, advisors, mentors, and sponsors near and far
Doubt or constantly complain about changes	Somewhat adapt to changing trends with uncertainty	Adapt easily to ambiguity as innovators driving change

POS	Role-players	Great Consultants
Clients' and colleagues' concerns and needs are not their problems	Offers surface support to clients and colleagues until it becomes too much of a personal inconvenience	Are personally and professionally empathic to their clients and colleagues
Not self-aware	Reactive in self-awareness; somewhat apologetic and constantly blindsided	Acutely self-aware of personal perceptions, biases, and worldviews. Empathetic to different schools of thought
Easily replaced; no unique selling proposition	Not memorable	Unforgettable

Great consultants wake up every day with a purpose to own and shape their own destiny. They purposefully create an environment for excellence not only for themselves but for their teams, peers, and clients. Great consultants fail too, but the difference is they do not give up. While great consultants might not know the exact destination, they are focused on progress. And they forge into the unknown with conviction.

One partner asked me to describe how I differentiate between POS, role-player, and great consultants. He completely agreed and took the definition one step further.

"Don't make any mistake about it. This distinction is seen across the partnership levels. POS consultants become POS partners. There are a handful of partners that inherited a book of business from a retiring partner but do not proactively sell in the market. Then all of a sudden when that annuity revenue dries up due to a change of their clients' market positioning, all of the partners feel the hit."

From this point on you get to decide every day what type of consultant you want to be. Decide to be great.

If you are a new consultant, reread the descriptions above and decide what kind of consultant you want to be. If you are an aspiring consultant, decide what type of consultant you will strive to become. I wrote this book for go-getters who want to be great. If that is you, keep reading!

More about Consulting Partner and Leader Interviews

I believe that being successful starts with emulating and role modeling successful people. With that principle in mind, I wanted to broaden the conversation about consulting best practices and asked leaders to weigh in on this topic. I connected with fifty-plus consulting partners and leaders representing thought leadership from over twenty-seven different consulting firms. Each leader has reached a career milestone that tens of thousands of consultants strive to reach but many will never see. They share their stories, unwritten rules, and habits on what it takes to be a great consultant.

The majority of the partners and leaders inter-

FROM THIS POINT ON
YOU GET TO DECIDE
EVERY DAY WHAT
TYPE OF CONSULTANT
YOU WANT TO BE.
DECIDE TO BE GREAT.

viewed represent thought leadership from 80 percent of the top ten most prestigious consulting firms in the world. I include twenty-one interviews as virtual fireside chats, so you learn firsthand through their experiences. The interviewees represent a combined 420-plus years of consulting experience, ranging from newly promoted partners to those recently retired. They are trusted advisors that shape and influence the landscape across eighteen industries in every corporate function in the Fortune 500 and beyond. Collectively the interviewees have conducted business in over forty-eight countries across six continents.

The majority of the partners and leaders interviewed represent thought leadership from 80 percent of the top ten most prestigious consulting firms in the world.

I indirectly or directly worked with approximately 41 percent of the consulting partners and leaders who shared information; the other 59 percent were recommendations of other leaders or consultants. Due to various firm guidelines and independence requirements as of this writing—combined with the fact that I am currently employed at a Big Four+ firm—69 percent of the consulting partners I spoke with chose to remain completely or partially anonymous.

One hundred percent of the leaders interviewed represent what I call first-class leadership. The leaders I interviewed understand that leadership is not about a popularity contest; it is about having the courage to lead. They know how to create impact for their clients and the marketplace while being authentic to their core values. These leaders inspire and challenge thinking. They have trusted relationships with clients to help them solve complex business issues. Each in their own right are living and breathing examples of great consultants.

The First-Class Leaders' Guide to What Makes a Great Consultant

Every single consulting partner and leader I interviewed discussed ideas centered on emotional intelligence habits and traits when defining key differentiators of a great consultant. While technical prowess, delivery capabilities, and industry expertise are important, these skills come secondary when defining what makes a consultant a memorable, trusted advisor. Figure 4 pictorially illustrates how the consulting partners and leaders interviewed for this book collectively view the attributes of a great consultant.

Five Common Myths, Urban Legends, and Complete Falsehoods about Consulting

The following are collective observations I gathered from the virtual fireside chat interviews I conducted with the consulting partners and leaders that debunk common myths of what success looks like for those creating a career in consulting.

To be a great consultant, you have to be solely focused on your personal brand within your firm, practice, and client. Most leaders interviewed focuses on clients

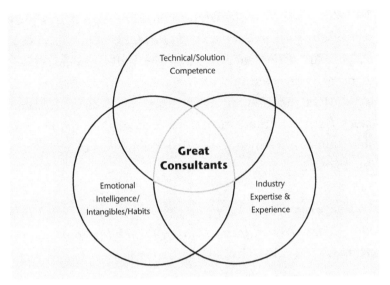

FIGURE 4. Attributes of a Great Consultant

and team, as well as actively managing their personal brand. Ninety-five percent of the leaders are regularly cited or featured in global, national, regional, and local media such as *CNN, Forbes, BBC, Bloomberg,* and the *New York Times* for their thought leadership on key business topics.

To be a great consultant and become a partner, one must have been a consultant their entire career at the same firm. Forty-three percent of the leaders interviewed are consulting boomerangs, which means they came into the profession, left for a variety of reasons, and then came back to the same or a different consulting firm. Of the nine boomerangs, four left consulting and came back to the profession several times over the course of their career.

To be a great consultant, one must always agree with the client's decisions and behaviors. Approximately 40 percent of the leaders interviewed discussed striving to be a living example of integrity, ethics, and values, which has resulted in either reprimanding or in some cases firing clients in order to protect their teams and stand up to unethical behavior, regardless of the short-term financial impacts.

To be a great consultant, one must have grown up in a consulting career doing strategy work for commercial clients. Only 19 percent of leaders interviewed have been in consulting their entire career doing strategy work for commercial clients. 81 percent have held roles outside of consulting and have a broad experiences. Examples of other career roles include former Fortune 500 C-suite executives, entrepreneurs, engineers, accountants, attorneys, government officials, and investment bankers in public, private, and non-profit organizations.

To be a great consultant, one must have earned an MBA at a top school. Higher education is absolutely paramount as a consultant. One hundred percent of leaders interviewed have a bachelor's degree, while 76 percent have an advanced degree. And of those with a master's degree, 41 percent have MBAs, and the remaining 59 percent have either PhDs, JDs, or other advanced graduate degrees. A handful also hold professional industry certifications such as certified public accountant, project management professional, or Six

Sigma. Out of the nine leaders interviewed with MBAs, 44 percent graduated from a top ten business school.

To be a great consultant, particularly for women, one must choose between having a family and having a career. Ninety-six percent of the leaders I interviewed are married, 56 percent were women, and 80 percent have children. Several consulting leaders we interviewed have more than one child; one female consulting leader interviewed has four children. While many of the leaders discussed the need to sometimes sacrifice, one hundred percent of them agreed that it is possible to have a career, marriage, and a family; you have to purposefully design and prioritize a life with a support system that takes into account all facets of your desired lifestyle goals, which looks different for everyone.

The Journey to Greatness Is Infinite

Numerous studies have shown that the journey of human ambition toward happiness is about progress, not perfection. The same holds true with the journey to greatness; success is not a final destination and failure is not a permanent state. Greatness is a way of being. One makes significant strides toward greatness by starting small. To go from good to great typically takes about a 20 percent pivot in your current approach.

Once you have identified key developmental areas, build in new habits to the point of unconscious competence—meaning, a skill you do without thinking about it. I simply call it the brushing your teeth test. One of the first things I do when I wake up in the morning is brush

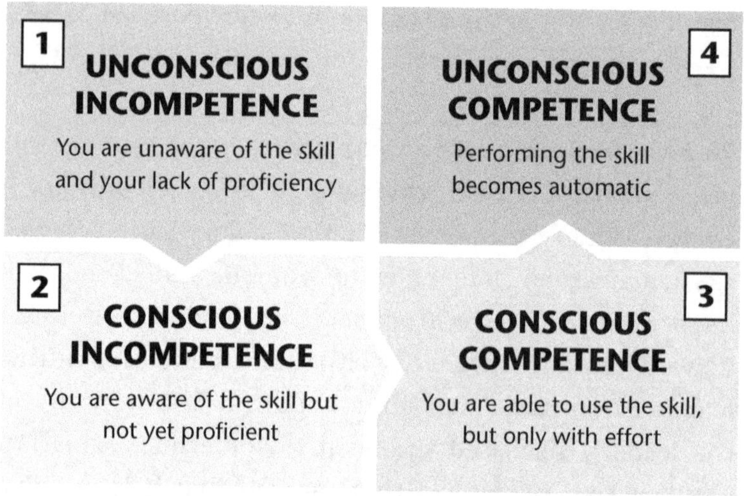

1 **UNCONSCIOUS INCOMPETENCE** You are unaware of the skill and your lack of proficiency	**UNCONSCIOUS COMPETENCE** **4** Performing the skill becomes automatic
2 **CONSCIOUS INCOMPETENCE** You are aware of the skill but not yet proficient	**CONSCIOUS COMPETENCE** **3** You are able to use the skill, but only with effort

FIGURE 5. Maslow's Four Stages of Learning Framework

my teeth. I do not have to think about it or put it on my calendar. Once you have mastered a developmental area into an unconscious competence, move on to the next area of developmental focus. And repeat.

Becoming a great consultant is a cyclical journey. It takes making a conscious decision that is congruent with your subconscious thinking. Our brain begins to rewire itself to support a decision made, which is why and how thoughts become things. Even after all of these years, I am also still on my journey to greatness. The road to becoming a great consultant is infinite; you never arrive, and there is no ceiling. You just get better at being great.

Creating a Pay It Forward Mentoring Movement in Consulting

In recent years a wide variety of online forums that help create conversations amongst consultants across the industry have been formed. While these forums are entertaining, there is a level of miseducation in some of the information being shared broadly. My goal with this book is to create a standard definition of what great consulting looks like in a non-divisive, empathetic way. I challenge other seasoned consultants to continue to elevate the profession responsibly to help shape the incoming generation. Pay it forward with one mentee or with dozens. As consultants, our jobs are to leave an organization better than the way we found it; this principle should also apply to the collective advancement of our profession.

The road to becoming a great consultant is infinite; you never arrive, and there is no ceiling. You just get better at being great.

Being the Career Mentor I Wish I Had

I do not claim to be the authoritative expert in consulting; I am an expert in being the mentor that I wish I had earlier in my career, and I wrote the book in that voice. I spent the first 5 – 6 years of my career seeking mentors, with a mental map that a mentor was going to look like an older, more experienced version of myself. That person never showed up. I rarely saw women, particularly women of color, in consulting leadership roles. After years of feeling lost, I decided to become my own mentor because I was determined to succeed in consulting. This meant I had to blow up my original definition of what a mentor looked like. Today, I use the following definition of what mentors looks like in action, which could be any race or gender. A mentor is someone who:

- takes you under their wings and shows you the ropes
- answers your questions in a non-judgmental empathetic way
- demystifies the noise of an engagement practice and client politics to keep you laser-focused on the bigger goal of delivering with impact
- talks you off the ledge after a terrible week that forces you to question if you are cut out for this profession
- tells you what you need to hear not what you want to hear
- is not jaded in their career advice despite their own personal hardships
- provides generous feedback when they notice that you have become complacent and can do better
- introduces you to influential leaders who share their personal stories to give you a different perspective of the profession
- shares articles, tools, or business books before you realize you need them
- spends a Thursday night or Saturday morning reviewing your deliverable and giving you feedback so that you look good on Monday

I am thankful that my decades of experience and stoicism in a demanding career that was not always kind have afforded me the opportunity to pass along these nuggets to you.

Let's get you started on your journey to greatness.

THE MINDSET OF GREAT CONSULTANTS

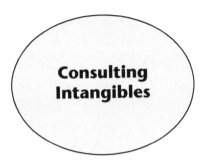

FIGURE 6. Intangibles are Core to the Mindset of Great Consultants

Great consultants are like great athletes and the journey to greatness begins with mindset. Mindset is based on a structured mental model of rules, values, and societal ideals that collectively become what I will call intangibles—abstract, invisible qualities or attributes that provide profound insight into an individual's character. One cannot place a specific metric on characteristics such as leadership, initiative, judgment, and organization. One cannot always see ethical or moral values with the naked eye. What many people fail to realize is your professional maturity and handling of intangibles make or break your consulting career. What is promising is that while intangibles are critical skills, they can be learned.

Cultivating intangibles is key. Possessing or knowing a concept academically doesn't mean you actively utilize it in everyday life. An unwritten rule of consulting is to practice intangibles daily to make them an unconscious competence. Intangibles could get lost or change to adapt to your environment. Just like an athlete that spends time in between games and in the off-season doing basic drills or keeping up a nutrition plan to stay in peak condition, it is in practicing the basic skills over and over again that we become great at whatever we are doing.

As Tony Robbins says: "Repetition is the mother of skill." Well-executed intangibles offer you the ability to exert influence at mastery regardless of level, technical skillset, or experience. It is the effort you put forth, how you show up, but most importantly how you make people feel when you leave the room. I touch upon intangibles in order of importance, and how they are collectively the building blocks for an amazing career in consulting.

1

Make Manners Your Competitive Advantage

Politeness is a sign of dignity, not subservience.

—THEODORE ROOSEVELT

Contrary to popular belief, chivalry is not dead and neither are manners. And great consultants use manners to their competitive advantage. Since consulting is a relationship-driven business, it's important to have a candid discussion on manners and etiquette.

> **At the end of the day:** recap a specific point; similar to *in a nutshell*

At the end of the day, etiquette is the core principle of good customer service. It is a basic skill that I wished was reinforced in the learning curriculums of professional services firms.

By etiquette, I'm not talking about knowing the difference between a salad fork and entree fork. I'm talking about good, old-fashioned manners, which sometimes can mean the difference between winning and losing business.

Christine Pearson, professor of management at the Thunderbird School of Global Management and coauthor of *The Cost of Bad Behavior*, says 96 percent of Americans report experiencing rudeness at work, and 48 percent say they are treated uncivilly on a weekly basis. A lack of couth could impact your ability to get simple things done and wreak havoc on your career without you even realizing it. Let me share some real-life examples.

Career Limiting Decisions

I was in a client meeting discussing resourcing and project extensions for my team several years ago. I had a pretty good relationship with Paul, my client, and noticed his hesitation when we got to one of the senior consultants on the team who I held in very high regard. I asked Paul what was wrong.

He paused. "Christie, I'm going to be frank with you. I'm not extending Bob's contract. I don't see a need for his role anymore at this next phase of the project. And from what I've been hearing, he's apparently extremely rude and inconsiderate to my team."

I was stunned and completely blindsided. Bob? He was one of the hardest working and most competent senior consultants on the team. He was the team lead and well positioned for a promotion at the end of the year. I never witnessed that type of behavior when I met with Bob and his team. When I probed further, it turned out that Bob had a split personality. When he met with Paul the client, myself, or leaders of our practice, he acted very differently than he did to anyone he deemed of lower rank than he was.

To everyone else on Paul's team and his own team, Bob acted like a bully. He exuded an air of arrogance and rudeness that rubbed people the wrong way. Any time Bob left the client's building, he failed to hold the door open for others behind him. Bob would see people running for the elevators but not hold it open. He left a mess in the client's break room expecting someone else to clean up.

Many employees at the client site could not stand him, eventually reporting Bob's behavior to Paul. Luckily, Bob was the only person on our team with such poor manners. It was unfortunate because Bob was smart and a technically competent consultant. Up until that point I considered him an invaluable asset to the team. It was an embarrassing and unnecessary issue that distracted from the team's work.

When I probed his team, they noticed his behavior but were scared to provide feedback to any leaders since Bob was considered an invincible rock star back at our firm. They didn't want to jeopardize their own career. After many discussions with leadership, we rolled Bob off the project. Word got around the practice about Bob getting rolled off; because of his bullying ways and his rude manners, he became dead weight. No one wanted to take the risk of staffing him on their projects. Months later, Bob left the firm.

Talent Divide in Organizations

In another instance I was speaking to a colleague seeking a new project opportunity when I was a senior consultant. Tim was a consulting rock star and a high performer. Every engagement manager in our practice wanted Tim on their projects. I was actually surprised he didn't select a project that was the type of work he wanted to do with less travel. He turned down what his peers consider a glamorous, highly-visible, once-in-a-lifetime project. The role would have provided direct access to top influencers of a particular industry. Everyone was trying to get staffed on this project. Why did Tim turn it down?

Tim, like any great consultant, did his due diligence to learn about the culture of the project. Tim heard from other colleagues that the engagement leadership team was extremely rude and pompous, notorious for running teams into the ground. Tim also found out that the client was demanding and just as rude as the leadership. Project leadership apparently allowed the client to walk all over the team and never said no to the client, no matter how questionable the demand, decisions, or behavior was. To Tim it was not worth the stress. The engagement leadership team was disappointed and surprised that Tim chose another project that required cross coast travel instead of the fast track to promotion project.

"Politeness is to human nature what warmth is to wax."

—Arthur Schopenhauer, nineteenth-century philosopher

Loss of Access to Key Stakeholders

Earlier in my career I had an executive assistant (EA) confess to "accidentally" bumping meetings of a senior manager off calendars of key leaders. Apparently Brett, the senior manager, passed the EA every day in the hallway and purposely made a point not to make eye contact. He only acknowledged the EA when the leaders were around. Brett constantly made urgent, aggressive demands of the EA via email or the company's instant message without saying please or thank you. Every communication was rude and a crisis ask that had to be completed immediately. To top it off, Brett frequently misspelled the EA's first name in his correspondence.

Unfortunately for Brett, the EA he continued to disrespect supported many of his close senior leaders. What was also unfortunate for Brett was that this lead EA oversaw a team of assistants that managed the calendars of at least fifty other leaders across his region. The

EA subtly paid Brett back for his rudeness by occasionally cutting off his access to key leaders.

That resulted in Brett and his teams constantly facing odd delays and hardships because decisions couldn't be made without going through the senior leaders, which resulted in avoidable late nights and last minute changes. Brett and his teams couldn't figure why it was so hard for them to get anything done.

Missed Revenue Opportunities and Strained Relationships

A colleague witnessed two executives lose a $5 million deal with the potential for an additional $10 million multi-year extension. While I'm sure there was more to the story, lack of manners clearly impacted their ability to collaborate fully. Senior leadership asked two executives whom had never worked together before to partner and bring the best of the firm's solution and industry expertise to the market. Given the longstanding relationship the firm had with the client, the team was well positioned to win the work.

Executive A rubbed Executive B the wrong way from the very beginning. In front of a ten-person proposal team, Executive A started texting in every meeting in the middle of Executive B's conversations. Then Executive A would finish texting and fire away questions already covered, interrupting the flow of brainstorming discussions.

My colleague sat next to Executive A for a couple of proposal meetings and watched her tweet, comment on Facebook posts, and text message pictures from her most recent vacation to someone. In the same breath Executive

A kept gushing how exciting it would be to pull off this win. Executive A's team was equally distracted during meetings. They rudely texted while their colleagues spoke, mimicking their leader's behavior. The awkward energy in the room was deafening.

As a member of Executive B's team, my colleague was horrified by this behavior, but no one dared to address it or say anything about it. Executive B was clearly annoyed but pretended it didn't faze him. The tacit tension between the two executives gradually increased. This affected their ability to collaborate, preventing them from doing their best work. While they got through the process and the proposal was submitted, a competitor ended up winning the contract.

Mastering the Manners and Etiquette Imperative

There's an old saying: *Nothing personal; it's strictly business.* In reality and particularly in today's business environment, this is completely false. Everything is personal in business. *Everything.* Particularly in relationship-driven businesses like consulting. A lack of manners is an undercurrent, like an airborne virus infecting client interactions, conference rooms, and team cultures. A survey conducted by Kessler International shared that 84 percent of those surveyed observed rudeness and lack of courtesy in their staff and another 65 percent felt that a shocking majority lacked a moral compass.

My goal in sharing those real-life examples was not to make anyone feel bad, paranoid, or guilty but to make you aware that how you treat people does matter.

MECE MENTORING MOMENT

❝Saying please and thank you, keeping a commitment ... showing the good manners that you are taught as a child ... turns out that these are good lessons for business. Have good manners, showing up to your promises, and always taking the high road—it will always pay off in the end.❞

–Paige Arnoff-Fenn, CEO of Mavens & Moguls

Your personal core values may be different from others. The higher up you are in the food chain, the bigger the stakes are, and the more expensive etiquette miscues are. Great consultants choose to make a different decision every time.

I'm not claiming to be the etiquette police or a manners expert. Great consultants live by the platinum rule: treat others as *they* want to be treated. It is not about you; it is about how you make others feel regardless of your personal beliefs.

Selected Etiquette Practices and Habits of Great Consultants

While many of the practices below are considered basic, I would be remiss to not highlight them as reminders. Great consultants are aware of how their personal biases may show up in interactions and adjust according to the environment or audience.

- Practice correctly pronouncing someone's name.
- Give someone a nickname as a result of an

established relationship with sincerity and mutual consent, not because you are too lazy to learn how to properly pronounce someone's name.

◆ Ask people how they are doing and genuinely listen to their response.

◆ Respect cultural nuances of both your firm and the client organization.

◆ Learn about the native culture when working in a different country. Honor and respect local customs.

◆ Choose your words and actions wisely. How you treat others is a true character test.

◆ Hand out more compliments than insults. The classic saying: *If you don't have something nice to say, don't say anything at all* still rings true.

◆ Write or email a timely thank you note; it is appropriate and highly underutilized.

◆ Practice shaking people's hands; it has to be firm, not limp or bone crushing.

◆ Refrain from divisive behavior in an attempt to shame or discount the opinions of others that are different from you.

◆ Refrain from constantly monopolizing a conversation or cutting someone off in mid-sentence in an attempt to rush through a conversation.

◆ Facilitate introductions between different groups of people that may not know each other.

- Practice the order of how you make introductions to people such as introducing the most senior person first or a woman first.
- *Please* and *thank you* are still powerful words. Use them genuinely daily.

Crucibles of Etiquette and Manners in the Digital Age

According to a study conducted by Robert Half Technology, 76 percent of surveyed executives said technology etiquette breaches greatly or somewhat adversely affect a person's career prospects. Below are selected digital practices and habits to reflect on.

- Refrain from using your phone in meetings.
- Do not hold phone conversations in public areas, particularly when discussing confidential personal or client matters.
- Think before putting a caller on speakerphone without their consent or knowledge.
- Obtain consent before using a camera phone to record a work conversation or meeting, particularly if confidential information is being shared.
- Don't respond to any hostile emails sent to you in the same manner you received them; be like Michelle Obama—when they go low, you go high.
- Think twice about friending or following colleagues, leaders, and clients on social media sites such as Instagram and Facebook.
- Be cautious on forwarding tasteless email

jokes, chain letters, or inappropriate memes amongst colleagues or business contacts.

◆ Refrain from sending real-time emails, tweets, or text messages when you are supposed to be listening or participating in practice or firm-wide town halls and meetings. It will be noticed and noted whether it is mentioned to you or not.

◆ Ask the sender before you forward emails deemed confidential.

◆ Refrain from replying to all on a broad email unless the response truly pertains to the entire distribution list.

CONSULTING LEADER INTERVIEW...

Fireside Chat with a Partner

Greg is a partner at a global management consulting firm with over twenty-one years of combined experience in both public and private sector consulting work. Greg's journey is an illustration of how everything in business is truly personal. He shares a powerful story of how temporarily leaving consulting—twice—accelerated his ultimate success in the profession. Greg also discusses his thoughts on life, faith, and embracing the journey.

Q. Please share how you decided to go into consulting. What attracted you to the profession?

A. I was attracted to consulting as far back as my undergraduate studies in college, when I was first introduced to consulting through the Big Four+ and the boutique strategy firms. I knew early on that I got bored easily and constantly needed new challenges. I was pretty intrigued by the diversity of experiences, the need for new challenges. And the thought of helping shape a company's strategy was very attractive to me as a career.

Fortunately, I didn't get a consulting offer and instead took an offer from a multinational technology company, working in their operational finance group for three years.

That experience was critical because I learned early on how to make accounting real and how business decisions translated into financial results. I also quickly learned how to visualize how business decisions flow through the profits and loss statements.

Looking back on that experience, going into operations finance was actually one of the best decisions I made. Sometimes career consultants do not have empathy for clients or understand the reality of their environments, what it actually means to sit on the other side of the client and deal with the political nuances that clients sometimes face.

In my finance role I only report on the business decisions that were made. That drove me to want experiences on the other side of the table to either make those decisions or help shape those type of decisions. It ultimately led me to business school. I then made the leap to consulting.

Q. There are junctures or moments in every career where you get to a crossroads and wonder if you should continue on. If you could share your thinking during those moments, what keeps you going during reflective moments or challenging times?

A. I've reached several of those moments in my career and haven't always stayed in consulting throughout my journey. There were moments when professionally things were going well but personally it wasn't. My career at the time was impacting my family life, particularly after my wife and I had a baby. I stayed in consulting but at that time decided to do it at another firm.

Then I had a real personal moment when *I thought: I don't know if God created me to help rich people get richer.* At that time, I had a moment of clarity and a unique perspective about my purpose that led me to leave consulting and go into community redevelopment work. It was a moment in time when I was thinking: *There has got to be more I should be doing with the talents that God has given me.*

Then there was another moment in my life where I said to myself: *I really love consulting.* By then I had matured, and my perspective evolved to where I realized consulting wasn't about rich people getting richer; it was actually about solving problems. Being in consulting I realized that I could create positive, impactful results in the client environment that could create jobs.

Then I made another decision to join a client—and then again came back to consulting. My journey has not been straightforward in consulting.

I am happy to have chosen this journey because the diversity of experiences helped me develop a broader depth of character I don't think I would have had by staying on a linear path. My experiences helped me have a deeper appreciation for the real community issues, which kept me grounded. One thing that keeps me going in challenging times is my faith in God.

Consulting is a cyclical industry; whatever happens in consulting typically happens in the industry six months later. During the trying times I think you get the greatest level of creativity when you embrace those challenges, leaning on the talents and experiences you were given.

Q. What was the one experience that shaped your values and how you do business in consulting today?

A. Earlier on in my career during the second consulting project, I was part of a team asked to conduct a sourcing and procurement strategy to come up with recommendations for a Fortune 500 organization. It became very apparent early on that the client hired us with an agenda and hired a third-party consulting firm for the sole purpose of supporting their objective.

What also became apparent was that our recommendations would go against the client's agenda. This project was right after 9/11 during a down cycle in the consulting industry.

When we presented the recommendations, the client was happy with the work but not with our recommendations since it didn't support their agenda. As a result we didn't win the implementation extension of the work attached to these recommendations.

During the presentation, the engagement partner realized that we would not win an extension and literally started begging for the extension. I realized at that moment that I would never demonstrate desperation in front of a client or my team. I understand we have a business to run, and if you are transactional in nature, relationships will be short-term. It was a moment of clarity, and from then on I became very aware of the importance of alignment of interest.

Q. What is the craziest experience you've had as a consultant?

A. Early in my career we had some executive sponsor pushing major transformations on a client. The transformation was one of the highest priorities on the C-suite agenda. The executive sponsor walked into the room, called the project team together, and said, "I'm no longer with the company due to the political backlash of pushing this initiative," and suddenly walked out of the room in tears.

That experience impacted and shaped me for a number of reasons. One, when a company is undergoing large-scale transformative change, a lot of times the catalyst of the change doesn't make it due to the politics of the change. Two, our work as consultants can have serious implications on people and families. While we could do spreadsheets, talk about deliverables, and use all of these buzzwords, at the end of the day, a lot of our work directly impacts people. It became deeply personal as I think about the work that we do. Third, all things ultimately lead back to people. I will never forget the face of this client walking out the door.

Boost Your Personal Brand as Low-Hanging Fruit

Winning starts with the beginning.

—ROBERT SCHULLER

> **Low-hanging fruit:** short-term solutions that can be implemented with the least amount of effort and greatest impact; a quick win.

Your personal brand is low-hanging fruit because it is the one area you have the most control over in your career. Yet people often underestimate how important it is.

A personal brand in its totality is how you show up in the world—your executive presence. It is how you present yourself, communicate, and influence others. According to Glassdoor, roughly 80 percent of recruiters and hiring managers use social media to look for and vet job candidates, making it extremely important to have a professional presence on the Internet.

Maximize Personal Branding Moments That Matter

An unwritten rule in personal branding as a consultant is to identify critical moments that matter in your day-to-day interactions, and take control of the narrative you create. These are the moments when your training, experience, skills, decisions, and habits need to come together to shape your image. Typical critical moments that matter for a consultant can include:

- how you present yourself image-wise;
- face-to-face interactions with your clients, teams, and leaders, including social activities;

- how you respond to critical feedback from a colleague, leader, or client that you deem offensive or surprising;
- how you address an individual who publicly disagrees with your recommendation or challenges your analysis;
- deliverables or work products submitted to your team, leader, or client for review; and
- how you act under pressure, in times of high stress, exhaustion, or disappointment.

According to Glassdoor, roughly 80 percent of recruiters and hiring managers use social media to look for and vet job candidates, making it extremely important to have a professional presence on the Internet.

Personal Branding Begins with Integrity

Integrity is the quality of having strong moral principles. It is the sum of the decisions you make when no one is looking. Living with integrity sometimes creates a short-term setback in exchange for long-term gains. Great consultants never compromise integrity given the negative, irreparable impact it has on a career reputation or a business brand.

Executive Presence Begins Now

Earlier I mentioned that personal brand is how you show up. To further elaborate, executive presence (aka how you show up) is the ability to project confidence and composure that results in establishing trust. The

MECE MENTORING MOMENT

❝I had a CEO client of a small business that hired us to do public relations work. We built a great relationship, and she would reach out to me to bounce ideas off her. She called me one day and said, "I need to tell you something confidentially. We are in talks to be acquired by a major corporation, and I'm not going to be able to talk to the press for the next sixty days in case this deal goes through. Can you not call me for a couple of months?"

I told her, "I think we need to put this project on hold. It doesn't make sense for us to pitch you to the media if you cannot speak to them."

She was willing to honor my contract, and I refused to do so.

The client said, "I've been in business longer than you have been alive. No one I have ever worked with would miss an opportunity to bill me and do no work. That doesn't ever happen." Her business was eventually sold to a very prominent company and industry leader. My client then goes to the company's CEO and says, "I have a signed contract with this small marketing firm. I don't care what you do with the business, but you must keep these people on staff and honor the rest of their contract. And you should probably have all of your companies using their services because they are best."

Given any opportunity to sing our praises, she would. She has sent me a ton of business over the years. She has been re-

tired for over a decade, and she is still sending me business. That one small gesture of pausing the contract has paid dividends for my company in ways that I could have never imagined. 99

–Paige Arnoff-Fenn, *CEO of Mavens & Moguls*

ability to read an audience or situation and adjust. It also includes key attributes such as decisiveness, assertiveness, and charisma. An unwritten rule is to focus on developing executive presence every single day regardless of level. Executive presence is not something you wait until you are becoming an executive to start focusing on. We own the impression we make on others for better or worse.

Creating the Brand of a Great Consultant

Image Is Key

According to *Scientific American*, studies have shown that dressing for success enhances your credibility and also influences your performance. The workplace is increasingly casual, blurring the lines of what is deemed acceptable or appropriate. Blend in with your client's dress style and culture, whether that means showing up in suits, wearing khakis or jeans, or jogging pants and sneakers. Make sure you look put together in whatever your style of choice is that makes you authentically effective. This will only enhance your ability to better connect with individuals. A survey conducted by

A survey conducted by OfficeTeam found that 80 percent of executives say clothing affects an employee's chances of earning a promotion.

OfficeTeam found that 80 percent of executives say clothing affects an employee's chances of earning a promotion.

Verbal Communications and Presentation Skills

Another element of executive presence is verbal communication. Great consultants master the art of verbal communication. If you are not able to afford a coach, join a local Toastmasters chapter or meetup group. Practice presentations and speeches in advance and out loud. Video record yourself and make observations on your verbal and non-verbal elements. Model your style after individuals who are articulate. TED Talks are a great place to start. Learn how to communicate the same message to multiple audiences. Have multiple elevator pitches and sound bites memorized. Learn to analyze stakeholder groups to determine what is important for them to be aware of. Obtain feedback from others to refine messaging.

Maximize Thinking and Learning Skills

An unwritten rule is to take time to discover how you think and learn to unlock key methods to maximize your core consulting skills. How you acquire, process, and interpret data is the foundation for creating techniques to mastering analysis skills that lead to developing sound client recommendations. Each person has their own unique way of thinking and problem solving, key building blocks to cultivate quantitative and qualitative skills. A great place to start is with the book *Frames of Mind: The Theory of Multiple Intelligences.* Author Howard Gardner provides a multi-dimensional perspective on seven key intelligence types: linguistic, logic-mathematical, kinesthetic, spatial, musical, interpersonal, and intrapersonal.

Leveraging the Power of Feedback

Professional maturity is an important component of executive presence. Consultants spend a lot of time sharing ideas, brainstorming, analyzing data, and reframing information. Great consultants crave constructive feedback because they understand the power of it. You have to be open-minded and agile to create ideas and deliverables with personal detachment. Being coachable and learning to aggregate different points of view is a critical skill. No matter how strongly great consultants may feel about their position, they learn to listen and adapt.

Become an Expert at Something Not Work Related

Remember when applying for college, you had to describe interests, hobbies, and extracurricular activities in the application? Admission officers wanted to get a glimpse of your personality outside of academic records. This concept still applies in the business world. When I've shared this with mentees, some look at me like: *Is this*

MAKE IT MECE

Top Ways You Hurt Your Personal Brand without Realizing It

❶ Not actively managing your online reputation or brand

❷ Not giving credit where credit is due

❸ Responding to emails or feedback with negativity

❹ Not double-checking your work before submitting it to leadership or the client

❺ Making sweeping statements that are false, unfounded, or steeped in personal biases

❻ Cutting people off while they are speaking just to have the last word or to usurp their point of view

❼ Making everything about you, your needs, and your career

❽ Not meeting commitments or having inconsistent follow-through

❾ Not managing the client, team, or leader's expectations of you and your performance

❿ Jumping to conclusions without having the full story.

woman insane? When am I supposed to find time to do my work if I take on a hobby? You have time for whatever you decide you have time for. If you decide on a hobby, you'll always find a couple of hours or days per month to devote to it. It's an unwritten rule that being a well-rounded individual with genuine interests or hobbies outside of work helps accelerate relationship building and your ability to influence. In other words, create a life outside of consulting so that you are not always doing or talking about work.

There are numerous benefits to having extracurricular activities. You'll be surprised at how you come back to work recharged and ready to do it all again. The easiest way to develop an interest is to decide what you're passionate about and become very knowledgeable about the topic. It doesn't matter what it is as long as you enjoy it thoroughly. Here are some thought starters:

- Become the go-to sommelier for recommendations on wine-dinner entree pairings.
- Take helicopter pilot lessons and learn everything from the cockpit perspective.
- Volunteer at a local shelter on a regular basis.
- Write screenplays, become a chess champion, or tennis player.

Whatever your passion is, become an expert at it and let it be known. The more unique your interest, the more memorable you become. Experience is king. If you have dined at forty-five of the top one hundred restaurants in your state and able to provide instant recommendations for any county, it's impressive. It will always give you an anchor for discussions with colleagues and clients alike.

Manage and Protect Your Brand

Understand how your online brand impacts your personal offline brand. Online reputation isn't only determined by the type of content that is on the Internet

Take a moment and Google yourself. Clean up any questionable content. Create a Google alert for your name or use online reputation management services to actively monitor.

about you. It is the sum of your online footprint; your thoughts, opinions, photos, and any other generated content. Manage your brand like you manage your credit score. Your online brand affects how others view your professional skills and capabilities, whether real or perceived. Make sure you invest time in yourself to curate the brand you want to project. Take a moment and Google yourself. Clean up any questionable content. Create a Google alert for your name or use online reputation management services to actively monitor.

CONSULTING LEADER INTERVIEW...

Fireside Chat with a Consulting Leader

Paige Arnof-Fenn is the founder and CEO of Mavens and Moguls, a global, million-dollar marketing strategy consulting firm with a clientele ranging from start-ups to Fortune 500 companies including Colgate, Virgin, Microsoft, and the New York Times Company.

Paige holds an undergraduate degree in economics from Stanford University and an MBA from Harvard Business School. She is regularly quoted in the media, was a monthly columnist for *Entrepreneur* and *Forbes* magazines for several years, was selected as a *Woman of Note* by the *Wall Street Journal* and a *Time* magazine opinion leader.

Paige started her career on Wall Street, and before starting Mavens and Moguls, she ran marketing at three start-ups that were either bought out or went public. In this interview Paige gives us a glimpse of her amazing career journey and how the power of a personal brand helped her chart the course to launch her own consulting business.

Q. Please share the moment you decided to start your business and go into consulting.

A. Unlike you, I didn't start out my career in consulting, and I never really thought about being a consultant. I joke that I'm a bit of the accidental consultant. Never thought I would start a company, and I never hired consultants. Although I had a lot of friends that worked at a number of the premier consulting firms, it just wasn't a path that I chose.

Out of college I worked on Wall Street and did several stints in big marketing roles at some Fortune 500 corporations. From there I stepped out of the corporate path and tried my hand at leading marketing functions for various start-ups.

September 11 changed the world and affected marketing significantly. Events of 9/11 immediately put all marketing activities on hold, and it was accelerated given the recent dot-com bust. Corporations buckled down to conserve cash, and the first thing most companies reserved on their budget was the marketing funds.

Fortunately for me, by the time 9/11 impacted marketing, I had been the head of marketing at three different successful start-ups and had good exit strategies during the buyouts. I got very lucky three times; when 9/11 hit I had just gotten bought out of my third start-up. My husband and I lived a very lean financial lifestyle, so we were in a very fortunate position in that I didn't have to go out and find a job.

At that time I had a lot of connections in the investment community given all the activities I had done recently with the three start-up companies that were familiar with my experience raising significant venture funds. A number of my connections began reaching out to me because they had laid off their entire marketing departments, but there were a ton of projects where they needed to help. Many companies had limited funds and were trying to figure out how to implement basic marketing activities while riding the crunch period.

My first instinct when people in my network kept asking me to help them with various projects was: *I know what you need, but I am not a consultant, and that is not the type of work that I do.* In my mind I was always on the client side, never the agency side, and more of an internal chief marketing officer (CMO) type.

People didn't outsource marketing as a function sixteen years ago the way they do now. And I kept being asked to do something that was not commonplace in the marketplace as it is today.

Since I also had a great network of marketing talent I worked with across the globe that had gotten laid off, I spent the entire holiday season after 9/11 calling and emailing people I used to work with to see if they were interested in some of the projects I had. Many of the marketing professionals I reached out to were just laid off and thrilled to get involved. So I started to pair marketing professionals to the various projects from the portfolio companies of the various investment firms. I jokingly refer to my network of marketing professionals as marketing mavens and marketing moguls once project requirements started coming in.

I didn't even realize that I was starting a company; I just kept connecting companies with good talent for various projects. Once several projects began to take off, it dawned on me that I probably should start to formalize all this. I didn't even write a business plan, but with my network I pulled together a website, created a logo, letterhead, and became incorporated.

Before you knew it, I had cobbled together a company and was running a consulting organization, acting as one of the first outsourced marketing firms in the industry. Most of my first set of clients were small, emerging businesses that needed skeletal, outsourced marketing support to help them get through the down economy.

It was a completely accidental career choice but turned out to be the best way to start a business because we were able to test the concept in real time.

Q. What an amazing founding story. Given the way you started your company, did you start to formalize with consulting methodologies or frameworks to deliver on the work or did you continue to grow organically?

A. We were very opportunistic. Because I didn't have consulting experience I really didn't know what a consultant was supposed to do. We didn't really have any widgets or productize our offerings. Everything we did was customized work due to the unique set of challenges of our clients. Most of the professionals in my company I had worked with or hired in my previous lives, so they had a similar work style and approach like me.

The feedback we would get from our clients was that they had never worked with a consulting firm like ours before. Both our heads and our hearts were much more aligned with their interests than that of other consultancies they had worked with. I've approached client problems from their perspective, without trying to cross-sell or upsell. I was giving them advice that I wish someone had given me. I really understood their needs extremely well given our past experiences.

It made us stand out from the beginning because we acted more like a partner with a good understanding of their environment than a vendor trying to sell them solutions.

Q. What is the one thing that keeps you going during challenging times as an entrepreneur?

A. Just because a client says no now, doesn't mean no forever. If a client turns you down and you take the high road, you become memorable for being classy.

Q. What is the craziest experience you had as a consultant?

A. I'm very active in the women business owner community in New England. In one of the groups, there is a very prominent woman, well known within the community as a tough person; she was not warm and fuzzy, a very no-nonsense but a very influential individual.

During one of the community events, she asked me to come out to her office with a proposal of our services. Overall we had a really great meeting. I followed up with her for three weeks straight—emailed her, called her. But she never responded to the proposal, and for months I never heard anything back. I knew I was going to see her at this women's organization holiday event because she was going to be the keynote speaker discussing the importance of supporting women-owned businesses.

I'm in the audience of this three-hundred-person-holiday event, and this woman began her fifteen-minute keynote speech. At the end of her speech, she says, "We as women business owners have to put our money where our mouth is. We need to stick together and support our businesses. And that's why I'm going to be putting my money where my mouth is. My company is going to be hiring Paige Arnof-Fenn of Mavens and Moguls for all of my marketing needs for the next year."

I was in complete shock. *Did she just say we were hired?* I found out like everyone else that she had just hired my company. When she said this, all eyes in the room were directly on me. After the speech, everyone kept congratulating me, patting me on the back, and sending me high fives. People were saying how much this woman hated everyone and everything. *If she hired you, you must be really good.* I was like a rock star at a concert. It was amazing! I got a ton of business from that moment; it was completely surreal.

Q. Knowing what you know now, what advice would you give your younger self?

A. When I was younger, I thought I wanted to be like Meg Whitman or Ursula Burns; I wanted to conquer the world, become a Fortune 500 woman CEO, and run a big multinational company. I had high aspirations to play in a very big sandbox, and I was in such a rush to get there. I was very impatient, and I wanted to be the youngest, the first, and the best on the thirty-under-thirty or forty-under-forty lists. Very anxious about being successful and getting there on the fastest path possible.

I'd tell myself to take a breath and chill out, understand that it's okay to enjoy each phase and learn what you need to learn at each part of your career. Don't be in such a rush.

My definition of success changed as I got older.

I began looking at success holistically in a different way from the executive roles I held at various companies and decided that is not what I wanted in my life.

Now I'm more focused on the big picture, wanting to do work that is fulfilling and meaningful on topics that I care about with people I respect.

If you told me in my twenties that I would be fifty-one and not CEO of a big Fortune 500 company, I would have probably thought I was a failure when in fact that is not the case at all. Turns out being CEO of a company that I created from scratch has been even more fulfilling.

You have to live your own definition of success, not someone else's definition of success. What you want to spend your life working on and what will make you fulfilled.

3

Network to Unlock Any Door

If you want to go fast, go alone; if you want to go far, go together.

—AFRICAN PROVERB

As the saying goes, your network is your net worth. Building a rich, dynamic network takes years and is a long-term investment. Ask yourself these key questions:

- Do I know at least five people who would hire me on the spot without even looking at my résumé if I needed a job?
- Do I have relationships with at least ten other people who I can ask for a referral, introduction, or recommendation without feeling awkward?
- When I look at my network, if my spouse, sibling, cousin, or child needed a job in a similar field, do I have enough capital in my relationship bank account to call in a favor on their behalf? Would that favor be handled urgently or be delayed?
- If I decided to start a business venture, can I go to my network and easily crowdsource $250,000 because people believe in me and my capabilities and know that I will pay them back?

> Networking: proactively interacting with people regularly to build relationships that ultimately further your career, brand, or ability to influence; the exchange of information with colleagues, potential business contacts, or like-minded individuals.

- ◆ If someone in my network needed a referral, recommendation, introduction, job for their loved ones, or to raise money for a business venture, would they come to me? Would they trust me enough to ask for help? And would I deliver?

These examples are the net result and impact of a strong, actionable network. Take another look at these questions. This exercise was intended to create awareness. If you are scratching your head and coming up blank, begin to make your network a priority. Now.

Great consultants intentionally focus on building and maintaining their network before they need to leverage it.

Great consultants intentionally focus on building and maintaining their network before they need to leverage it. Great consultants know it takes years to curate an actionable network that will pay dividends for life. You have to want to work on your network, because, like exercise, no one is going to force you to manage your network or chastise you for not making time to do it.

A study conducted at Cornell University demonstrates the power of networking in professional services. They surveyed 165 lawyers at a large North American law firm, and their research showed that the "success of lawyers depended on their ability to network effectively both internally (to get themselves assigned to choice clients) and externally (to bring business into the firm). Those who regarded these activities as distasteful and avoided them had fewer billable hours than their peers."

Paige Arnoff-Fenn, CEO of Mavens and Moguls, shares her thoughts on how to create authentic relationships when networking. "People always say that I'm such a great networker, which in my mind is an odd thing to say. I don't think what I do or say as networking. I'm just being me. It's just who I am; I like meeting and chatting with interesting people. I am naturally a gregarious, curious person who loves problem-solving and asking a lot of questions. People are generally appreciative that I take the time to get to know them, understand their needs, and how I seek to help them out. I don't network or spend time with people I find offensive or all that I could get out of them is work. If someone doesn't treat my team or me well, I don't want to spend time with negative people."

There are tons of great books available on networking, so I won't go into the basics. Instead, I share networking tips critical to becoming a great consultant that I wish someone had told me earlier in my career.

Tapping into Networking Power

Twelve Types of People You Need in Your Consulting Network

Studies have shown people model the behaviors, habits, and ideas of the people around them. Great consultants surround themselves with like-minded individuals who play various roles in their ecosystem. The following table provides an overview of 12 types of roles/people you should seek to identify in your consulting network.

TWELVE TYPES OF PEOPLE YOU NEED IN YOUR CONSULTING ECOSYSTEM

Role	Description
Associates	People that you have an informal, casual relationship with at work, school, academic, hobby, or association connections.
Clients	People in your chosen industry who are in positions of power or decision making authority. Past, present, or future prospects (rising future leaders) can also be included in this category.
Coaches	Paid professionals that support you in targeted areas of your life or for a specific objective based on their areas of expertise.
Connectors	Individuals with their own large network or tribe of followers with a canny ability to connect you and help you make introductions.
Elders	Individuals with significant historical knowledge of a particular industry, firm, or organizational culture.
Go-Getters	Influencers, rising stars, rock stars, thought leaders, or movers and shakers of all backgrounds. These are individuals who are out in the world making things happen. Great consultants are go-getters!
Mentees	Individuals that you offer support to based on your life experiences.
Mentors	Experienced professionals who offer guidance to help you make informed career decisions. Please see introductory chapter for a detailed description of a mentor.

Role	Description
Peers	Like-minded individuals within your network with similar goals, values, habits, and aspirations. Contrary to popular belief, peers can be older, same age, or younger; commonality and shared vision is what truly defines a peer—not age.
Realist	People with a realist point of view that surface truths and help ground you in various areas of your career and life.
Sponsors	Influential and powerful mentors or allies who take a vested emotional interest and investment in your career.
Superfans	People in your network who are the biggest fans of the brand that is you.

Planning for Networking Success

An unwritten rule to networking is to genuinely expect nothing in return. When you network for the sole purpose of getting something back, it will reflect in your attitude and interactions. It will show up in your decisions to respond or not respond to a request. And people sense it. Creating expectations means you will get upset if someone doesn't say thank you fast enough or doesn't help you when you think they owe you. Let it go. Expect nothing and allow the universe to do the rest.

Before you begin a new project, or when you're setting your career goals, create or update a relationship management plan. A plan creates clarity. Highlight or identify the people you need to know as well as how you plan to stay connected and cultivate relationships.

Sponsors: Secret Weapons to Fast Track a Consulting Career

According to the Harvard Business Review, having a sponsor can confer a statistical career benefit of 22 to 30 percent in the form of monetary increases, engagement assignments, and promotions. Women and professionals of color particularly benefit from obtaining career sponsors. The Center for Talent Innovation found that 85 percent of mothers employed full-time who have sponsors stayed employed longer compared to peers. Minority employees are also 65 percent more likely to be satisfied with their rate of advancement compared to their unsponsored peers. Big Four+ partner Karyn Twaronite recommends finding sponsors earlier on within your consulting career. I personally found out about the concept of career sponsorship nine to ten years into my career. Don't let that happen to you. Understand that mentors and sponsors are like friends; they come in your life for a moment, a season, or a lifetime. Do not be upset or disappointed if mentors or sponsors come and go. Actively manage relationships, but let it ebb and flow naturally.

The 2 + 1 Rule for Career Sponsors

It is always in your career's best interest to have more than one sponsor. In Sylvia Ann Hewlett's research,

ADAPTATION OF HEWLETT'S 2+1 RULE FOR SPONSORS

Current State	Sponsor Approach
Boutique consulting organizations of less than ten employees	Have one sponsor in your firm and two outside sponsors in the same industry.
Entrepreneurs/ independent consultants/ boutique consulting firm owners	Two sponsors in the same industry and one sponsor in a complementary industry/sector.
Consulting organizations with ten to five thousand employees	One outsider sponsor and two insider sponsors—one in your line of sight and one in a different (influential) practice or competency.
Global organizations with five thousand-plus employees	One outsider sponsor and two insider sponsors—one in your line of sight and one in a different (influential) country or HQ.

the 2+1 Rule introduces the concept of securing at least three sponsors. If you are in an organization with fewer than ten people, you are most likely best served having one sponsor in your firm and two outside of it in the same industry. In larger firms you'll want one outsider and two insiders: one in your line of sight and one in a different department or division. This rule pertains to every career stage, from entry-level to executive. I highly recommend Sylvia Ann Hewlett's book for a deep dive on how to identify, attract, and manage sponsor relationships.

Great consultants are always building consulting karma by being a mentor and/or sponsor to many others. What better way to cultivate your network than by helping others in their careers.

Get in the habit of creating and updating your LinkedIn profile, website, or blog. As of this publication, LinkedIn is a popular site for business connections and network management. A recently added LinkedIn feature allows you to download your entire network into a spreadsheet and leverage that information for relationship management exercises. Get in the habit of sending out LinkedIn invitations in addition to exchanging business cards.

Cultivating a Network

An unwritten rule: state your intent of the relationship goals upfront. Do you want to get to know someone better? Let them know. Do you see someone as a mentor and want to focus on strengthening the relationship? Let them know. Make sure you are both on the same page about the relationship you desire. Do not assume that an individual knows what type of relationship you are seeking with them.

+ Be present when conversing. Have a set of go-to, open-ended questions to start meaningful conversations.
+ Leverage memory techniques to internalize

information to remember facts about people (birthdays, anniversaries) and practice these techniques until they become an unconscious competence.

◆ End each conversation in a way that allows you to pick up on it in a future discussion; steer away from transactional discussions.

◆ Great consultants respect and value every human interaction made. A budding relationship with a Fortune 500 CEO does not outweigh the respect and honor given to the parking valet at the hotel you stay at every week.

◆ When traveling, carve out networking time to connect with friends, coworkers, or former classmates. Even if connecting means a thirty-minute hotel lobby meetup.

◆ Strategically join one or two professional organizations, associations, internal firm networking meetups, etc., without wearing yourself too thin.

◆ Be aware of body language, and respect people's boundaries.

◆ Stay in touch. People move in and out of our lives. Do not just say you will keep in touch. Actually do it.

◆ It is easier to rekindle past relationships than build new ones. All it takes sometimes is one outreach to reset a former relationship. The holidays or an anniversary is a great excuse to do so.

Great consultants get to know people on a personal

level. Big Four+ partner Marcelo Fava, views consultants in his practice as "four hundred friends, four hundred families, four hundred stories," which illustrates his vested interest in the success of each and every consultant that he is responsible for. Create the habits to keep the needs of your network front and center in every interaction.

Do not be offended if someone you admire doesn't have the time you are seeking to network. Be thankful they respect you enough to be honest, and ask them to refer you to others they may know with a similar background. Networking relationships have to be reciprocal in nature and not awkward, forced interactions. Just move on.

CONSULTING LEADER INTERVIEW...

Fireside Chat with a Consulting Leader

Jennifer Maddox is a strategic transformation solution leader at a global management consulting firm with over nineteen years of consulting experience. In this role Jennifer advises clients on delivering large-scale business transformation initiatives across a variety of industries such as retail, healthcare, and non-profit. In this interview Jennifer demonstrates the power of cultivating relationships throughout a consulting career. Jennifer shares her amazing career journey of working in consulting while being married with four children and how she has been able to balance a successful career through a strong network of relationships.

Q. Please share how you got started in consulting. Is it everything you expected it to be?

A. I started my career out of college doing accounting work for a large healthcare software development company. One of my girlfriends said: "I'm going to move to Denver, Colorado. Do you want to come with me?"

And on a whim I said okay. I loved Denver so much—I was living on the East Coast at the time, which was very different—and decided to move there myself. I applied for a job from the newspaper to be a consultant at a Big Four+ firm and got a call to interview in their Denver office. My interview was with a consultant who eventually became a partner that I still work with twenty years later.

I was hired given my experience implementing an ERP system as an end user, and that was my start in consulting over twenty years ago. I had no kind of expectation of what that meant; I just knew it was super cool, really interesting, and hard, challenging work. I loved the travel, the constant change, and ability to be flexible. My family lived in Virginia, so if I wanted to go home and see them from Colorado, I could factor that into my travels.

When I started working with clients, I figured out fairly quickly that I was good at building relationships with people. The ability to build relationships and that trust helped me tremendously to become a good consultant.

While on my path to move up the ladder, I

ended up getting pregnant with my oldest son. I had to scale back, and my view of work changed when I became a mom. I ended up taking a part-time role, working only three days a week at the firm. That worked well, and I was back on track. Then I got pregnant again eighteen months later. Again, a total change in path—with one it's pretty manageable; with two, all of a sudden you're like: *We have to look at daycare options, nannies, and what it costs versus what I would bring in.*

I ended up leaving consulting after my second son was born and made the decision to stay home for five years while my husband—who was also in consulting at the time—decided to work for a client.

During that five-year period, I maintained my relationships and my network. I advise new or aspiring consultants that if you decide to be a stay-at-home mom, never drop your relationships and contacts because you never know what life is going to bring, particularly with tools like LinkedIn.

I made a conscious effort to meet the partner that originally hired me for coffee once or twice a year. I maintained all my friendships and my network with those other consultants by keeping that up; I always had a foot in the door.

After some time I started consulting again part-time and then had another child. So now we have three boys all within five years. While doing work for a national beer company, we ended up having our fourth child; we have three boys and a girl.

Back to the drawing board and back at

home again, but I didn't stay home for long. Two opportunities and four years later, a role presented itself with my first partner, and I jumped at the chance to follow her to my current firm.

I'm very fortunate to have an extremely supportive husband because he understands the profession since he was a consultant.

Q. What advice would you give younger consultants seeking to get staffed on a certain project or join a specific competency or sector?

A. If you want to get on a certain project, industry, or competency, it always goes back to relationships. Go out of your way to get to know people, do some work for them on the side, and show your value. Keep yourself educated on the industry or competency you want to get into. Always do research. Always read ahead of time. Don't come in with a bunch of questions that you can get the answers to off the Internet.

Prepare yourself and figure out the type of people you work well with. It's one thing to want to get on a cool project, but it's another if the people on the project are difficult to work with. You're going to have a miserable time. It's also worth it to work on a project you're not that interested in, but you love the people you're working for because you are going to learn a ton from them. Just have a good experience.

Maybe you're going through something in your personal life and don't need a stressful person to work with at the moment, and you need an easier gig. Figure that out about yourself. I think a lot of young people need to become self-aware. Learn what you're good at, what you struggle with, and where can you develop more. I think a lot of it comes with maturity and years of experience versus somebody telling you to become self-aware.

What I love about certain younger consultants is the teaming. I have one person that's working for me, and he'll ask me at the end of every day: *Hey, Jen, I'm about to sign off. Is there anything I can help you with?* And I'm like: *You're amazing. I'll let you know.* I love that. He'll do that throughout the week too. If we work on a project together or if he sees I'm stressed out—*What can I help you with, Jen?* He's a first year out of school, and I plan on taking him to any project because he always adds value.

Become valuable to somebody.

Q. In your opinion, what's an impactful, quick win that younger consultants should consider doing toward becoming a great consultant?

A. Asking: *Can I help you with something?* without being asked is a quick win. Be aware of your surroundings and your team. *What is the sentiment on the team right now?* And it's not even just the person you are working for. If your coworker is stressed out, help them and be a better team member. Another quick win is high work quality; check for spelling and grammar.

Q. What are your tips on managing family and a demanding career?

A. I have been employed at four consulting firms and was an employee out in the industry for a brief period. If you're thinking about a life change—whether it's getting off the road, getting married, having a baby—there's always an opportunity for you.

Look for other opportunities at your company whether that means going part-time or taking on an internal role. That way you keep a foot in the door, and you're in a better spot than leaving altogether. Going somewhere else means you're going to have to start from scratch because you lose your network and don't have a reputation.

You have to find the right person who will allow you to do that and be your sponsor. Finding that person means building relationships. So you've got to build relationships with people.

The other thing I would say about this is, the grass isn't always greener. What's interesting is that if somebody told me that twenty years ago, I would be like: *You have no idea what you're talking about. I'm going to do what I want to do. I still want to see what else is out there.* Despite all of the great advice I give a young consultant, sometimes people just have to go through the experiences themselves; that's how you learn.

Q. Knowing what you know now in consulting, what advice would you give your younger self?

A. Give yourself a break. Don't be so hard on yourself in terms of how smart you think you are, how you look, how you present yourself. I think we are way too hard on our younger selves, especially in this day and age. Am I skinny enough? Am I pretty enough? Am I smart enough? You become smarter and better with age because you get all these life experiences, and that's more impactful than being even book smart I think.

Just work hard at trying to develop in the things that you want to develop in and be self-aware about the things that you need to develop in.

Travel, travel, and travel as much as you can. Go see the world because you're not going to have those opportunities once you become a parent; when you're traveling for work, all you want to do is get home and see your kids.

4

Balance Life as a Consultant

Consider the bigger picture. Think things through and fully commit.

—EPICTETUS

The Consultant Lifestyle

If you're seeking a traditional nine-to-five, forty hours a week type of role, being a consultant may not be for you. When I was first out of college, my friends would call to check-in or vice versa. About three years into my career, my phone stopped ringing. Conversations went from: *What are you doing this weekend?* to *What city and state or country are you in now?* The scary part about work taking over my life was that I enjoyed what I was doing. I enjoyed the thrill of the chase, tackling new challenges, the build, and working with smart people to make an impact.

A 20,000-foot view: looking at the bigger picture of a particular situation.

"The world is a book. And those who don't travel only see a page." —Saint Augustine

The Heart of a Road Warrior

Ahh ... life on the road. The notion of traveling for work sounded ultra-glamorous in college, one of the main reasons I chose a consulting career. I grew up in Boston, and besides the occasional road trip to visit family in Montreal, I didn't travel much as a child. I wanted a high growth career that took me to different places all over the world. It's amazing that after all these years I still enjoy travel. Call me a dreamer, but with each trip I envision infinite adventures, opportunities, and possibilities.

But there were moments in my career when hitting

the pavement week after week for years on end wore thin. No matter how much one enjoys travel, it will take its toll when you are in the constant throes of it, averaging 250 days annually on the road year after year. I then created a weird love-hate relationship with work travel. When I was traveling, I wanted to be home. When I was home, I wanted to travel.

Great consultants have thick-skinned patience when it comes to traveling. They do not allow travel delays or hiccups to affect their well-being or attitude. Once at the client or engagement site, it's game time. Great consultants know how to put travel woes aside to give their best to the client and their team.

Earn the Airlines Miles and Devise Life Management Plans

Don't let life just happen to you on the road; you have to purposefully design life plans. If you let work and travel take over every aspect of your life, you will burn out and become resentful of the career. Plan out your weekends in advance. Schedule quality time with family, friends, or hobbies. Think these things through in advance, and let everyone in your life know what the plan is.

Sign up for major airline, hotel, and car rental loyalty programs then centrally manage accounts. Learn the ins and outs of key travel programs. Strategically plan vacations and side trips as allowed with the loyalty programs. I create a reward travel goal with every project or key deliverable milestone. I track my travel points appropriately, which gives me a celebratory award I look forward to. I have also been able to gift plane tickets or hotel stays to friends and family as needed, which is a great feeling!

Find a prioritization approach that works for you. I use Stephen Covey's time management framework from his book *First Things First.* I spend the first half of each day focused on not urgent, important activities. It has become a life and career game changer.

- Take advantage of the digital tools and hacks when available.
- I could be halfway around the world and answer my doorbell. I check my stepson's homework and have a working session with him.
- Always have a suitcase packed and ready to go. I invest in two sets of toiletries, so I don't have to worry about forgetting to pack my favorite shampoo or deodorant. I have rotating pairs of clothing, shoes, and accessories.
- Invest in a good pair of silencing headphones to meditate or use while working in flight.
- Always have a downtime plan while traveling. Travel with just-in-case work or reading that does not require internet connectivity.
- Maintain firm and client confidences while traveling. Consultants work on very confidential projects and information leaking to the wrong person in the wrong forum can potentially have a devastating effect on the markets. Be extremely cautious when using your laptop or mobile phone in public or having a client or team call discussing strategy.

- Mindfulness or meditation techniques are extremely helpful. I then like to envision my interactions, what success looks like for me at the end of the week, etc., and stay in a positive state.

- Travel light. Evaluate 'just in case' activities. If you haven't read a book or cracked a notebook open in a fifteen-day cycle, revisit priorities. Refrain from traveling with dead weight.

- Be mentally prepared to travel. Flights get delayed or canceled. Planes sit out on the tarmac. Your luggage takes a while to show up, and cabs get lost. It is part of the journey of a road warrior. Expect and embrace it.

Focus Energy on What You Can Control

Earlier in my career, I spent a lot of energy focused on what was happening to me on matters that were out of my control. I got upset from the craziness of traveling and carried that energy around. It created an atmosphere that made it difficult for me to get things done. Travel today has become easier. I do not allow delays to affect my well-being. I have built-in workarounds, buffers, and activities planned in case of any unexpected dead time.

Create Life Hacks on Your Own Terms

After many years in this field, I've learned how to create room to spend time with my family and have a career.

Is my style the textbook definition of work-life balance? Probably not. But it works for me. Seek out work and life hacks. It may take several tries of differing techniques and points of view, but if you focus on it, you will find tactics that work for your lifestyle. One of my heroes of the life, work, and career tactics is the king of experimental hacks, Tim Ferriss. I highly suggest you check out some of his work. Below are selected practices based on how I've created some semblance of balance.

- Set aside time to reflect and rank what is important in your life.
- Once you have identified your priorities, stick to them by creating boundaries in your career. Honor boundaries; if you do not, no one else will.
- Learn the difference between non-chargeable hours and value-added hours. Just because you spent fourteen physical hours in the office or at the client site, doesn't mean you bill fourteen hours to the client. It's important to know the difference and spend your time wisely.
- Even with boundaries, at times you have to be flexible as needed with your engagement or practice as an exception to the rule.
- Leverage the power of anticipation. Accept that things will sometimes not go as planned: you will miss that flight or have a deliverable that is taking longer than originally scheduled to complete. If you constantly plan for both sides of the coin, it helps mitigate unnecessary stress or false expectations.

GIVE UP THE PURSUIT
OF PERFECTION;
INSTEAD, FOCUS
ON THE PURSUIT OF
EXCELLENCE.
SEEKING PERFECTION
IS AN EXHAUSTING
HAMSTER WHEEL OF
DECEIT.

Find ways to celebrate. Go and explore the world. Immerse yourself in other cultures. Give yourself permission to be silly. Spend time with your significant other, or curl up on the couch with a good book and hot chocolate. Volunteer. Visit friends or family you haven't seen in a while and take in some good laughs. Go to a spa or to the movies—whatever brings you joy outside of work.

Focus on Your Health and Wellness to Fine-Tune Performance

While consulting is a very rewarding career, you have to be mindful of the mental and physical toll if you allow it. If you want to create a long-term career in consulting— or any demanding profession—longevity is key to your overall success. Try to avoid running at full tilt without the proper gates in place.

The Dangers of Workaholic Tendencies

In Asian countries people working themselves to death is a real phenomenon. In Japan it's called *karoshi*; in China, self-induced suicide from overworking is *guolaosi*. According to the *Power of Full Engagement* by Jim Loehr and Tony Schwartz, "It is not the intensity of energy expenditure that produces burnout, impaired performance, and physical breakdown, but rather the duration of expenditure without recovery."

Over the course of my career, I know of five cases of extreme illnesses such as heart attacks and lung collapse where overworking exacerbated preexisting medical

MAKE IT MECE

Maintain Optimum Health and Wellness

- Develop self-care health and wellness rituals. Work with a nutritionist or physician if needed. Prevention is key to good health.

- Food is the biggest lever for you to pull and keep your body in tip-top shape.

- Seek and schedule professional mental health support if you need it. There are even counseling services available via SMS text. Most large firms also offer employee assistance programs as a standard employee benefit.

- There are online exercise programs accessible via laptop or mobile phone you could use in your hotel room if you do not have access to a gym.

- Take mandatory mental breaks throughout the workday, even if it is for five minutes. Try exercise techniques like Braingym.

- Seek fun ways to regularly train your brain with enrichment activities such as chess, crossword puzzles, Sudoku, or apps like Lumosity.

- Drink tons of water, consume supplements/vitamins as prescribed, and eat whole foods. Regularly detox or fast to reset your system as prescribed.

- Purchase ergonomic-friendly business and travel equipment.

- Find ways to declutter and de-stress in all areas of your life.

- Stop and listen to your body.

conditions. I have also seen some consultants take better care of deliverables or a cell phone than their own health. Creating a framework of accountability for health and wellness in partnership with your physician will pay exponential dividends in the long run.

Refrain from developing life habits and being around people that deplete your natural energy or health. This includes excessive drinking, consuming artificial foods, or associating with negative people. These elements over time show up as foggy brain, increased anxiety, and lower than expected performance. It shows up in your decisions and presence when you're not operating at full capacity.

CONSULTING LEADER INTERVIEW...

Fireside Chat with a Partner

Kris Pederson is a partner and strategy practice leader at a global management consulting firm. A Harvard Business School alum, Kris has twenty-five years of management consulting, auditing, financial analysis, and corporate board experience. Kris was recently awarded the coveted Consulting magazine's 2016–2017 Lifetime Achievement Award.

In this interview Kris uses the analogy of a business doctor to describe the profession, share how motherhood has changed her as a leader, and provides insights on how she stays in shape while on the road. Kris demonstrates how she keeps a twenty-thousand-foot view of life front and center when it comes to managing a career, family, and prioritizing her health.

Q. Please share how you decided to go into consulting. Is it everything you expected it to be?

A. As with all of my colleagues graduating from business school, I figured that I would do my time as a consultant with this crazy lifestyle for three to five years. And then one of our clients would hire us; we'd get out of it or launch a business at a great level and go from there. I am still in it because it's so much fun. That's what indeed keeps us going. It's the never-ending fast track, and it never ends. That makes it exciting, and I learn something new every single day.

I am around amazing people that keep me learning, so it's an ever-learning situation that is inspiring. The project base work is really fun too. We work on cases. On the strategy side, cases are anywhere from six or eight months to a year. That was fun earlier in my career because you got to engage with so many different projects.

Now as a more senior partner running a practice, I get to hear about the whole portfolio of amazing work our consultants are doing. That's just fun. It's crazy, but it's really fun and invigorating, and it's an always continuously learning world.

Q. Share the best career advice you received from an unlikely source.

A. I think it would be from my mom. She would always say: *Make sure that you really love it.* My mom always has my personal wellness on her mind. Sometimes I would say to my mom: *This week I will be in Tel-Aviv, next week I'm in London. I am killing myself on this, so I can't make that dinner, Mom, because I will be ... wherever.* And she would just look at me and say: *You're killing yourself. You're at the place in your career that you don't have to anymore. Do you really love it?*

I think when it gets to be not any fun and you don't love it ... it takes so much out of you that you have to make sure you really love it. Maybe that's the trite thing to say and think about, but it's such an all-encompassing career, I think making sure you truly love it is critical. Otherwise, this is such a great springboard to so many other roles. When it starts not to be fun and when it starts to be too hard on relationships then use that springboard. Or keep loving it and figure out ways to make it work for you, which I feel like I have done over a long career.

Q. Describe the one career experience that has shaped your values and how you do business today.

A. Being a mom to my daughter, Jordan. When my daughter came along, it changed everything for me. Going from the workaholic life where my friends were all my colleagues, definitely married to the job to *Oh, my goodness. I now have this life. I have a daughter; I have a husband now.* So this notion for me of building a more balanced working world really became my purpose. I think it absolutely changed me.

Honestly, I think she's why I am still in this all-encompassing profession. It forced me to think about how to do the job differently, how to balance, how to not always have to be gone, how to call into a meeting versus needing to be there, how to split the difference on a two-day meeting that's not critical for me, to say I will be there the first day and be remote the second day.

When Jordan was born I also looked for roles, even if not the nirvana role, where I could add value but not have to travel so much. I was a partner for a couple of years at that time and my mentor, Peggy Vaughn, helped me land the next nirvana role that I could do from home. I still didn't want to travel to clients, because Jordan was two. My husband was working, so I did a quasi-staff role with limited travel. That was a great thing that my mentor did for me.

Q. As you grew up in consulting, what is the most common, career-limiting blind spot you have witnessed in your peers and colleagues?

A. I think the blind spot that consultants—often strategy consultants—have is that the best consultants are those who gain consensus for their ideas with colleagues and clients—not the ones with the very best ideas.

Young consultants want to be the smartest persons in the room. Maybe you are, but first-year consultants, clients are smart people. If you come in with external analysis suggesting something and you position it like you know something, it's a complete turn off when you come in with that data for a conversation sharing insights versus being smart. Having meetings where you are just talking, listening, asking really good questions. If you have something you want to share like research you did, present that in the context of sharing. I see so many young consultants crash and burn because of an arrogant approach versus being insightful and personable.

Young consultants that are tell-you-how-smart-they-are arrogant rarely succeed. Most of them fail miserably and get out of the profession because they have all the answers but nobody wants to be around them and hear from them.

Q. What is your secret travel tip to help create a sense of work-life balance while you are on the road?

A. I am a fanatical exerciser. I am fanatic about doing something every single day. When I am on the road, I will sacrifice an hour of sleep to get in the gym. That has been so important to me being incredibly fit, getting that in the morning. Turn my music on and running on the treadmill. I've turned it into two things. First, it's my time for myself to turn on CNN headline news when I am on the elliptical, get that half hour catching up on the news. And the other thing is, there was a tip in a magazine article about keeping your brain stimulated to prepare for a big presentation, get on the treadmill and think about it. I thought that was really cool because part of my routine when I work out is to bring my presentation with me. I go through the presentation every morning when I am on the elliptical. That could be my little secret. I get my exercising in, I am prepping, I get it in my brain, I am full on, and there are no distractions for that thirty-five to forty minutes. I am fresh and ready to rock and roll for the meeting right after I get out of the gym.

Sometimes, I take the whole PowerPoint presentation with me. Sometimes, if I am just going to do a speech, I take my one-page outline and make myself say it while I am working out, just in my head. I always do that instead of sitting in my room just going through the presentation while I am eating breakfast. I also have a bike in my home office, so if I have to listen to a broadcast meeting or answer emails, I get on my bike. When I fly abroad, I get off the plane, I go to my room, put on my exercise clothes, and the first thing I do is hit the gym. It's consuming; I think about it all the time. I consistently sneak in exercise because it is hard to get in enough exercise in this profession. It's been my habit for over twenty years.

5

Celebrate Moments with a Happy Hour

The more you celebrate your life, the more there is to celebrate.

—OPRAH WINFREY

Jennifer Maddox, a strategic transformation leader, says it best. "I think it's not just the celebrations and dinners; it's the relationships you build with your teams and how you celebrate them personally, with your words and actions."

Even though this chapter is called happy hour, I am not talking about drinking alcohol as a means for celebration. While drinking is one way to celebrate, to thrive in this profession, you have to create time to celebrate in a wide variety of ways. An unwritten rule is to create happy hours to regularly celebrate big and small wins on a weekly, sometimes daily basis. I wish I had begun to celebrate often earlier on in my career. I would go weeks at a time, sometimes years, grinding to the ground. While I made great progress along the way, I reserved celebrations for major life milestones. Life became harder. I became unhappier and started burning out.

> **Happy hour:** a marketing tactic of offering reduced price food and beverages at restaurants and bars during a pre-determined increment of time during the day.

"Receiving positive feedback from clients or co-workers is always something to celebrate. When you get a thank you email, star it or label it so you can come back to it in a low moment and remember why you do what you do, even if the major accomplishment is one you're still waiting for."
                                                              —Melody Godfred

Only celebrating major life milestones sometimes means celebrating once a year—if even. Great consultants celebrate often, multi-dimensionally, and they celebrate others. Celebrate moments like when you caught a flight and made it home just in time to tuck your kids into bed. Or when you cleared your inbox. Or had a very successful client meeting.

After I started allowing myself to celebrate more frequently with others and for others, life began to change. Regular celebratory moments create momentum to face challenges.

Take time to recharge and refresh with friends, family, and colleagues. Make sure you don't check your emails or do work while celebrating!

According to Dr. Alex Korb in *Psychology Today*, there is neuroscientific evidence that "gratitude, particularly if practiced regularly, can keep you healthier and happier. Feelings of gratitude directly activated brain regions associated with the neurotransmitter dopamine," which controls the brain's reward and pleasure centers. "Increases in dopamine make you more likely to do the thing you just did. So once you start seeing things to be grateful for, your brain starts looking for more things to be grateful for."

Conversely, when you don't celebrate, life begins to wear you down. You start dreading flying out to work, disliking your team, the work, or your firm. Suddenly you're ready to quit when all you probably needed was downtime to reflect and cherish key moments. Incorporating frequent celebrations changes your mindset on life and helps you operate on a higher energy plane.

ALWAYS FOLLOW RULE 6; DON'T TAKE YOURSELF SO SERIOUSLY.

— Benjamin Zander and Rosamund Stone Zander,
  The Art of Possibility

Be generous and present in your celebration of others. Appreciation and gratitude begets more to celebrate. It's a simple equation. Take time to celebrate both big and little things because consistently celebrating with gratitude makes life worth living.

CONSULTING LEADER INTERVIEW...

Fireside Chat with a Partner

Marcelo Fava is a partner at a leading management consulting firm. With over eighteen years of consulting experience, Marcelo was born to Argentine parents in Cleveland, Ohio, grew up in Argentina, and after earning a degree in political science from a university in Argentina, earned a master's degree in public policy from Duke University.

In this interview Marcelo highlights how he made the transition from the public sector to consulting, shares his most memorable project experiences, and discusses how he helped build a consulting practice from the ground up to over four hundred consultants.

Q. Share how you decided to go into consulting. Is it everything you expected it to be?

A. I got into consulting by random accident. I am originally from Argentina, and my background had always been in the public sector, local government, and politics in my hometown. After graduating with my degree in political science, I had moved to Buenos Aires and worked at the Department of

Treasury for the federal government. My goal was to come to the US and work in the public sector here with one of the big government agencies in Washington and then eventually go back home. While I was at Duke, I had an internship with the Government Accountability Office (GAO).

As graduation from my masters was getting closer, I had an offer from a federal government agency. But all the consulting firms were recruiting at my school, and they did a really good job getting everyone's attention on what a career in consulting meant in terms of the diversity of experiences. I decided to give consulting a shot for two years and then go back to Argentina or work in the public sector here in the US. Eighteen years later I am still in consulting, so I never left.

Consulting clearly exceeded all of my expectations. The opportunities you have to learn new skills, acquire deep content expertise in particular industries, and work on the biggest problems facing Fortune 500, Fortune 1000 companies are unparalleled.

Q. **Share a story of your best project team experience and worst project team experience.**

A. My best project experience was at a major wealth management, global company. They were doing an entire (front, middle, back office) transformation of their business, technology, and operations; they decided to outsource most of the large components of their infrastructure to a few third parties.

I was lucky enough to land the program director role and had over forty people from my firm working with me. There were about three hundred people in the program. I was a senior manager and not yet a partner or principal, but I was able to set up the team the way I wanted to. And it was a very, very diverse team; we had people from all sorts of backgrounds, experiences, orientations. And this project was in the Midwest.

Here's a good and funny story that illustrates the diversity of the team. One day we went out to eat a late dinner after a long day of work; we had a Latino (me) and an Asian lady, an African-American lady, and a couple of white guys.

The server comes over, and she says: "Are you all friends?"

I guess she had never seen a team like that before—it was a small town in the Midwest. But the point is when you're able to put together a team with that kind of experience, expertise, inclusiveness, and diversity that's when the best outcomes are produced. Our clients loved that; they actually talked about it openly. And we still have solid friendships with many clients there. That was about ten years ago now, and we are still good friends with them. I know about their kids, they know about my kids. We exchange messages and cards for the holidays, birthdays. Some of them have moved on, going to other firms and different things, but the friendships never change. We were there for almost two years working with them day in and day out, and it was the most rewarding experience on a personal and professional level.

My worst project experience was the formation of a joint venture of two companies after the financial services crisis in early 2009. It was my worst project experience because there was a lack of proper understanding of what the clients wanted to achieve and what we as a firm wanted to achieve. We had to put a team and proposal together in short order in one weekend; there was never a very detailed proposal in terms of expectations, expected outcomes, and how everyone was going to work together.

There were a lot of leaders from my ex-firm on the engagement, and we just wanted to win the project so bad that we simply went with the flow. Two weeks into the project the whole team was miserable; I was certainly miserable, and the engagement team was in poor shape. We clearly did a poor job focusing on what the right outcomes needed to be and how we were going to get there working together. It was two different companies, two different cultures, one from each side of the joint venture, the third-party law firm, and us as consultants. We were just caught between a rock and a hard place, and we couldn't really add any value. That was just too much to coordinate, and the communication across all the teams was very poor; eventually we were let go from the engagement. So the bottom line is when expectations and outcomes are not well-defined in advance, and when there isn't a clear leadership team in place, the chances of success are small to none.

Q. What would you say you've learned from both of those experiences?

A. What I learned is that you have to sit down and slow down when you're starting engagements, when you're putting teams together, when you're working with clients on high-visibility topics. Ask all the hard questions up front: Do we have all the right people with the right skills? Do we have the right expertise? Can we really help them?

It's not about making a sale; anybody at the end of the day can win an engagement. But not everybody successfully delivers an engagement while achieving the right outcomes. You really have to focus on the value that you bring to the client.

Thinking back to my worst project experience, I think the root cause was that we just wanted to win it. Every other competitor was there, it was in the news every day, and we just wanted to be part of it. And that was the mistake we made. We brought in the wrong people with the wrong expertise—people were not very collaborative. You just have to slow down. Think long and hard about how you as a consultant are going to add value. Our clients expect the best from us, and we should give that to them. And it's not about getting some revenue, or getting some people engaged; it's all about adding value. That's the main lesson learned.

Q. Describe the one experience that has shaped your values and how you do business today.

A. I would say two mentors at two different firms helped me with that. One mentor was a lady with a PhD in psychology. She grew up in a very small and poor town in Texas, and she was a partner at one of the firms that I worked for. She was all about taking the high road; no matter what—when things were bad, when there was disagreement with the client—always take the high road. Just sit down, talk about what went wrong, why we didn't meet their expectations. Sometimes clients are unreasonable, but you still have to sit down and make them understand that. And she always got it done, always took the high road even if it was going to cost some money. Clients are always going to remember your attitude when things weren't going well, not how you behaved when things were going well. My other mentor has a similar style even though he had a different background. The value they both taught me was always doing the right thing, always take the high road, turn the other cheek, and be the better person.

Q. Share your most significant accomplishment to date in consulting that you are the proudest of.

A. I came to my current firm about seven and a half years ago to specifically build a team within a sector of financial services that we didn't have much expertise in. I came in as a senior manager, and I now lead the entire sector for the region. We went from a handful of people to over four hundred professionals across the US, have grown revenues seventeen times over from where we started. I am proud of being able to sit in this chair and lead an entire team of four hundred individuals that we didn't have before. That's four hundred lives, four hundred families, four hundred sets of friends. That is a lot of people and being able to offer flexible opportunities they deserve makes me want to get up every morning and do my best for them. Being able to have this opportunity to influence the lives of so many people in a positive way is something that I never expected when I was growing up back home in a rural town in the middle of nowhere in Argentina. It's more than just building a book of revenue; it's about the stories of all of the people that are now part of a great journey.

Q. Throughout your career, how did you build your personal brand that has really helped you?

A. Your personal brand is going to have to go along with your passions. What is it that you really enjoy doing? One of my passions is coaching sports. So I used to coach both of my daughters in soccer when they were growing up, and I helped out with my older daughter's school volleyball team as an assistant coach. I enjoy coaching sports because it's all about helping people find their strengths, make them more aggressive, make them take risks, make them forget mistakes and keep playing, trying harder every time. Helping them see what they are really good at and what things they need to work on and cultivate.

Same thing in consulting. You have to give your team members feedback on the things they don't do as well, and at the end of the day, it is about helping them find their passion. You only exceed your own expectations by finding your core strengths. A lot of times you find people that are lost, they don't know what it is they're good at. Helping them find what they're good at is one of my passions.

I have many stories where people had been placed on some project, and they come in and say: I don't think I can do this. You sit them down and give them examples of why you think they can, they start believing in themselves, and they go and get it done. Then they come back fully energized, and you see their careers take off. That is priceless. That is why I do this; it is truly uplifting.

Helping people find their strength and giving them an opportunity to prove that they're better than they think they are because every single one of us has tremendous skills is something I truly value about consulting. What you are good at needs to go hand-in-hand with your passion. My passion is to work with people every day whether they are clients, whether they are my team members, whether they are competitors. I love sitting there trying to understand how we do things better and how we help clients.

Q. What is your secret travel tip to help create a sense of work-life balance while you are on the road?

A. I'd say a couple of things. FaceTime is probably the best thing in the world. I FaceTime my wife and daughters twice a day—before the girls go to school and after they have dinner. I don't care where I am; I don't care who I am with. I think it's important for them to know I am present, I am thinking about them, they are a treasure to me, and I am grateful to have them in my life.

The other day I was taking my daughter to a volleyball tournament, and we drove for four hours. At one point during the drive, she said, "You know what, Dad? Sometimes you're not around a whole lot, but it's like you're always there."

"What do you mean?"

"You're always there. You know which test I am having, you know when I need to go to practice, you know when something went wrong at school, and you know because we are always talking, and it is like you're always there."

Leverage technology. Text them a picture. *Hey, look where I am*, or *Remember when we came here?* You have to be present and being present means thinking about them and staying in constant contact with them. I also write them cards every quarter at the end of the season. They remember all the messages; they remember the fact that I went to the store, thought about them, and wrote them a few lines. And then they replicate. They start doing the same things to you. You have to find those little things, and it takes a second. That's my tip: just leverage technology and be present.

Q. Any last remarks on becoming a great consultant?

A. You have to have a personality, be open-minded, like to work with people, enjoy working on hard problems, or have quantitative or statistical skills. People should give consulting at least three to five years to decide if they really like it. You have to go through some engagements that are not going to be as good because that's going to better prepare you for your future life.

We all come to consulting one day, and we all leave either because we go to another job or because we've retired as a partner. We are all coming and going; no one is doing this thing forever. For people that decide to come, I recommend giving it a little bit more time. Don't just leave at the first thing that doesn't go well because that's going to help you down the road.

6

Commit to a Consulting Career

Diligence is the mother of good fortune.

—Benjamin Franklin

Consulting is a demanding profession that is hard to sustain. Before you begin on any new journey, ask yourself why consulting? What type of experiences do you want? Why do you want to solve problems for a particular client or work at a specific firm?

Why Consulting as a Career?

Consulting is unique given the many different pathways and choices available within the profession. Consulting can help you gain significant experiences in a short amount of time. Consulting can be just the interim career step you need until you figure out your next move. Consulting can also be a long-term, life journey. As illustrated in

Due diligence: an extensive analysis or study of a particular business scenario to determine the most optimal solution; commonly used with merger and acquisition or investment business problems.

the various consulting leader stories throughout this book, success in consulting doesn't have to be a linear career path. You can always leave and come back to consulting as you see fit for your career.

I knew I wanted to be a consultant since college for reasons that still ring true today:

- ◆ I enjoy solving complex business problems.
- ◆ I wanted variety in the type of work I do, the people I work with, and the challenges I helped solve.

- ◆ I wanted to make a significant impact on the business world and make my clients successful.
- ◆ I wanted to work in an environment that forces me to stay current on the latest trends and world events.
- ◆ I wanted to become a business badass.

What Type of Consulting Experiences Do I Want?

Once you have determined why you want to go into consulting, decide the best way that you would like to obtain those experiences. An unwritten rule in consulting is decide early on how to be positioned, both internally in a firm and externally out in the marketplace. Use the positioning curve in Figure 7 to help you best determine your marketing position.

From a positioning perspective, I have always been on the transformation side of both strategy and implementation consulting engagements. I decided it was best that I positioned myself to focus on transformational programs in the HR function because it was work that I found interesting, clients I enjoyed, and was a growing field, particularly for technology organizations. In the last two years I pivoted to an internal consultant role that has allowed me to gain the perspective of the client side in order to be a more effective consulting leader.

Why This Client? Why This Firm?

Decide on your desired consulting experiences, what types of firms to seek employment with, which indus-

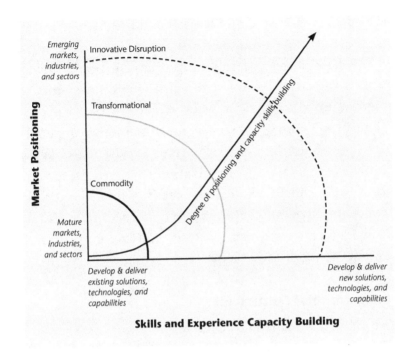

FIGURE 7. Positioning Curve

tries and types of clients you would like to work with. Which firms provide these opportunities that best align with your needs? Here are things to consider when conducting due diligence toward working for a particular client or at a consulting firm: explore formal and informal channels to conduct due diligence about targeted consulting firms or clients, attend public firm events or webinars, search the Internet, and connect with current firm employees.

Whether you are an independent consultant or work for a large firm, make sure you know your competition and clearly articulate your value proposition regardless of level. While being focused on a broad array of knowledge areas helps cast a wider net, depending on the specific industry and market conditions, there may be value in niche areas of expertise.

When I was conducting due diligence for a consulting firm, I wanted to work where my points of views and contributions were valued, work for prestigious brand, and learn from some of the smartest people on the planet while having various experiences. Know your *why*. Choose an organization that will meet your long- and short-term career needs when recruiting. Make employment decisions based on the total package. Consider elements such as firm culture, subcultures, and maturity of the practice, not just compensation.

Importance of Cultural Fit

An unwritten rule is to conduct historical research on the various firms and practices. Understand a practice's core values, culture, and rituals by tracing back to its founding roots and the evolution of its journey. This is particularly true when there have been spin-offs, acquisitions, or other consolidation activities within the last ten years. In a millennial branding study, 43 percent of HR professionals believe cultural fit is the single most important attribute to understand during the recruiting process.

The cultural fabric of an acquired firm absorbed into a publicly-traded company will be vastly different from the culture of a small, family-owned business that consolidated with a large private partnership. Those differences surface in the political climate of an organization in a myriad of ways including leadership appointments, decision-making processes, and what behaviors

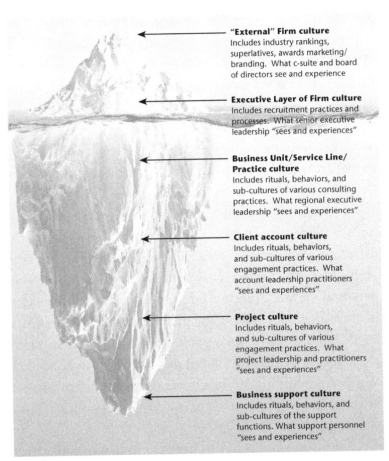

"External" Firm culture
Includes industry rankings, superlatives, awards marketing/branding. What c-suite and board of directors see and experience

Executive Layer of Firm culture
Includes recruitment practices and processes. What senior executive leadership "sees and experiences"

Business Unit/Service Line/Practice culture
Includes rituals, behaviors, and sub-cultures of various consulting practices. What regional executive leadership "sees and experiences"

Client account culture
Includes rituals, behaviors, and sub-cultures of various engagement practices. What account leadership practitioners "sees and experiences"

Project culture
Includes rituals, behaviors, and sub-cultures of various engagement practices. What project leadership and practitioners "sees and experiences"

Business support culture
Includes rituals, behaviors, and sub-cultures of the support functions. What support personnel "sees and experiences"

FIGURE 8. Learn What is Beneath the Cultural and Subcultural Layers of a Firm

are rewarded. Same applies to independent consultants conducting due diligence on new clients.

Importance of Understanding Subcultures

While a prestigious firm may have a great reputation, what makes or breaks your experiences are the local projects, leadership teams, and practices you are exposed to. Understand the iceberg model of firm cultures. The culture displayed externally is seen in the rankings and at recruiting events. The culture may look very different underneath the surface. The lower you go into an organization, the more you see the subculture in action. Sizing up the subcultures of a firm is what you want to get a handle on during recruiting phase. Network aggressively to get an initial impression of the practice, projects, or leaders that you are being recruited into.

It is common to know two different people that work for the same consulting firm but end up having vastly different experiences. You want to join a practice that aligns closer to the external firm reputation and/or your personal values. Another unwritten rule: in some cases it may be worthwhile to wait for another opportunity at the same firm to open up in a different practice than to go into an area that is not aligned with your values. While transferring out of a particular practice or project is an option, it could take years and a lot of political positioning to do so.

Jennifer Maddox, a transformation consulting leader, says it nicely: "Prepare yourself; figure out the type of people you work well with. It's one thing to want to get on a cool project, but it's another if the people on the project are difficult to work with because you're going to have a miserable time."

Maturity of the Practice and Its Offerings

Weigh your options based on the current stage of your career, future goals, and maturity of the practice, firm, or client environment you are seeking to join. An unwritten rule is to recruit with a specific consulting practice or client environment based on both career and experience fit. Although a consulting firm may be well known, understand the perception and position of its offerings in the marketplace.

For a seasoned professional—someone with eight-plus years of management consulting experience—going into a mature practice may not always be the ideal scenario. Current timing of market conditions plays a big factor in career decisions. If the external market has peaked and you join a practice that is the market leader in a specific space, chances are there is internal saturation. It will be tough to differentiate—or get promoted—in that environment and increases chances of hyper-competition among peers.

For an individual with solid expertise, joining a firm forging into new territory is a strategically good option to consider. The opportunities to use your expertise to shape and influence in unknown territories while building your brand might be a risky yet rewarding tactic.

For less-experienced consultants—five years or less—a mature practice is usually an optimal environment to learn a tremendous amount in a short amount of time.

Understand Your Earnings Potential

Seek credible sources to gain insights in your local market for your earnings potential. While blogs, online forums, and word of mouth provide general direction, your earnings potential is situational. Speak directly with recruiters who understand the local markets to give you a more accurate figure. Research the financial health of the firm and practice. Bonus structures, raises, and promotions are funded based on the financial health of the practice or the firm. When you are at the point of the interview process to discuss compensation, get specific. In some firms you may not have access to a particular bonus structure until after you have been employed for a year. Understand the fine print of the offer, particularly where there are variable pay bonuses, stock options, college tuition, and other discretionary benefits.

CONSULTING LEADER INTERVIEW...

Fireside Chat with a Partner

Karyn Twaronite is a partner, global diversity and inclusiveness officer, and member of the US executive leadership committee at a leading global management consulting firm. Karyn is responsible for maximizing the diversity of professional services employees by striving to continually further enhance her firm's inclusive culture across 150 countries in areas including the Americas, Europe-Middle East-India-Africa (EMEIA), Japan, and Asia Pacific.

Karyn is a thought leader and frequently consults with clients on diversity and inclusiveness matters. Her insights have been featured in the *Financial Times*, *Forbes*, *New York Times*, and dozens of other publications. In this interview Karyn shares thoughts on what it takes to succeed in consulting, provides helpful advice for working parents, and explains how inclusive leadership helped shape her career. Karyn also shares thoughts on how to conduct due diligence during the recruiting process from a diversity and inclusiveness perspective.

Q. Please share how you got started in consulting and what prompted you to come into this profession. Has it been everything you expected it to be?

A. I knew early on that I wanted to work for a large, successful, multinational business. I joined the accounting side, particularly in taxation, because I knew that I wanted to become a CPA and taxation was something that interested me. Working for this type of firm allowed me to see a variety of clients and provided me with training, learning opportunities, and the ability to work around the world. I also get to collaborate with really smart and interesting people every day. It absolutely has been everything that I expected and hoped it would be.

Q. What was the one skill you perfected that made all the difference to accelerate your success?

A. We all work at being successful every day. Asking good questions and really listening to responses is critical. Listening helps show someone that you value and respect their opinions.

Earlier in my career, I was given permission to ask questions so that I could get better at my job and learn more. As my career developed, I continued to be curious. I asked questions of clients as well as colleagues of clients so I could learn about their business and be the best service provider that I could be. Asking questions, listening, and observing how people work and lead over the years played a pivotal role as I developed my acumen as a team leader, client server, and client-facing person representing my firm.

Q. What is the one secret travel tip that helps you create a semblance of work-life balance while on the road?

A. I think it is really important to stay super organized and connected to my team so they plan their work in advance. It's also helpful to be organized at home so that my family plans for my absence. They say 95 percent of human happiness is managing expectations. I believe it's really important to manage the expectations of my husband, my son, or others that may be helping us such as my parents.

Since I've started traveling significantly due to the nature of our business, I've always kept my son involved with my travel plans. I tell him where I'm going, when, and who I am going with. It's helpful for kids to see the good side of working and to understand that it's not just a hardship or something that takes their parent away from them. He understands the benefits of working and begins to see it as enriching and intellectually stimulating. And yes, work can be complex and strenuous, but there are also really interesting learning opportunities when encountering so many different cultures, people, and stories.

Every time I come home I bring pictures and funny anecdotes from my trips. My son always asks me, "What did you learn? Who did you meet? And do you have any good stories?" He cannot wait for me to get home. He gets to experience my work through his eyes.

Today, even though he is a bit older and more mature, he still looks forward to hearing about my travels. It gives us real fuel for an ongoing dialogue. Having a traveling parent is tough; I know firsthand as I grew up with one. But while it may be difficult in many areas, it also provides a true point of connection.

Q. For aspiring consultants looking to get into consulting and currently recruiting, what is a diversity topic or issue that is often overlooked in professional services organizations like consulting firms?

A. Aspiring consultants should authentically reflect on what aspect of diversity and inclusion is important to them. What is an important value to me might be different for someone else. I suggest they ask questions like: *Can you tell me what your diversity and inclusion program is like? What aspects of diversity are important to your organization? What type of differences do you value? How does diversity and inclusiveness work* *at your firm?* Words really matter. By asking questions you get a deeper understanding of how much a company values diversity and inclusion (D&I).

It's also important to understand that diversity is about all types of differences. It isn't just about gender or placing a label on one population; it's about people. Diversity is about whether you will be valued for being an individual. It's about who brings their differences and opinions to work.

I also suggest comparing your values to the values of the diversity programs of the firms where you're interviewing. Are you going to be valued for being an individual or for conforming? Can you bring your whole self to work? Try to find a supportive and inclusive environment where you feel comfortable enough to be yourself, and you will be far more successful.

Q. **What is the one pressing hurdle service organizations like consulting firms must still face to overcome issues regarding diversity and inclusion?**

A. Just like other multinational companies, consulting firms face the complexity of diversity and inclusion. They have to meet the needs of very sophisticated companies and clients while providing value and innovative thinking. Consulting firms have to stay one step ahead and have the best answers to solve some of the world's biggest challenges, all while being able to work across differences—function, technical, and even borders—to maximize solutions.

Q. Any last remarks for those interested in becoming a great consultant?

A. If you're going to work in consulting, expect to work in a matrixed organization on a number of different teams and with a lot of different bosses. It's important to look for an equitable sponsor in your career, someone who will help you advance within the firm and reach your full potential. Work hard to earn that sponsorship early on. Consistently seek to outperform yourself—triple-check your work, do extra bits of research, slow down, and really assess what you are delivering. Show your loyalty and commitment to your team, to your efforts, and to your solutions.

PERFORMANCE AND CONDITIONING OF GREAT CONSULTANTS

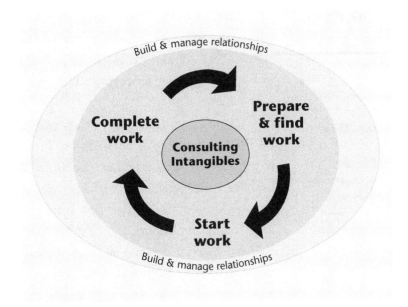

FIGURE 9. The Lifecycle of Consulting Habits, Rituals, and Decisions

Similar to athletes, great consultants follow a nutrition and training regimen designed to create an optimal conditioning environment for career success. A great consultant's nutrition plan consists of (1) the right mindset steeped in the consulting intangibles, (2) a healthy lifestyle for mental capacity building, (3) the right tools and support system coupled with (4) a cultural environment with the right emotional contagion.

Conditioning includes a consultant's collective experience and skills such as exposure to various business problems, client engagements, industries, and project activities. Consultants must learn to upskill, acquire clients, secure projects, manage relationships and expectations, complete deliverables, and close out projects in a cyclical fashion in alignment with the marketplace.

Great consultants have purposeful habits and conscious decisions to build experiences. Experiences become a body of knowledge. Body of knowledge becomes expertise.

The illustration represents the total performance conditioning of the way great consultants work, build skills, gain experiences, and acquire knowledge.

Great consultants have purposeful habits and conscious decisions to build experiences. Experiences become a body of knowledge. Body of knowledge becomes expertise. Expertise becomes a fulfilling livelihood.

An unwritten rule of great consultants is to become purposeful in every aspect of the profession through the conditioning found in daily habits and decisions. Your ability to condition with the right mindset, right habits and decisions, in the right environmental conditions maximize every consulting career and your life. In this section I shared selected conditioning practices, rules, and habits great consultants create to achieve career breakthroughs.

7

Make the Most of Downtime

You don't need permission to chase your dreams.
Go Execute.

—GARY VAYNERCHUK

Great consultants rarely spend time on the bench. But when they do, they treat bench time as a golden window of opportunity to regroup and reflect, network, and get ready for the next adventure. As you can see from Figure 10, to be a great consultant one needs to create habits out of each element and downtime is the perfect time to do so. Similar to an athlete, great consultants treat bench time as practice runs for their next game.

The bench: downtime spent in between consulting engagements; also known as the beach.

Make Bench Time Purposeful

Treat bench with the same level of respect and rigor as a client engagement. Be visible in your practice or local office, work your action plan, and build or strengthen your network.

Create Visibility and Make Connections

Go to your local office every day you're on the bench and connect, even if you don't know anyone or have immediate members of your practice located in your local office. If you are an independent consultant, go into your office or become a member of a shared workspace center such as WeWork or WorkBar. Six degrees of separation guarantees you will make meaningful connections over time.

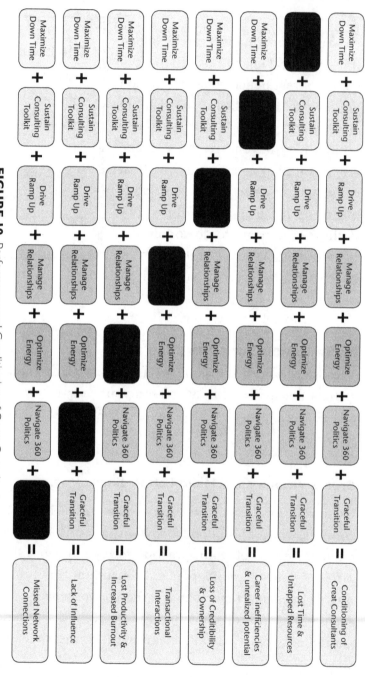

FIGURE 10. Performance and Conditioning of Great Consultants

Do not underestimate the power of familiarity. The more interactions with an individual increases the likelihood to build rapport. Over the course of my career, I've been staffed on three projects and got pulled into one proposal effort just from being visible while on the bench.

Have a Plan of Action

- Learn a new skill, refresh a certification, complete expense reports, write an article, or contribute to a proposal.
- Don't underestimate the importance of mindfulness. Reflection is powerful to help evaluate performance and identify career developmental needs.
- Research and learn about the state of the business, practice leadership, and emerging trends.
- Share information you learned with others.
- Be prepared to travel at a moment's notice. On multiple occasions I was staffed at 6:00 p.m. for a new project and ended up flying out on a 5:00 a.m. flight the next morning.

Build and Strengthen Your Network

- Meet or reconnect with key stakeholders that you have not recently crossed paths with.
- Begin scheduling networking activities and meetups before downtime even begins. Do

not wait until you are on the bench to do this groundwork. Bench time can end abruptly at any time; every hour of downtime is critical.

◆ Stay connected with your local leadership, resource management, HR teams, and any other internal firm contacts. Consultants that stay connected with their internal firm network land unique opportunities and experiences.

Fast Track Your Growth with the Right Projects and Right Leadership

Bench time ends once you are staffed on your next project assignment. Great consultants take the opportunity while on the bench to intentionally get staffed on the right projects with the right leadership culture based on experience and skills development needs. Projects range in scale, size, and length. You could be on a project for two weeks or two years, with two team members or hundreds. The right engagement for you may be different today than it will be three years from now or it was two years ago. At each stage of a consulting career, great consultants determine and seek out the experiences to accomplish career goals or meet firm or client requirements. Seek out engagements that provide these opportunities.

"I believe luck is preparation meeting opportunity. If you hadn't been prepared when the opportunity came along, you wouldn't have been lucky." —Oprah Winfrey

The kicker is finding these golden engagements. Early in your consulting career, you may not have much control over the types of engagements you are staffed on. Project assignments are made based on the needs of the firm, practice, and ultimately, the marketplace. Over time as you build your brand, network, and tenure, you will have more control over engagement selections because you have built solid relationships and areas of expertise. Sometimes getting staffed on an engagement is the luck of the draw; you just happen to have the right skill sets available at the right time. Great consultants:

- Find out who the good engagement managers are in their practice area.
- Do their homework. They know the key challenges and latest industry trends. They attend town halls or industry webinars, carving out time to learn about firm offerings and solutions.
- Network with current members of different engagements to determine any opportunities that may be on the horizon.
- Contribute to practice development and proactively contribute to future proposals or white papers for the clients.
- Figure out the difference between how projects are led versus how projects are staffed at your firm. At the firms I worked at, the expectation was for consultants to reach out to the managers and senior managers for staffing decisions on projects, not always partners.

CONSULTING LEADER INTERVIEW...

Fireside Chat with a Partner

Craig Berkowitch is a partner and vice president of operations at ArchPoint Consulting, a boutique management consulting firm with a global footprint. A Cornell University alum, Craig has more than fifteen years of consulting and industry experience advising clients on complex business transformations across a wide variety of industries.

In this interview Craig discusses how he transitioned from governmental public affairs to consulting, his most pivotal career experience, and shares how he has built a personal brand.

Q. Share how you decided to go into consulting?

A. I learned about consulting after I graduated from undergraduate. I was doing a series of informational interviews with consulting firm alumni who really introduced me to the field of consulting. I always had in the back of my mind that it might be something I would be interested in doing, but I wanted to get some real-world experience under my belt first.

My first job out of college was in Washington, DC, in government public affairs and public relations. That was a great experience giving me a view of how Washington works and then also honing in on my communications skills. We did a lot of work for labor unions, so we were the only unionized public relation firm in the country. At twenty-five years old, I was chairman of the bargain union, doing collective bargaining. It was actually a very, very contentious experience. I knew it didn't really work out for us. I can't imagine that was working well for anybody, so that's what really piqued my interest; it was all about cooperation and empowerment, doing things together, not opposing each other. That's really why I took to that topic. Then I took to that skill set. By that point I knew I wanted to go to business school, but wasn't ready to yet.

My second job in the early '90s was at a think tank whose mission was to help create a human capital development system for the information-based economy. At the time the economy was beginning to shift away from a manufacturing base toward an information base. The organization's founder had the hypothesis that the credit education system in the United States—school-to-work systems, training, and even management systems for the industrial economy—was not going to be the same that we would need for an information-based economy.

One of my projects was looking at high-performing workplaces. Through my research I became intrigued about the changing nature of the workplace and how the ability to push information down to the lowest part of the organization could be very empowering for people but would really change the entire paradigm of labor-management dynamics. So I knew at that point I had found what

I wanted to do and that was help organizations make the kind of changes they need to succeed in the twenty-first century.

I went to graduate school and got an MBA and a master's in industrial labor relations, studying organizational behavior and human capital. One of my summer internships was at a consulting firm, and that's how I got started.

Q. Is consulting everything you expected it to be?

A. Yes. Consulting is at the heart of what I do and why I love ... helping people with their most pressing challenges. It's amazing when you do this for as many years as I have, you see so many patterns and behaviors. Things that people can't necessarily see for themselves are so obvious, and to be able to turn those observations into insights and help people solve that challenge is tremendous and rewarding.

Q. Share a story of the best engagement manager you have worked for and the worst engagement manager you have worked for. What did you learn from both experiences?

A. Mike, the best engagement manager I worked for, was leading a $30 million dollar major transformation project for a consumer goods organization. It was his first major engagement, and he had thousands of people on the team. What struck me about Mike was that he was very humble and the power he had was his ability to be thoughtful and to listen. I thought that was such a great combination because it wasn't about showing people how smart he was or about his ego, it was about the client, their problem, and the consulting team. That was always the priority. He never made himself the priority, and he was very evenhanded. He had a calm demeanor. I felt like he had such a wisdom about him. People wanted to follow him—not just consultants, but clients—so I think that's the best.

In terms of the worst engagement manager, I can think of one person. What made him the worst was his inability to listen; he was very quick to judge, was explosive, and had a temper. Would dress people down and embarrass them. And then would be completely different in front of the client—a Jekyll and Hyde characteristic that was unbelievably frustrating.

Frankly, I never felt the team was at the forefront of his thinking. It was always about the next sale. The hardest thing about him was his unpredictability; you didn't know if you were going to get Dr. Jekyll or Mr. Hyde. He created a culture of fear, and people would really think hard if they were going to bring him some bad news.

I think it should never be about you, and you have to put ego aside to do this job well. To be successful is to make your clients shine and your team shine. The spotlight should be on the people working for you and the people you are serving.

They should get the credit, kudos, and rewards of their good job. If you do that, your reward is the feeling of satisfaction that will come. That's what I've experienced.

Q. Describe one experience that has shaped your values and how you do business today.

A. The most pivotal experience was actually getting laid off right after September 11. I was doing very well professionally three years after business school. Although I wasn't a seasoned professional at the time, I knew I was doing really well because of the rating and bonuses I was getting. The work I was doing was great, my clients were happy, my project managers were happy, and I was asked to do projects. I knew that was my currency; if you get asked to do high-profile projects, your reputation will get you moving forward.

I was asked to work on the most strategic project in the entire firm. We had a new CEO who wanted an assessment of the firm to develop the strategy for the next five years. I was asked to join that team, and I was also asked at the same time to join the team of the new global partner of a particular practice, who I worked for on a project. So I had two internal projects that were a dream for me. I honestly didn't get the fact that I was at risk because I was doing internal work. I was so consumed with: *I'm doing such important work, how could I ever be at risk?* That's the inexperience.

The economy turned in 2000. We had a round of layoffs, and again, I was doing such high profile stuff, I didn't even think twice about it. I felt bad for people that left including my boss. My boss got laid off. But I never thought I would be at risk. And then right after 9/11, we had another round, and I was let go. I was shocked.

It made me understand there is no such thing as being indispensable. It didn't matter how important I thought it was; there is always going to be somebody who could make a decision based on numbers. That made me understand the numbers and the billings and the revenue generation drive the business. If you do good work and you are bringing in the money, then you are at a much better position than if you are not. The good work wasn't enough.

Q. Throughout your career, how did you build your personal brand that has really helped you?

A. Just by being true to my values, who I am, and what I love to do. It allows me to really care about the work and the people, both on the client side and the team side. I think when you are focused on serving clients and growing team members, people want to work with you. I think it's a lot less about the content. Of course you need the content for people to see that you bring value. A lot of the values I bring are helping people come to their own answers.

Q. What is your secret travel tip to help create a sense of work-life balance while you are on the road?

A. I always make sure to call my family every day. It's usually before I go to bed. It doesn't seem complete unless I am connecting with my family on a daily basis even if I am in another city in another part of the country. Keeps me grounded.

Q. Any last remarks on becoming a great consultant?

A. There are so many areas where you can consult; find the area that you really have passion about. A competency for learning is important to become a good consultant. At every stage of your career, you will be learning new ideas and have to be open to learning. If you have that service mindset, I think the job becomes very rewarding. As soon as it becomes about the title or about the money, you get lost and disoriented allowing for a really hollow experience.

8

Build a Consulting Career Toolkit That Lasts

The best way to predict the future is to create it.

—Unknown

As with any profession, you must learn to do your job effectively and efficiently. As I recounted in the introduction, I showed up at my first project unprepared. Building a living toolkit over the course of your career will be critical to your success.

> **Straw man:** an early draft of an idea that is specifically designed for people to poke holes in.

What Is a Consulting Career Toolkit?

Great consultants are in a constant state of 2X-3X growth, meaning that every one year of consulting experience is equivalent to two-three years in industry. To sustain such growth at an accelerated pace, great consultants require an ever-evolving consulting toolkit—a collection of information, resources, and materials that create a competitive edge. The tools of the trade for a consultant are knowledge and expertise.

Benefits of a Consulting Career Toolkit

The benefits of having a consulting career toolkit are immeasurable. You create a platform to quickly access the latest information on a myriad of topics and knowledge areas. Building and maintaining a robust consulting toolkit that is curated based on past, present, and anticipated future career experiences, can help you create a brand of differentiation.

"A man and his tools make a man and his trade."

— Vita Sackville West

In consulting, access to information in close proximity and speed to execution is power. I've created and maintained a consulting career toolkit for most of my career. I recommend creating your toolkit on a personal laptop and using online repositories like Google Drive or Dropbox with consulting firm agnostic tools and reference materials.

Take inventory of the core skills and experiences you will need to gain competence in a specific area of technical, domain, or industry competence. Build out the resources around those skills to support your developmental goals. The mechanics of a consulting career toolkit has information ranging from basics to advanced levels of skills and information.

Great consultants constantly have a pulse on the broader trends in the marketplace and industry. Great consultants tap into particular knowledge areas based on the projected needs of their clients. Being knowledgeable helps great consultants proactively read articles and journals, ask questions, conduct analysis, connect dots, and bring insights into client conversations.

A consulting career toolkit never stays static; it is a living knowledge base. I typically refresh my toolkit every two weeks with various pieces of information I think will be helpful in the future. Periodically review and refresh your toolkit. Reviewing the same information in a different state of mind can result in a totally different perspective.

- Subscribe to the latest top publications and associations of your selected industries to know what is happening.

MAKE IT MECE

Straw Man of a Consulting Career Toolkit

- go-to industry or solution white papers and reports
- template library of sample deliverables, project plans, reports, work products
- analysis tools and templates
- materials from previously attended courses and workshops
- business books including audiobooks and book summaries
- magazine or journal subscriptions
- bookmarked websites, blogs, apps, and other online sources
- (insert your own tools and resources)

- ◆ Create a personal email account; set up alerts, RSS feeds, Google alerts; or leverage social media channels to stay abreast with industry news. Sift through those emails to find gold nuggets several times a month to include in your toolkit.
- ◆ Follow applicable government legislation and financial news that may impact your industry.
- ◆ Learn and understand the language of business and consulting. Listen to public shareholder meetings and leadership webinars; listen to business podcasts and read business journals.

- Hardware and software maintenance minimizes crashes from happening at the most inopportune times. Optimize your computer's hard drive performance, capabilities, and have backups to ensure you always have timely access to the toolkit.
- Take the time to set up an ideal filing structure and get in the habit of keeping files organized.

CONSULTING LEADER INTERVIEW...

Fireside Chat with a Partner

Joe is a partner who advises Fortune 100 clients in the mutual fund, hedge fund, and private equity space at a leading global management consulting firm. With over twenty years of experience and a background in both accounting and product management, Joe shares how he got started in consulting, his must-haves of a consulting career toolkit, and the back-to-basic concepts of what it takes to be a great consultant.

Q. Please share how you got started in consulting. Is it everything you expected it to be?

A. My career started in consulting in 2000 working in investment management. Key industry-driven projects such as the Euro and Y2K introduced me to project-based work when I was just coming out of school.

What I soon realized was that the project work was more fascinating than the day-to-day work. In the day-to-day life in investment operations, you come and do cash, settle trades, corporate actions, and pricing. And that was your day. It was scripted. But project work was neat.

In 2000 I was recruited by one of the Big Four+ consulting firms. I remember not knowing what exactly this entailed, but I thought it was going to be project after project. What I didn't know was that there were three-month projects, but there were also three-year projects. At the end of five years, Sarbanes-Oxley hit, and my practice was sold to another consulting firm, and I was part of that acquisition. I then left for five years to run product management marketing at a software company, and that was another really cool experience because it taught me sales. I knew when I took that job that it was going to be a great learning experience. I was going to gain a lot out of it, but I always knew I would go back to the consulting business as that was where I wanted my career to end up. Since I've come back to consulting, I haven't left again since.

It's a job that is as demanding as anything you'll ever work in, but provides freedoms to guide your own career. There are so many different paths to it; you can jump projects without really changing firms, and jump around in various industries. If you want to learn, grow, and work with people, I think it's a great career. I'm going to hit my millionth mile on Delta this year due to the extensive travel. While there are some downsides to the career, largely it's a great job.

Q. Describe a career lesson learned that shaped how you do business today.

A. Probably one of my proudest moments is when we sent one of our staff, who was about twenty months out of school, to training on systems development life cycle (SDLC) and was so excited about connecting the dots with her experience and training. She was like: *I know what a go, no-go decision is!* I remember how a retired partner taught me that, and now my job is to pass that skill down to younger consultants. It is critical.

Point one: Be a teammate. If you're done with your work and walking out but the person sitting next to you is still there, asking to help them goes a long way. It will pay itself back. I remember I had a proposal due and needed a qualification, and it was five o'clock on a Friday night.

I emailed a colleague and asked, "Do you have this? Can I have a quote?"

He said, "Well, I'll send it to you Monday."

"Hey, don't worry about it, I got to have it done tonight."

And he responded, "Give me half an hour. I'm on the train. Let me boot my computer up."

I will never forget that. Being a team player is something that will get you further in your career than sometimes knowledge, power, or positional power. That relationship power and not worrying about who gets the credit will propel you.

Point two: Take time to teach people on your team. If you learn something and hoard that skill, you are an army of one. If you teach four other people on your team, you're an army of five. Now you've got more depth. Share skills as fast as you can, and build the skill.

Point three: Know where you want to go in this career. So many times you sit and talk to young people or people who are going through the ranks and you see them struggling to decide where they want to go. I have been—to use your phrase—bumped on the head; I've been through that. Sometimes you don't have the answers, but you have to have the courage to take the first step. When you chase your goal, you just have to keep focus and move toward it, sometimes not knowing how it will all come together. But you do the best of figuring it out as you go, gaining clarity into what it has to look like on the other end.

Have a goal, be a good teammate, teach people what you know, and people are going to teach you back. If you do that, you have a good approach to get where you want to go. Maybe you'll get there faster.

Q. What are three must-haves in your consulting toolkit?

A. I created a lessons-learned document earlier in my consulting years and have been updating this living document for over a decade.

Point one: First and foremost, you've got to really focus on communicating. And communicating is listening and really understanding what you're being asked to do, asking questions, and trying to meet that goal. A lot of that is done by talking to people.

Don't have a kickoff meeting, go hide in a corner, and come back with a PowerPoint. Build the dialogue with clients, keep talking, keep asking questions, keep having ideas, and keep sharing thoughts. Be able to run a meeting. So many times you see younger people go to a meeting and not have their bio ready or know how to introduce themselves. It is really easy. (1) Tell them what experience you have that puts you in the chair, and (2) what your role is on the project. Those are two simple things. Write down the things that you're going to say about yourself. This is the first impression you're going to make, and you might as well do it well.

Communication is important, all the way from the bio when you start to after you leave and get feedback on how you did. If you do it, you empower your client to help you—if you listen. Some people think communication is written and verbal—can they write or can they speak? But to me at least it's a lot about listening too.

Point two: I think commitment is important. If you are in the undecided population about a consulting career and you're not fully engaged and not fully committed, your work is going to show that. And most clients who have been dealing with consultants for a long time, they'll be able to tell. We're never going to be perfect, everybody gets that, but you can never fault somebody who's working hard. If you're trying and working hard, your clients, teams, and peers are going to see it.

Point three: Reach high and take risks. Work on the proposal that you don't know, or go with the solution idea that's not the easy one, or take a look at the new software platforms from an up-and-coming provider and not the market leader, not the one that everyone else is buying. Try to do the cross-service line project; go beyond the big project. Those things shape and build you. If you don't ever take those big risks and try to reach for the stars by doing something that's way outside your comfort zone, you're never really going to benefit from it.

Sometimes I hear people say: *Well, I like that ten- to twelve-week strategy work, and that's absolutely fun work.* But you should do the one- to two-year projects every once in a while. It keeps you fresh, it helps build you and creates lifelong friendships, and in some of those projects, you will build a lot of new skills.

So, I think that if you communicate, if you commit, and you take risks to reach out and do things that are uncomfortable, you'll end up getting a lot of skills in this job. If you're in consulting for the long haul, those are big things and are not easily done. All of them I think are tough.

But when you really care, you really try. You turn your computer back on when you're about to shut it off, or you do work when you are on the plane. All those things show you are doing the right thing. It might not always be fun, but at least there will be days when you will leave work and know you did something, you did the right thing. You always take pride in what you have done.

Q. How do you identify and manage relationships with mentors, sponsors, or a board of personal directors?

A. I grew up playing sports and always feel as though managing teams is a strength area. I remember when somebody in college asked: *Are you the captain?* I said: *No, I'm just the one that teaches my teammates accounting in the student union at night. I'm really not that good; those two guys over there, they're really good.*

Where I struggled was managing and finding mentors. I haven't always had those mentors although I have had a couple of great ones over the years. But some of my mentors rolled off and went on a different career path, and then I had other great ones that were point-in-time mentors. I think the toughest in a consulting firm is to find the person who's going to coach you and mentor you. Because there's a lot of great coaches and a lot of great mentors, but you have to find somebody for you.

A great asset for leading and coaching staff is when you manage people differently as not everybody's the same. You have to recognize that some people are going to be motivated by positive feedback; other people are going to be motivated by a challenge. Other people are going to be motivated when you get after them a little bit and say: *Come on, I know you can do better; you know you can do better.*

The people all in for consulting will self-select. They want to learn; they will find you and ask for help. They'll be the ones on your teams who sign up and commit to do a proposal and do the stretch projects. At the end of the day, they're going to stand right next to you. You'll select people who have the same values you have but they don't have to think the same. The more perspectives you have on the team, the better you will be.

I think managing amongst a team is about listening. It's taking the time to talk it through with people and get everyone's input when you whiteboard and things like that. It is about defining solutions and explaining them in simple terms. Also, when we define new solutions, if we are really good, we'll run it by three of our friends. If we sell it to them and they agree, then we just got it. If they come in and say: *Well, we don't agree* then we start over. That's listening. In leading teams it's just including people in the conversation and listening to their perspective and then finding that right answer.

Managing up … you have to seek people out, and it's the toughest part of the job. My personal wiring is to always go do my job. I grew up in a steel town. You go do your job, and at the end of the day when you are done and did your job right, that will be success. In consulting, sometimes you have to let others know that you did your job right.

Find somebody you want to follow. They are probably not going to reach back and pull you along; you have to follow them. Sometimes you have to chase them; sometimes you have to ask fifteen times. Sometimes you have to go work with them, but there's a number of different ways. But find people and don't be passive.

Sales is a contact sport, and I think in a lot of ways finding mentors and coaches is a contact sport too. You've got to go find the people you think have similar beliefs and passions to yours and chase them, follow them. They may not always know that you're looking for a mentor.

Q. What is the craziest experience you have had as a consultant?

A. I was supposed to take a five-hour trip from Irvine, California, to Tampa, Florida, that ended up taking a day and a half. I got on an airplane in Irvine, and I landed in Los Angeles thirty minutes later, and this was not planned. I then took off for Atlanta; we landed in the middle of the night. I slept in the airport, and the next morning I flew from Atlanta to Tampa. It was just one of those things where we had mechanical issue after mechanical issue after mechanical issue.

Q. Wow, that is insane. Did you get points for the inconvenience of that trip?

A. That's the thing; I never even complained! I should have. I was so tired at that point. One of the consulting lessons—which I had not learned—is to go after your points. Some people tell me they get off the plane and say they left their iPhone charger and get five thousand points. Craziest experience for me was always travel.

Q. In your opinion, what are three impactful quick wins that an individual should consider doing to become a great consultant?

A. If you want to make an impact on your team, go help some other people. Go say: *Can I help you?* How many times in consulting have you heard somebody ask you for help? You don't usually find the people asking if they can help you. It is the most powerful thing.

There's one young guy; he's still in consulting. We've worked together across two firms. I remember when he would send email that said: *I've got four hours in a hotel in Minneapolis; is there anything I can help you with?* I always remember him. I would run through walls for that guy.

Q. Any final remarks on becoming a great consultant?

A. It's all about back to basics. Keep it simple.

9

Ramp Up on an Engagement

Life begins at the end of your comfort zone.

—NEALE DONALD WALSCH

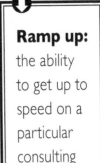

Ramp up: the ability to get up to speed on a particular consulting project or at a client site.

The first hours and days of your project determines your credibility with clients, teams, and leadership, as well as sets the tone of the brand you will build on that particular project.

Ramping up on a project was not something that I truly understood until I watched great consultants in action. I remember starting on the same day on a new project with other consultants. I learned the same answers to questions, attended the same meetings, and read the same documents. But then something happened. Within less than seventy-two hours, consultants began immediately talking the language of the client and building rapport. They started working through the problems asking insightful, spot-on questions. Within a week, some consultants were able to begin immediately delivering value.

I was so impressed that I decided to become the type of consultant that could show up and start dropping gems of value as if I had worked in the client environment for years.

I became obsessed with figuring out what some of these consultants were doing differently than I was. By observing them in action, asking questions, and by trial and error, I learned that a project's ramp-up begins before you ever arrive at the client site. It's a skill I work on to this day by using the following strategies.

Twenty-Four to Seventy-Two Hours before Your New Engagement

The main thing to do before you begin any engagement is research, research, research.

Organizational Research

Within seconds you find a treasure trove of information on the Internet. Assess the information you've pulled together to get a pulse of the client's organizational history, products and services, past successes and failures, and competitors. Get a glimpse of a client's culture with employee reviews on sites such as Glassdoor. Teams may provide onboarding materials or the contractual statement of work.

Stakeholder Research

Look up key client sponsors and other stakeholders online. Learn about the engagement team on the ground by speaking to current or past engagement team members. Gain an understanding of the personal and professional backgrounds of key stakeholders as well as the political landscape of the client organization.

Debrief Your Research Findings

Great consultants take on the mindset of a client during the ramp-up phase and throughout the project to ensure the client's worldview stays front and center. Become laser focused on mentally consuming large amounts of data. Absorb as much as you can. Read through project materials provided, make notes, and jot down key questions.

Your First Two Weeks on a New Engagement

Whether it is your first engagement or your twentieth, create reputable first impressions on every project.

Great consultants know that the first ninety days matter. Be particularly sharp, comprehensive, and insightful. Image wise, look the part to appropriately acclimate at the client environment. The first seven to ten days on a new project makes or breaks your entire experience on an engagement. It is very important to be aware of the habit loop you create on a project. Habits are usually established within the first seven days of a project and are diffi-

Purposefully create and maintain good habits during the first few weeks, whether the project is six weeks, six months, or several years.

cult to break. Purposefully create and maintain good habits during the first few weeks, whether the project is six weeks, six months, or several years.

- Play sponge at the beginning of an engagement and do not make any assumptions. Be open to learning and not being afraid to be wrong.
- Ask insightful questions in your client interactions and team meetings. Do not start trying to solve the problem yet while investigating and validating initial hypotheses.

- Great consultants know that they have to understand the organizational dynamics of the project as a first priority. This includes organizational charts, stakeholder biographies, key players, important alliances, cultural norms.
- Reassess the current political landscapes. Compare your initial external research with internal project information. Understand where your team sits within the paradigm of influence.
- Dig deeper; understand client personalities, motivational triggers, and pet peeves.
- Learn the unwritten rules of your team and the client site. Explicitly ask if no one offers this information to you up front.
- Look for opportunities to share learned insights with your team, leadership, or the client.
- Make sure you know your role on the project as it relates to the rest of your team.

Harness Empathetic Intention during Ramp Up

Before you even show up at the client site and meet your team, leverage the power of intention. Do not just let life happen to you; script it. Decide beforehand what your legacy and impact will be on a project. Even if it is your first project ever at this firm, practice, country, industry, or sector. Even if you don't know much about the client's environment, challenges, or expectations. Focus on the variables you do have control over.

MAKE IT MECE

You get to decide what kind of team player you want to be and the types of relationship you'd like to cultivate with the client. You also get to decide the type of performance reviews you want written about you. Visualize it. Say it out loud. Write it down. Internalize it. Most people start a new project with the wrong mindset or emotional residual from their previous engagement.

If you start a new project thinking: *I hope I will know what I'm doing*, your actions will convey this mindset. When you are unsure, you make unconscious decisions in an attempt to cover up those insecurities which potentially amplify insecurities further. People will lose confidence in you, even though you just walked in the door.

If you start a new project thinking: *I hope I get along with everyone*, your actions will manifest awkward conversations that become interpersonal challenges.

Great consultants seek to create a legacy and impact on every client, project, and team.

Instill Confidence

Your goal at the beginning of an engagement is to create a sense of comfort and confidence in your professional abilities with clients and colleagues. Usually a lack of knowledge creates uncertainty, which is why doing a lot of upfront research will better position you right from the beginning. Establish that you are a reliable, coachable team player willing to learn and know how to have fun. Part of instilling confidence during the ramp-up period is to cultivate, strengthen, and sustain relationships. Big Four+ partner Kris Pederson states, "If you are going to be on a project team at any level, make the effort to get out there and build those relationships in person. Meet your partner in person, meet your superiors in person, get with them, have dinner, look eye to eye and build that one on one engagement, and then it makes the whole virtual engagement model, the flexible model, work so much better."

CONSULTING LEADER INTERVIEW...

Fireside Chat with a Retired Partner

Randy Martin is a retired partner at Deloitte Consulting LLP, after spending thirty-plus years in the management consulting profession. He has extensive global experience delivering projects in Latin America, Europe, and Asia. Randy has recently established his own consultancy focused on the non-profit, charitable, and social enterprise sectors. Randy is also an adjunct professor at Emory University's Goizueta Business School as well as the non-profit initiative leader for Social Enterprise@Goizueta.

In this interview Randy shares experiences and lessons learned that helped shape his career, recounts his recent trip to the White House, and provides guidance on how consultants create a successful career.

Q. Share how you decided to go into consulting? Is it everything you expected it to be?

A. Like many people, I fell into consulting. I intended to pursue an academic career, and I went to Harvard University for graduate school in sociology. Instead life intruded upon me; I ended up getting married. With a child on the way, I found myself in a position of needing to really make some money. I began as an independent consultant doing work for the state of Massachusetts as part of a research team. I started doing consulting in the mid-1980s for a couple of years, and then I found myself really enjoying consulting. I decided if I weren't going to be an academic, then this was the second-best career for me.

I started marketing strategy consulting work with small boutique consulting firms for the high-tech industry back at the time it was taking off. I really enjoyed it, and eventually one of the small boutiques was bought out by a Big Eight firm. I ended up working at one of the big audit tax consulting firms for about six years and then ultimately joined Deloitte and spent twenty-one years at Deloitte.

Consulting was a very fulfilling career, especially before the massive projects like big technology adoption projects, which were interesting in their own right, but I much prefer the more interactive work with client leadership. As consulting projects got bigger and bigger, they got a little bit more structured and routine. I continue to do a little bit of independent consulting now that I've retired, and I only work for nonprofits or social enterprises. I just pick the work that I do so I have a meaningful social impact through the work I do.

Q. Describe the one career experience that has shaped your values and how you do business today.

A. I started my career in consulting doing a lot of workshop based initiatives, working with leadership groups, management groups, and generally working with organizations that were going through change. A lot of managers and leaders were struggling with how to lead during times of change and ambiguity. One thing that kept coming out of those sessions is that I really had a lot of gratitude for being able to help people work through what were clearly difficult situations for themselves personally and professionally. What I learned from those interactions over many years was that you had to treat people with both respect and integrity. I've always prided myself in that I always respected people; it's not my place to judge them. I build good relationships with my clients and project staff.

The other piece I learned when I was in college, where we got steeped a lot in philosophy and theology. I had a Jesuit professor who had us read a book on Gandhi. In the book, Gandhi was being interviewed, and he was asked: *If your ends are just, can't you engage in violence to achieve those ends?* And Gandhi said: *The means are the ends in the making.* In other words, how you do something is just as important as where you're trying to go. I always adhere to that viewpoint; how you do your consulting and interact with people is as important as what you're trying to accomplish. And I still live by these things.

Q. Share your most significant accomplishment to date in consulting that you are the proudest of.

A. I think there are different ways to answer that question. I've done a lot of different types of consulting. Early on in my career, when I was conducting workshops and retreats, it was pretty intense. Just watching people gain new insight and see themselves in a new light was always extremely gratifying.

I recently conducted an executive retreat for the leadership group of one of the largest nonprofits in the country. It was an offsite retreat for an organization going through a tremendous amount of change. After three days we had the group just reflect on what happened over the three days.

One of the executives, who I knew was struggling because they'd been there for a long time and this was a major change for them, said, "I thought I had changed; I realized that I hadn't changed. And now I can see that I need to."

Those kinds of experiences are just really gratifying. So that's one type of impact.

The other type of impact is seeing the impact of an organization. I had led a pro bono effort for my previous firm a couple of years before I retired. The organization was struggling with how to be relevant in minority communities. It tended to be mired a little bit in the past in terms of not keeping up with serving certain demographic groups. A lot of the communities in which they were located as an organization had become heavily Latino, African-American, and refugee. I led an effort to help them develop an overall strategy and blueprint for serving underserved communities. That's work I continued to do on my own for several years, and I still work with them to this day on their diversity and inclusion leadership council that reports to their board. For me, watching this organization gain momentum around diversity inclusion and make a difference in these underserved communities was extremely gratifying. This organization was invited to the Obama White House for a day of panel discussions around what this organization was doing in the areas of social responsibility, diversity, and inclusion. They invited me as one of the few non-employees of the organization to go to the White House and participate in this discussion. I think it was very gratifying and meaningful work.

Q. As you grew up in consulting, what was the most common career-limiting blind spot you have

witnessed in your peers, colleagues, or junior staff members?

A. I think people go into consulting because they like to problem solve. They rush to answers and solving things. Sometimes you have to let your clients struggle through figuring something out on their own. I think one of the things I always tried to focus on was: *How can I structure the way we do our work? How can I structure the questions I ask in a way that helps move my client and their thinking to a point where they can understand the solution themselves?* Just telling them a solution isn't really necessarily going to create their buy-in to that solution if they haven't experienced certain things to get there.

I know sometimes consultants are hired to provide a solution, and that's fine if that's what the project is. My focus had to be more on changing attitudes, mindsets, and behavior. I have always adopted that partnership working model with my clients to help them move in a certain direction.

As the cost of consultants gets higher, there's always a lot of pressure on consultants to just give the answer. You have to resist doing that. That's one blind spot I think consultants need to be aware of. You know what it actually takes to change behavior and really make a difference.

Consultants are hired for various reasons; you just need to be clear about what you're being hired for. And if you're not sure, you need to clarify it.

Q. What was a trade-off or sacrifice you had to make in order to be successful?

A. That's just something that consultants struggle through, right? I say the one thing you have to do is define your relationship to the organization that you're in. Meaning, how much of your time, energy, mindshare, goes to the consulting organization that you work in versus for you personally. I wish I had learned to ask that question sooner in my career than I did.

At some point in my career, I kept thinking: *Well, once I get done with this project or once I get done with that, then I can focus on whatever it was that I wanted to personally focus on.* And then I realized I'd been saying that for about ten years. *This is my life, and if I don't figure out how to do the balance now, I'm just not going to find it.* I remember that insight just kind of hit me. I just started picking and choosing and started to find more balance, which made me happier, but it doesn't come without consequences, right? At some point in my career, I sacrificed the pursuit of success for the pursuit of balance and being happier with myself.

Q. Share your tips and best practices of how you ramp up on a new project or at a new firm.

A. There are similar skills in terms of ramping up on a project and getting into a new firm. I think you need to listen and be observant. And I know that's easy to say, but you really have to go in with a posture of trying to absorb as much as you can through listening, through observing, through talking to people.

A lot of my background is in anthropology, and I think you know going into a new organization whether you're going to work there. Go in as if you're going into another society that has its own culture, norms, and unwritten rules. It has its written rules, it has policies, it has all this stuff, and you have to be attuned to all of that, absorb it, and really understand that as quickly as you can.

The other piece that's really important is having self-awareness. You have to understand how what you do affects the people around you, how you're influencing the area itself because you're part of the interaction. Unless you understand that, I think it's hard to be attuned to either your client or the organization you're participating in.

Q. In your opinion, what will consulting look like in the next ten years, and how should a young consultant prepare?

A. Things are changing so fast I'm not sure I have a good grip on that question. I think a lot more consulting might be done remotely; the model of flying big teams all over the place may not be as relevant as it was for quite a while. There are a lot of people with good skills and knowledge. I wonder if there is going to be an opportunity to shift more toward bringing in independent consultants than a bigger firm. I think maybe there's going to be a bit more specialization. There's always a role for the big firms when clients need a lot of resources. With the technology, we'll be able to do a lot more in a shorter period of time.

Q. What is your secret travel tip to help create a sense of work-life balance while you are on the road?

A. We traveled a lot when I was young and lived overseas a number of times. I guess I didn't really ever have that strong sense of missing being home so much. I was always comfortable being in hotels. Just try to stay connected to what's happening at home.

Q. Any last remarks on becoming a great consultant?

A. I teach a course on management consulting at Emory University, and what I share with my class is that at the end of the day, all you have is your reputation. You've got to treat people honestly and with respect. Even if it's inconvenient in the short-term, it's really very important in the long-term. Doing things with integrity is something that's really important. Just be authentic and honest in your dealings.

10

Make the Best of Life in the Team Room

Players win games; teams win championships.

—BILL TAYLOR

I believe 85 to 90 percent of consulting experiences are shaped by the culture of your engagement team. Period. While you may have great experiences attending training workshops, town halls, conferences, or happy hours, those interactions make up less than 15 percent of your total experience as a consultant. You have to make

Team room: working location of a project team.

the most of your project team experiences by learning from past team experiences, being a team player, and learning how to maximize relationships with different team member personalities.

My Best Team Experience

One of the best teams I ever had was on a very large account on an IT commerce portal engagement with hundreds of consultants. I was part of the testing work stream with eight other consultants. We all had varying skill sets and backgrounds. It was one of the most diverse teams and inclusive environments that I have ever worked in.

From the onset, we worked together well. We met as a team to work on key deliverables and processes. There was an air of ease with the culture of our work stream. We held structured, standing meetings to discuss progress. From the beginning, there were clear roles and responsibilities. The work stream lead shared updates from other work streams and the broader program. There was a sense of trust on our team. Granted, we had one or two individuals with egos, but over time they seemed to smooth things out.

As the project progressed, the work got intense. The problems became more challenging and the client more demanding. Despite the hours getting longer, our team bonded even closer. Although we worked hard, time flew by. We had an inherent interest in seeing each other succeed, helping each other complete work products and deliverables.

We were consistently praised for producing amazing quality work and creating innovative approaches to the system's testing practices. We seemed to get better and better as a cohesive team. During downtime the work stream lead scheduled knowledge sessions in the form of account updates, technical writing classes, or guest speakers from other parts of the program. We created a co-ed softball team, and everyone played one night a week regardless of skill level. A couple of games in, we even got team T-shirts.

I remember being excited to get on a plane every week and go to the client site. Not only was the work we were doing cutting edge, I had an amazing, trusting team. Even though it was over thirteen years ago, those moments still bring a smile to my face. I learned so much on that project while making friends for life. It was so sad when the project came to an end.

My Worst Team Experience

My worst team experience was the ramp-up of a global transformation engagement. From the onset the senior manager workstream leaders didn't trust each other.

Their insecurities played out in competitive battles every day. This dynamic resulted in a permanent fracture that created insider-outsider clique dynamics. It was the most diverse, non-inclusive project team environment I have ever worked in. The creation of cliques led to an inherent lack of respect for the contributions or voice of everyone on the team. People would leave the team room for lunch or for the day, only to be severely criticized and belittled for unfounded reasons. Ideas not thought of by members of the insider cliques were automatically considered crap.

Tensions ran high and long hours felt like days. There was clear favoritism and constant acts of spitefulness, and an air of arrogance combined with insecurities and fear. One could walk in the team room and feel the tension. A project team of less than ten people had the negative energy of thousands. Folks were cautious not to ruffle feathers, and everyone kept their heads down working.

When asked to think of creative solutions, it turned into heated debates over which project lead had the better idea. There wasn't a clear path forward of what success looked like, and the scope of our effort changed several times a week. To top it off, a number of high-level executives continued to rotate through the team room unannounced asking questions. Everyone pretended everything was fine.

I was exhausted every day I left the team room and dreaded going back every week. I fantasized about coming down with some sort of illness or getting hit by a car, just so I had an excuse as to why I didn't have to go back to that team room. But I never found a good enough excuse. It was the worst project experience of my life and the first time I thought about leaving the consulting profession altogether.

The project was originally short-term and was highly visible in my practice, so I sucked it up. Then I kept getting extended. What was supposed to be a three-month engagement became the longest year of my career. Over the course of that year, the dynamics of the project changed as various leaders came in, which did help. Having lived through the earlier days of that project left emotional scars that were coded in my DNA for life. I was mentally exhausted and spiritually disengaged. I was relieved when I finally rolled off that project. I never wanted to see some of the people on that project ever again in my life. Reminiscing about that experience years later still makes me cringe.

In both instances the scope of the project was innovative with a clear, significant impact for the client. The only difference was the makeup of both leadership and individuals on the team. What happens in the team room makes or breaks your consulting experiences. There is an axiom that people do not quit companies, they quit leaders. In this profession, consultants do not leave consulting firms; they quit practice leaders, project managers, and engagement teams.

There is an axiom that people do not quit companies, they quit leaders. In this profession, consultants do not leave consulting firms; they quit practice leaders, project managers, and engagement teams.

How Great Consultants become Great Team Members

According to Adam Grant's *Give and Take*, every time you interact with someone, you have a choice. In his book Grant shares how you get to decide what type of person you will be to that individual: a giver or a taker. Giving aligns with most religions and societal values. Givers are more successful by exerting powerless communication. Great consultants become great team members by always giving. They display this regularly by showing vulnerability, sharing, active listening, asking questions, and showing authentic curiosity about the interests of others.

Most Common Personality Types on a Team

An unwritten rule of being a great consultant and team player means accepting people for who they are, not who you want them to be. Celebrate and leverage people's strengths. Accept weaknesses and learn how to support your team to create highly effective relationships.

Below are eight common personality types that I have come across based on my experiences on a team: dominant, slacker, spotlight/credit stealer, complainer, team parent, drama queen/king, passive-aggressive, and the brain.

Descriptions of Common Personalities, the Judgment-Free Zone Edition

In explaining common personality types, I do not do so judging personality types as either good or bad. On the contrary, I view each personality type as human behaviors that every person has the capacity to possess. I see myself in many of the personality types described depending on situational context or environment. These archetypes are not linear; some individuals can display a hybrid of one or more personality types. I've also included how I learned to build effective relationships with each personality type over the years.

The Dominant

This is the super-organized and sometimes more cerebral than personable individual on the team that tries to force everyone to join them at 7:00 a.m. for breakfast at the hotel. It is usually to make some obscure point such as eating a healthy meal in the morning as a collective will increase the team's output by 10 percent. Or force everyone to stay for dinner on a Monday night after putting in a thirteen-hour workday on travel day to get a head start on brainstorming a deliverable that is not due for months.

The dominant always wants to be right and in control. They will never let a discussion move on unless they have been adequately acknowledged as having the right answers. If they are in fact wrong in an argument, they secretly look for ways to make team members pay for calling them out. The dominant usually have good intentions that rub people the wrong way. They just feel more comfortable when operating in an environment in which they have the most control. Show appreciation for dominants by leveraging their strong organizational skills and need to be right. Help them channel this trait into a meaningful project moment that matters by having them facilitate the client meeting or owning the deliverable.

The Slacker

This individual will do the least amount of work and exert the least amount of effort on the team. The slacker strategically finds ways to maximize their exposure and positioning at the right moment. On the outside looking in, slackers sometimes appear indifferent to the client's problems or the firm's brand. Colleagues may question why a slacker decided to become a consultant or how they got through the rigorous recruiting processes. The slacker is usually the expert schmoozer and expert relationship builder. Because of their ability to build rapport with others, the slacker brings laughter and fun to any environment that keeps them staffed and clients happy.

Slackers will distract from their lack of action because they have great storytelling ability, crack memorable jokes, and make the right comeback one-liners at the right time. In other words, slackers have perfected the art of bullshitting. They only produce at critical moments to appear as if they are actually staying busy and getting stuff done. People usually love slackers because they are fun to be with. Do not get it twisted; slackers are extremely bright and quite strategic. They just do not believe in putting forth any extra effort than what is minimally required of them.

Do not corner a slacker, try to publicly blow their

cover, or take on a project they originally owned and publicly demonstrate that you have done it better. Slackers become very aggressive and find ways to bite back if threatened. Instead, figure out ways to collaborate with slackers by building rapport and trust. Make sure there are clearly defined roles and responsibilities when working with a slacker. When you have gained a slacker's trust, you can do a lot of influencing on your teams and with clients. Slackers are the best individuals to brainstorm with because they usually find the easiest path to get to the crux of complex solutions. Be careful though. Once you have lost credibility with a slacker, it is hard to get it back.

The Spotlight or Credit Stealer

This is the individual on the project that seems to make everything about them. They focus most of their time trying to make moments opportunistic for their career to make themselves look good to leaders or clients, sometimes at the detriment of burning relationship bridges. They find subtle ways to steal credit of ideas, analysis, work products, or recommendations to reframe as if they were the original creator. Spotlight stealers that obtain a little bit of authority leading a team can be challenging for a team to work with. They are the first to take credit for great ideas and also the first ones to throw someone under the bus when something goes wrong. Do not take the actions of the spotlight stealer personally. It is typically mishandled and misdirected ambition that drives this behavior.

I have found that beating the spotlight/credit stealer at their own game is the best way to nip this behavior in the bud to diffuse this tactic. Once a spotlight stealer has their needs met, they seem to adjust appropriately. By shining the spotlight on them publicly by giving them credit for helping shape ideas, they, in turn, feel flattered and automatically return the favor. Create accountability upfront and throughout your interactions with them.

The Complainer or Slightly Paranoid

Because of their dark and cynical nature, this individual typically feels like everything is rigged against them and everyone is out to get them. To the complainer, life is not fair, and the client is not fair. To them the engagement manager or leader is never around or providing enough guidance to the team, the client is not providing enough information, the food in the café always sucks, and the deliverable assigned to them was done so intentionally to make them fail.

The complainer always suspects an ulterior motive despite a lack of evidence. Nothing ever satisfies the complainer. Show appreciation of the complainer by listening to them and being empathetic. Strategically investigate some of their claims, particularly when it is related to the project or a client interaction. The complainer helps identify potential risks or blind spots. Usually if there is a sense that something may go wrong, the complainer called it first. They love reminding people of that.

The Team Parent

The team parent is always looking out for every team member. They're usually the one who brings everyone bagels in the morning and passing out candy in the afternoon. The team mom or dad always has gum, cough drops, or any other random toiletry someone may need. They make sure everyone has access to the needed client files and the calendar invites to standing meetings. The team parent is dependable. They usually get team members up to speed in case they missed anything. They ensure everyone makes their flights and has enough support to complete their work. The team mom or dad is not necessarily the manager but sometimes is. They are often the unsung heroes of the team, and you don't know how you do without their care.

Take care of your team parents. Remember their birthdays, anniversaries, and kids' birthdays. Have the team pitch in to treat the team parent for lunch, dinner, or their favorite sports or musical. If the team parent needs help with a deliverable or research, go out of your way to roll your sleeves up and help them out. Just like a real parent, the team parent wants to be appreciated for their efforts even if they do not explicitly say it.

The Drama Queen or King

The drama queen/king (or prince/princess) is very melodramatic, exaggerating situations and stories. The drama queen/king has the ability to display a full range of emotions on any given business day. They are easy to spot because similar to the Slacker, they do not like to put forth a lot of unnecessary effort. It's the individual who swoops into the team room, plops their bag down, and before you can look up, begins to recount an insane travel story. Find ways to convey trust and confidence to the drama queen/king that they are enough. Acknowledge their stories and the attention they need briefly, but do not feed into it. Redirect the high energy they bring by channeling it as an opportunity to brainstorm ideas as a team.

The Passive-Aggressive

The passive-aggressive generally has a lot of pent-up annoyances and opinions not explicitly shared, such as secretly not agreeing on the team's direction of a deliverables, or having hidden pet peeves based on the actions of team members. But the passive-aggressive does not share what is on his/her mind. Instead, the passive-aggressive finds ways to sneak in subtle zingers during a conversation or in their actions. They sometimes sabotage others at a moment's notice. Work on building trust and being collaborative. If the passive-aggressive is quiet, call them out to participate in the team dialogue. Self-deprecation occasionally works well with some passive-aggressives. Find ways to give them the space and permission to be honest to tell you what is on their mind.

The Brain

This type of individual is usually quiet and keeps their head down. The brain is the first one in the team room and the last to leave. Due to their introverted nature, they like the quiet stillness of being in the team room before everyone else shows up. Whenever there is drama in the team room, the brain is nowhere to be found. They are often the backbone of the team, brilliant, quiet, and humble. You need a file from fourteen months ago that the client gave the team? Chances are the brain still has the notes and can rattle off the content and structure of the document you are looking for. The brain will show up to a team happy hour, nurse a fake drink for ten to fifteen minutes, and then bolt at the first opportunity. The brain tries hard to be social, but their jokes tend to land flat and conversations awkwardly short.

Engage the brain by acknowledging their knack for precision and thoroughness, but the key theme is to give them space and time to do so. They will not stick their neck out on unfounded hypotheses. Do not piss off the brain by asking them to do a client presentation without at least twenty-four hours advance notice. The brain loves to marinate in the thrill of the research, build, design, and data analysis. The brain is usually the best person on the team to lead the research or analysis components of a project; they love it.

CONSULTING LEADER INTERVIEW...

Fireside Chat with a Partner

Nalika Nanayakkara is a partner and practice leader at a global management consulting firm. Originally from Sri Lanka with over eighteen years of consulting experience, Nalika currently advises many of the top ten global asset and wealth management institutions in the world.

In this interview Nalika shares her journey in the profession, the traits she looks for in consultants, and the importance of building trust as well as creating a teaming culture of empowerment and trust.

Q. Why did you choose to go into consulting? Is it everything you expected it to be?

A. Right out of undergraduate school I worked in investment banking at a Japanese bank for three years. In this role, we helped Japanese firms looking for investments and joint ventures in the US. It was a great experience, but then I went to business school. Coming out of business school there were a couple of options; one was investment banking. I didn't think that I wanted to continue on that path. Another option was going to industry, and the third was consulting. I'm sure there were other options, but these were the three big options for me.

Honestly, I chose consulting because I like the dynamic environment and opportunities that come in a consulting firm. When there are emerging trends within an industry, consulting firms do the research. As a senior I got a lot of opportunities to get hands-on with things that are cutting edge in the industry.

The second reason I chose consulting was the diversity of experience. I enjoyed financial services, so I wanted to gain experiences at a number of financial firms and not just work for one. That's why I joined, and honestly, now that

I'm a practice leader, I love my job. You know, it's really like you're running a small business. My firm is a huge, global firm, but it's run like a bunch of small businesses where the practice leaders are really empowered to make the right decisions for our teams, our clients, and the firm. I really enjoy being part of a big firm and being able to run my own show. I don't know what I expected the profession to be, but I love my job.

Q. What was the one skill you perfected that made all the difference throughout your consulting career to help you build your brand?

A. I don't know if it's a skill, but at the end of the day, I think it's trust. When I was a senior, no matter how much the work—whether it was grunt work or not—I went out of my way to do the best job I could. Whoever depended on me to do their work could trust that I would get it done.

When things are going well, you know everybody's happy with no issues. But when stuff hits the fan, when people start pointing fingers at each other, throwing each other under the bus, that's when you have to be a leader. For me it's really being trusted by others and being able to trust other people. I think that's what makes a successful consultant at the end of the day.

Q. In your experience, what are common themes or decision points of why people leave a firm?

What made you stay at those same points in your career?

A. If you have the right culture of empowerment and purpose, honestly, the retention rates are going to be very high. I will tell you that in the last five years at my firm, the people who left our team have been a handful. And sometimes we've had to coach people out because you have to if you want to maintain a certain kind of culture of high-performance and a culture of teaming as well. Not everybody is a fit. In terms of people we've been disappointed to lose, I would say it's a handful. The reasons that they've left are ... I think consulting is exciting because you always do something new. You go to a client, you implement something, and then you leave. There are some people who don't want to build something and leave; they want to own it.

There's been one person, I could have cried when he said he was leaving, but he went to a client, and he's a great client for us, gives us a lot of business, and that's the reason he left. And then, there are probably a couple of other people who've left because of a life event, particularly women, at the senior or manager levels. They've left because they wanted more predictability in their schedules, which I totally understand.

Honestly, those are the main reasons I've seen people leave. I had a child as well, but I didn't have the same desires to leave consulting. For me, my career is intertwined. It doesn't feel like work, so I haven't had the desire to leave.

Q. What are some of your expectations of the dos and don'ts of client deliverables?

A. I worked with someone at my former firm, it was his first job out of school. He was looking for billable work. I was a senior manager. I didn't have any work, but we were doing this project related to client reporting, and there were these huge stacks of papers that needed to be properly aligned and allocated to certain types of client reports, and within those you had to recategorize them to the right context. The client actually wanted them in binders. And you can't just stick them into any binder; you have to be very thoughtful about it.

We needed someone to do it because we didn't have the capacity, so I asked this consultant to do it. Grunt work, putting reports into binders.

When he came back with the output, I was floored. I mean, this was phenomenal. He had really thought about the types of reports, the type of sub-reports, what went together, what were unique, what weren't, what was global, what was pertaining to a particular asset class—I could not believe what a great job he had done.

He left that firm shortly thereafter. But when I came to my current firm to build a practice involved in asset management, I made a list of people I wanted to convince to join the team, and he was number one on my list. Doing whatever you can and giving your all. If you can do that over and over again consistently, that's going to make you successful.

And the second piece, this may not be intuitive, but you have to be social. Consulting is not something where you go away and do something great and come back with the results. Or you go away by yourself or with a team. It's a social enterprise. Teaming means not just collaborating. You give, and you get back; others give. It's not just that you have to like people. You've got to be social. That's something people probably don't understand when they're coming into consulting. It's not just doing analytical, high-caliber work. To get the best out of each other, you have to actually like each other. And that is easy to do if you are a social person and have that DNA in you.

Q. What actionable steps can younger consultants take to build and master the art of influence toward becoming a trusted advisor?

A. Trust is not a game; it's not an art. If you treat it like an art or a game then it's short-term. Trust is in the long-term. You have to be genuine, meaning you have to be yourself. You cannot try to do things because the latest book on management skills told you that that's what you ought to be doing. You can, but that will be short-term.

Second, you have to be fair. You have to really care about the outcome, not just for yourself but for the other side, which could be your peers, people who work for you, people who are above you, or your clients.

The third thing is you have to be generous. On

a Sunday if you know that something needs to be done for a client on Monday you could say: *Oh, it's good enough.* Or you could be like: *You know what? I really have to perfect this. I really have to go above and beyond.* That means you have to generously give up your time on Sunday to do that.

It's being genuine, being generous, and being fair. Those are the three things people should care about. If you want to be a trusted advisor, those three things have to come together over the long-term.

Whether it's a firm or the world, that's how we're going to be successful. But if you do that thinking: *I'm doing it to be successful*, that's probably not the right reason. Again, giving has to be core to any culture. In our practice we built a culture, and we hire the people who have those three attributes. But then we also bring in people who have the potential, and then they learn by experience, and they see it and observe that it works really well and they adapt to that culture.

Q. How did you advise younger consultants throughout your career to gracefully push back, to fight for what they want?

A. It has a lot to do with leadership. When I think about our practice, we're a metrics-driven culture, so for utilization you might have to go to a project for six months, maybe one year. Not just me, but my leadership team would never force people to do something they thought was just not helping them grow personally or professionally. We'd make sure that they had practice development or were working on a thought leadership that gets them excited. And then beyond a year we would definitely not post them to be on a project like that.

I don't think it's so much about the pushing back; it's all about picking the right leaders. People tend to jump around because *Oh, that practice sounds so exciting.* But when people leave firms, they leave leadership. Just like that. You should figure out the leadership, the peers, the type of culture you want and other things naturally progress from there.

Obviously you know if you're in a not-so-great environment and you're being asked to do things over and over again that you don't want to do. You have to stand up for yourself. That's just a given. But when they're jumping around, people should pay extra attention to leadership and pick the type of environment and the type of leadership and culture they want to be a part of, not just follow the shiniest object.

Q. Let's say a consultant just joined a firm, how would they know to do this due diligence? What would be some tips you give people to figure out the leadership styles before they make the commitment to work?

A. What you need to do is find opportunities to work with people in the context of something, whether it's the project or an event you're putting together. When you're actually working with someone, you know how they react to unexpected situations, so that's leadership by experience. And the other piece is talk to your peers, talk to other people and ask them for honest feedback about different leaders. When things are great everybody's happy; when things go south, it's easy to tell a bad leader from a good one.

People know who the various leaders are based on experience. They know if a leader doesn't go out of their way to support their team members, is MIA when you need them versus another leader, has your back during tough times, and will be in the trenches. You've got to do your own due diligence and ask people that you trust, and then you make the decision to align yourself with one practice or another.

Rather than chasing what you think is the most exciting practice on paper, you should make your decision based on the type of leaders that brand attracts.

Q. Describe the one experience that has shaped your values and how you do business today.

A. I don't know if it's an experience, but having mentors that you could trust. You knew that no matter what they had your back and vice versa. That relationship piece kept me in consulting and shaped my view of how I treat my peers, how I treat people in the practice, how I treat the most junior person to the most senior person, and how I treat clients. Again, for me, it's a lot about trust. I don't manage up and manage down; I don't think of it that way. It's about who I trust because trust results in loyalty and loyalty results in everything else.

11

Achieve Breakthroughs by Managing Relationships

Management is nothing more than motivating other people.

—LEE IACOCCA

Great consultants spend just as much time building and sustaining relationships as they do building expertise. The consultant that wins is the one with a lot of friends. If you have not read the book *How to Win Friends and Influence People* by Dale Carnegie, I highly suggest you pick a copy up on Amazon. It is the best $10 you'll spend. If you already own it, you may want to pick it back up and read it again. Then refer to it regularly.

Manage up, manage down: the ability to manage multi-layered relationships such as junior colleagues, peers, and senior leadership.

Earlier in my career when I was spending a lot of time refining my technical skills, I wish someone had told me to also focus on my people skills. To be successful in consulting, all types of people—your team members, leaders, clients—have to like and respect you. Period. You have to be able to team and work with people that have very different worldviews. Great consultants manage expectations and relationships through good project management skills, asking good consultative questions, managing optics, navigating organizational politics, and dealing with conflict.

Managing Expectations and Relationships

At the end of the day, your job as a consultant is to be able to manage expectations and promises. This means

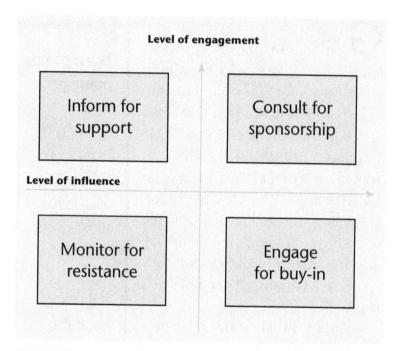

FIGURE II. Use the Stakeholder Management Matrix with every Project

that you need to manage the expectations of your clients, your leadership, your team, and your firm. Key to managing expectations and promises is your ability to follow-up and follow through. To do this well you have to have a clear understanding of your role and the roles around you as well as spoken and unwritten rules of the environment you are operating in.

Managing relationships and expectations is a dance. Manage up too much and you may be seen as a kiss ass; manage down too much and you may be considered a micromanager or bossy.

- ◆ Be mindful of not setting false expectations.
- ◆ Address questions, issues, and action items as

soon as possible; allowing open items to fester
derails your best efforts to manage relationships effectively.

◆ Take ownership of mistakes and course correct
immediately. Do not throw your team under
the bus.

◆ Actively share the spotlight and give credit
generously, especially if it was a team effort.

◆ Be authentic when offering ideas, suggestions,
and feedback. People sense disingenuous interactions a mile away.

◆ Be empathetic to the needs of your teams and
clients.

Leverage the stakeholder management matrix for
each engagement in Figure 11. Identify your stakeholders, prioritize them, and then plot them on the
matrix. Determine how to best manage relationships
using an action plan based on where each stakeholder
lands on the matrix. This is an interpersonal skill that
you must nail to be successful at any level in consulting.
Great consultants lead with empathy to effectively
manage relationships.

Hone in on Project Management Minimalism

Consulting is typically comprised of short or long-term
project-based work. Great consultants have a good grasp
of core fundamentals of project management, which
provides a systematic approach to follow up, monitor,
and analyze project activities and deliverables development of an engagement. Great consultants learn to lead

MECE MENTORING MOMENT

Great Consultants Ask Crunchy Questions

❝Earlier on in my career, I was given permission to ask questions so that I could get better and better in my day job so I could learn more. But then I also found it really helpful to ask questions of clients as well as colleagues of clients so that I could really learn about their business to be the best service provider that I could be. The last thing is, asking questions, listening, and really observing how people work and lead helped me to determine which of the leaders that I worked with over the years whose skills I really wanted to learn from and take on myself as I built my own acumen as a team leader, client server, and client-facing person representing my firm.❞

—**Karyn Twaronite,** partner at leading management consulting firm

with insights and analysis that project management techniques provide (such as tracking earned value or benefits realization of a project), not the administrative processes.

A secret weapon of good project management? Documentation. As one of my early managers stated: "If it is not documented, it does not exist." Failure to have organized methods or sound project management practices impacts the team's culture, creates rework and quality issues, and increases the likelihood of failed projects.

Managing Optics Is Critical

To manage client dynamics effectively, you need to understand and embrace the concept of optics. Positive or negative, optics are perceptions of behaviors or course of action. Optics shape the narrative and perceptions of you, your team, and your firm.

Leaders and managers on consulting teams have to not only manage the work and client relationships but the team and firm's brand. For example, showing up at the client site driving a luxury rental car can be misinterpreted as excessive travel expenses even if it was a free upgrade. Over time the wrong optics distract from the team's efforts and can potentially set off a negative chain reaction that is difficult to recover from. Below are a handful of traditional optics I was taught to manage to, which may or may not be applicable in today's environment.

- ◆ Junior consultants must stay on-site or in the team room until your immediate leader, manager, or the partner leaves the office.
- ◆ If you are at the management level, stay on-site until your client leaves the office.
- ◆ Do not have more than a couple of people meet with the client in person; there is an optic of too many people being paid to listen to the same information. One person listens to the conversation and brings back the information to the rest of the team.
- ◆ There should always be at least one team member on site during business hours even if others on the team are traveling or on vacation.

MAKE IT MECE

When new consultants start complaining about optics, I provide an example: think of the optics managed at a restaurant. If the server taking your order and bringing your food is constantly sneezing, you would have doubts about the meal you are about to eat. Even if that server doesn't have a cold, your first thought as a client is that they do. That doubt takes away from your dining experience. Consulting is no different in the sense of optics. While I've listed illustrative examples, make sure you know and understand the optics that your team needs to manage. The client's industry, geographic location, leadership, and culture will also influence how optics should be managed.

◆ Never leave the team room if everyone else is still working even if you have finished your assigned tasks. Be a team player and ask if anyone needs your help. One day you will need their help.

Are optics fair? No. Are some optics absurd? Probably. But they are what they are. Like a restaurant, a hotel, or a dry cleaners, clients come to expect a certain level of customer service.

There are tons of resources available out there to help you manage your team, peers, and managers. The key point to take away is that you need to do this in a deliberate way with every interaction. You must level set expectations, honor deadlines, and make sure everyone is aware of what you need. Don't become a problem solver on paper; walk the halls, talk to people. Brainstorm ideas, thoughts, and challenges as a team.

Lean into Organizational Politics

I hear younger consultants rejecting the idea of organizational politics. The *"I hate politics* or *I don't play games"* stance is a common position. That mentality already puts you in a losing position to miss out on key information and resources. Anytime you have a group of people, competing priorities, and limited resources (budget, talent, authority) politics will emerge. It does not matter if it is a business, church, industry association, sports team, or family. Politics is life, and it is everywhere.

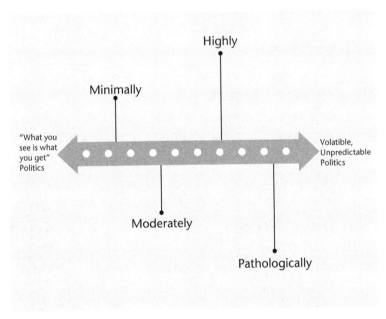

FIGURE 12. Illustration of Reardon's Four Types of Political Environments

According to *The Secret Handshake: Mastering Politics*, there are four types of political environments: minimal, moderate, high, and pathological. The continuum ranges from a nonpolitical *what you see is what you get* politics (minimal) to an extremely volatile and unpredictable politics (pathological).

Knowing the various types of political environments and your political "tolerance" is key to understanding how to best select practices or client environments you are best suited for. I'm not saying that you have to become an outmaneuvering political ninja. Great consultants are acutely aware that they are involved in organizational politics whether they choose to be or not. They own their experience by observing, monitoring, and navigating political landscapes. Great consultants become politically competent by embracing and accepting organizational politics for what it is, not what they want it to be.

Dealing with Conflict

Part of managing relationships is learning how to manage conflict. Kathy, a partner at a top strategy firm, provides some helpful tips on dealing with conflict within a team. "I quickly get everyone on the same page because that type of behavior is very destructive and has a way of magnifying if left unresolved. I always feel that I have to listen to everyone, find out what the issue is, and decide what makes the most sense for everybody. There's a difference between alignment and agreement. I don't have to get everyone to agree because I won't, but I can certainly get alignment—when I get it to 80 percent, I

MECE MENTORING MOMENT

Our industry is very male dominated, so women have to have a thick skin. Can't take things too personally. Although I never had any problems throughout my career, I find that other women in consulting have had experiences with sexual harassment. I've had a colleague tell me it happened to her at a different consulting firm, and that's one of the reasons she left. It's a very real undercurrent that no one talks about. But it's a real concern that has come to my attention recently.

–Anonymous female partner

can deal with the rest later. I like to have everyone feel like they're adding value, so I make sure everyone has a chance to demonstrate their value added to the team and has a chance to be that superstar."

CONSULTING LEADER INTERVIEW...

Fireside Chat with a Partner

Michael is a MBB[1] partner at one of the top strategy consulting firms in the world. In this interview Michael discusses how he became interested in consulting, the importance of building trust as the foundation of relationship building, and guidance on the key skills of great consultants.

---

[1] An acronym that stands for McKinsey & Company, Bain & Company, and the Boston Consulting Group

Q. Share how you decided to go into consulting. Is it everything you expected it to be?

A. When I was in undergraduate studies in the '90s at Duke University, I didn't fully know what consulting was. Since I studied engineering and computer science, my desire was to solve really hard, difficult problems. When I graduated, I started a very technically rich software company where we solved complex logistics optimization problems. We grew the company and eventually sold it. What I learned from that experience is that my passion was solving problems.

I went back to business school with the intent of understanding how I could solve broader business problems, not just specific technical problems. That's how I fell into consulting. I started to learn that consulting was the business problem-solving element that I really enjoyed from doing work for my own software company. And consulting gave me the platform to do that for many more clients with a very diverse set of problems.

When I originally got into consulting, I thought the end-all, be-all was running a profit and loss for a major company. I originally got into consulting with the intent that I would learn some skills over two years to end up at a major Fortune 1000 company.

Fast-forward ten, eleven years. It's been a great road, and I'll tell you it's been more than what I could have expected. It's afforded me the opportunity to work with some really bright minds and great companies. It's afforded me the opportunity to influence younger minds and the ability to pass on some of my experience and knowledge to people coming out of undergrad or graduate school. It's afforded me the opportunity to help build a business within a business—I have my clients plus my focus areas of expertise. When I think about the diversity of what I get to experience on a daily basis, this is way more than I could have imagined, originally coming in thinking I was just going to get to work on very interesting problems.

Q. What are some of your leading practices on managing up, down, or across within an organization?

A. If you're going to be an advisor to anyone, they have to really trust you, and trust doesn't come with the brand of your company. Just because I have a great company name doesn't mean that you as an individual are going to trust me. It gives me credibility, but it doesn't give me the right to ask for you to trust me. The question always comes: *How do you build trust?* I would say it starts with integrity and being there for someone and being really perceptive and listening and building a relationship with that person. This can be in your personal life, your professional life, upward, downward, and laterally.

But if you want to build trust, you have to start by asking questions, learning more about the individual, not the company. The client isn't the company. The client is the individual. Learning more about what's important to them. What motivates them, what some of their challenges are. Then when they start to open up small things to you, you have to offer them really heartfelt advice. It's not about selling someone something. I'm not trying to sell you a solution. It's about you opening something up to me; let me see how I can be helpful to you with the challenge that you've opened up to me.

And if we do that well, we start to build a relationship. When I was a young consultant, I was thinking about my project leader or partner I was working with. I said: *Let me build a relationship with this person, let me understand what's motivating them and their challenges, let me understand how I can be helpful to them and let me be genuine in how I'm helping them.* And I've used that as one of my platforms to make sure I'm successful in managing. It's just making sure I have those good, established relationships with trust being the foundation.

Q. Describe the one career experience that has shaped your values and how you do business today.

A. I had the opportunity to work with a client who I would say was unethical, bombastic, and destructive. Destructive to their own employees, destructive to my teams, and destructive to me. I had dialogue inside my firm about this company, which was not living up to the values that our firm espoused. This client was not going to be beneficial to us other than being a financial channel to make money. We had to make a difficult choice: was this worth us continuing to work? What shaped me was having this dialogue about our values, having others actually be very perceptive on thinking through our values, and the making a choice to say it's better to walk away.

And we walked away from this client. We told them: *We cannot serve you because of how you are operating. You have to change yourself and then change your culture, which we don't believe you're going to do.* And so we were able to walk away. That shaped me going forward. It's not that you're going to walk away from lots of clients, but you have to at some point live your values. It's not all about money; if we no longer serve our staffs or serve our own personal health and life in a supportive manner, we have to make tough choices that allow us to walk away. That shaped how I think about working with my clients. I'm going to be extremely supportive, but I also have to detect and understand your values. And if your values are completely out of line, I have to be willing to say: *I can't serve you.*

Q. Share your most significant accomplishment to date in consulting that you are the proudest of.

A. I was afforded the opportunity to participate in diversity and inclusion (D&I) initiatives, how to pivot from historical unconscious biases. I was asked to take this on by peers. Was proud to use my consulting toolkit to come up with a set of initiatives that resulted in additional diverse candidates at my firm. I had a personal passion, and it really turned out to be an impactful program.

There are many, many client opportunities I'm proud of, but I think some of the things I'm most proud of actually are outside the client. I was afforded the opportunity to be involved in diversity inclusion efforts for our firm, and I've learned just through my own interactions that a lot of people weren't very aware of things like unconscious biases, the challenges of how you actually pivot from historical decision making.

Things like the beer test. If I was stuck in the airport with someone, would I want to have a beer with them? That helps drive my decisions. All these embedded, natural biases that were in the consulting industry and inside my firm that I was asked to take on. And by the way, I was asked by largely white, male partners to help with thinking about how to improve diversity, in both absolute numbers of black and Hispanic staff but also diversity of thought to where anyone from any background, ethnicity, race, and sexual orientation would feel very comfortable being inside the firm, enjoy working there, and feel like they were supported.

And I was most proud of being able to use my consulting toolkit to analyze what were some of the challenges that our firm faced, and then come up with a set of initiatives that the firm would back, which they did. It resulted in a pretty phenomenal change in terms of the numbers of black and Hispanic staff that we brought into the firm. In our engagement survey we had a dramatic improvement of black and Hispanic staff feeling more engaged and supported by the firm. It wasn't just about one single thing that helped cause the improvement but a series of things that I was able to put in place. It was a testament to the research and tools you have as a strategy consultant to apply those, not just to our clients but to ourselves for an issue that I was personally passionate about and to have the support of my firm to do the things that they felt were necessary to help us pivot on the diversity and inclusion front.

Q. As you grew up in consulting, what was the most common career-limiting blind spot you witnessed in your peers and colleagues?

A. I'd say number one is understanding the principle of clients come first. In a client service world, we don't have full control over the workload that we take on, and there's a misbelief on young consultants: *The partner didn't scope the work appropriately, or the manager didn't manage it.* There is an element of our work that is a high-intensity career path. The work can be highly volatile at times, and the young staff just doesn't understand that. They're coming out of college where they've had much more flexibility over their daily life, and now they need to work fifteen–sixteen hours a day to actually solve some of the problems while also learning the key skills they need to solve the problem. So the newer consultants are generally naive about what it means to enter this career path, so that's probably number one.

Number two is, in consulting we are all about the answer. While there are a lot of hours expected early on, that's not necessarily rewarded; what's rewarded is insight and answers being delivered at a fast pace. Younger staff is often waiting for the partner or the manager to give them the answer; what they want to do is potentially use Alteryx or some new tool to come up with some analytics or regression model. But what is the answer that you can get from that work? They're not taking the broader perspective of the client who has hired them for the problem. What you're finding is that the early associates and consultants are acting much more like analysts and failing to understand they are consultants and advisors when they need to get to an answer.

The third is a problem with our university systems. Top universities are graduating people with degrees who are lacking some of the rigorous analytical skills to do the job well. I recommend to young people not to shy away from classes on econometrics, advanced applied statistics, advanced calculus and mathematics, and programming to get deep, rich technical and analytical skills you need to come up with facts.

People are graduating just woefully unready for the real work that we do. And then are finding themselves unable to compete and do some of that work because they lack the early training they could have gotten in college. Those are probably the three big pitfalls I see.

Q. At critical junctures in your career when you saw your peers and colleagues decide to leave the profession, what kept you going?

A. I think one of the things was, I had a set of sponsors. I call them sponsors rather than mentors because sponsors actually have ownership for your success, where a mentor is just giving advice. My sponsors were there when I ran into rough points, were very good at spending time with me to share their experiences along the journey, and just allowing me to express my frustrations. They were very keen on being helpful. Once I got past the frustration, my sponsors were helpful and said: *Let's figure this out together so that we can succeed*, whether it was a client interaction problem, a proposal management problem, a managing the team problem, or an answer problem.

Whatever the problem was, having sponsors that were passionate about you as an individual and wanted to see you succeed at the next level, kept me going in those critical moments and kept me in this career.

Q. Any last remarks on becoming a great consultant?

A. I worry about the younger generation coming out of college. When recruiting the top talent of the top universities, I find that juniors and seniors are too focused on things like: *I have to go into consulting so I can be successful* because a certain set of consulting firms are viewed as setting you up for long-term career success in what you want to do in life. They believe that to their core, and they've mapped out everything they need to get into a top consulting firm then get sponsorship to go to the top business school, come back to the consulting firm, potentially stay there and go into private equity. I mean you can talk to them at twenty years old, and they have their careers all mapped out till they're fifty. And they believe it.

People that think like that are often the least successful in this career path because they have lost any creativity and authenticity of who they are.

We talk to people getting an engineering degree, and they actually want to be a programmer and build mobile apps. That's their passion. But they've been told by their friends to go into consulting because that's the best career path. They're so unilaterally focused on the image of what successful looks like versus being successful in life. In all honesty, if they work for a mobile app company or start their own, that life experience will teach them so much more. Then when that engineer gets into consulting, they will be such a better asset to the consulting firms.

It's the same for people that want to go and volunteer for the World Food Program and help out in some countries in Africa. They don't do it because they're told: *Go into consulting.*

If I had one message, it's to figure out what you're passionate about, go do those things that you're passionate about, and then when the time is right, consulting will be here if you want. You can always come to consulting. We will hire you, and you'll be better off from your life experiences. You'll be happier. Don't just go through life thinking there is one path to success based on seminars at your undergraduate institution. That's just insane, and it's going to lead you to be less happy as a person.

12

Nail Your Deliverables Each and Every Time

Quality means doing it right when no one is looking.

—HENRY FORD

I truly appreciate the art of a well-constructed deliverable or work product. Great consultants put in considerable thought and energy into storyboarding, research, insights, quality of content, and the look/feel of a deliverable for their clients.

Deck: a PowerPoint presentation. Also known as slide deck.

Storyboarding and Research

Before content creation, take a moment to storyboard or outline your thinking. Have a clear understanding of what is the purpose of the content you are creating. Great consultants visualize how they see clients consuming this information. Socialize ideas with managers, peers, leaders, and client. You don't want to go full steam ahead in the wrong direction. Some selected practices:

- ◆ Take time to storyboard a logical structure before getting started.
- ◆ Have cited and accurate information, data, and verifiable resources. Your data must have journalistic integrity. As of this writing, blogs or crowdsourced knowledge sites like Wikipedia are not viewed as credible content sources.
- ◆ Don't plagiarize content. You not only put your personal reputation at risk, but you also put your firm's brand at risk. It's not worth it.
- ◆ Once you have a storyboard, save time by building out the deliverable with an appropriate template.

Insights and the *So what?*

The *So what?* is an important consulting concept that refers to the impact of a particular recommendation, insight, or observation. Clients pay big bucks for insights and expertise. It doesn't matter how pretty your content looks or how structured your report is if you are not sharing valuable information. Always nailing the *So what?* is where you elevate from being a vendor to becoming a trusted advisor.

Great consultants nail the ability to think critically, problem structuring, root cause analysis, and synthesize data using sound judgment.

There are a number of consulting techniques such as being MECE that help you nail insights. With every interaction strive to share data to help your clients view their organization through a different lens. Give them a different way of approaching a problem—one steeped in research and key analysis. Great consultants nail the ability to think critically, problem structuring, root cause analysis, and synthesize data using sound judgment.

Nailing the *So What?* Is More Than a Science

I remember the first time I had to understand the concept of the *So what?* It hit me like a ton of bricks one Tuesday night. I had just been promoted to senior consultant and was given a stretch role: subsection lead of a request for proposal (RFP) response to win new work for our client. It was the first time I was responsible for creating and shaping a portion of a proposal. I had to send a rough

draft of my section by the end of day for review edit. (The end of day in consulting time is code for 11:59:59 p.m.) The plan was to iterate one more time before an 8:00 a.m. morning proposal meeting.

I took what is called a *boil the ocean* approach—essentially like a school research paper. I spent hours researching emerging trends in the marketplace. I looked at a number of previous deliverables my firm had delivered. I reviewed past RFP responses in similar areas.

After doing all the research, I created a quick outline and started creating the document. It was dense, but I felt like I was very thorough, and that was the right approach. I provided specific examples of the concept, shared best practices out in the market, and tied that back to how we could do that work. I was laser focused, and it became a temporary obsession for five hours straight, after already putting in a day's work on the project. I didn't eat, drink, or move from my computer other than to print out documents, to take notes, and continue pulling my thoughts together.

I produced a single-spaced, twelve-page MS Word document. And I proudly sent it to my manager forty-five minutes early, which in my mind meant that I underpromised and overdelivered. After I submitted the proposal section, I sat back in my chair, crossed my arms, and waited patiently for the reply email to sing the praises of my document's thoroughness.

My manager sent me an email: *Can you call me?*
Hmm, that's odd, I thought.

My manager was hardworking and fair but pretty blunt so *Can you call me* at a quarter to midnight was not a good sign. This is how that conversation went.

"This is George." (Who else would it be at 11:45 p.m. at night? But I digress ...)

"Hi, George; it's Christie."

"Hey, Christie. I reviewed your draft and wanted to talk to you about it."

"Sure. What's up? What do you think? Let me know if you would like for me to walk you through the logic of what I was thinking—"

"Thanks, but before you do that can you point me to the section of your research that gets to the so what? It's longer than I anticipated, and I couldn't quite tease it out myself."

"The what?"

"The *So what?*"

"Can you elaborate a little bit, George?"

"Sure. While your document is well put together and has a lot of data—I could tell you did a lot of thorough research—you don't make a clear point of what all this data is trying to tell me. In other words, what's the insight that the client will learn regarding how we address their problem?"

"I think there's a lot of insight. Just look at all the facts about the market, about how we could do things differently, of how—"

"Yeah, but what's the point you're trying to make?"

"That we could do the work proposed because we have done this work before. We have demonstrated our ability to add value, particularly given the 35 percent increase of realized top-line growth the client has seen over the last three years since our team has been on the ground with our current solution. Based on my research our work and expertise are in alignment with marketplace trends that would give them a leg up to take on a dominant market position in this new space using another one of our solutions."

"Well, then, say that. And instead of saying it in twelve pages, I need you to say it in two concise pages. And I need to see the two pages by 6:00 a.m. tomorrow morning before our 8:00 a.m., in case it needs another pass before the proposal meeting."

He gave me a couple of other thoughts and then hung up. I remember thinking: *This is not what I had planned.* First of all, I was hoping to get some sleep. Second, I was completely off base with my document. I stared down the barrel of my deliverable, trying to think of other ways I could have approached it. I went back through, pulled out the key points and insights that we wanted to make, and then over the next two and a half hours, whittled my entire document down to less than three pages, which included an exhibit.

Great consultants take the time to teach new consultants what the *So what?* concept looks like in action. It will pay dividends in the future.

I sent it in and called it a night about 3:15 a.m. I met with my manager at 6:00 a.m. the next morning. It was a much better iteration, but we needed to pare it down again. By the time we submitted the proposal to the client, my section was about one full written page with an exhibit, and I was exhausted. The good news was we won the work, but I learned about the So what? concept the hard way. I was thankful for George taking the time to coach me through that moment because it has stayed with me for the rest of my career since. Great consultants take the time to teach new consultants what the So what? concept looks like in action. It will pay dividends in the future.

The Look and Feel of the Deliverable, a Teachable Moment

Once you have your insights, it is critical to nail your clients' and firm's aesthetic preferences. Some consultants will take one look at a document and in five seconds decide if it is crap or worth reading based solely on the look and feel. Make sure your content is packaged correctly. This is a frustrating concept if one comes from an academic or corporate environment that culturally does not place importance on the cosmetics of a document. But in consulting, the second most critical component of a deliverable next to insights is the look and feel. In some consulting firm cultures, the quickest

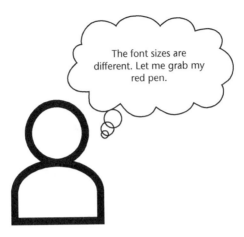

way your content can lose credibility is if it does not look cosmetically aesthetic or "client ready." I was in the early stages of my consulting career when I learned this important lesson and unwritten rule.

I was on a six-week project to provide support to a partner and his two senior managers. The project was to develop a growth strategy for an automotive client. I was in my second year as an analyst and I didn't know the importance of an aesthetically sound deliverable. Jesse, the partner I was working with, was relentless and unforgiving in his expectation of delivery. Jesse would storyboard the slides on the board. He then collaborated with his senior managers on the raw content for the deliverable. My job was to take the raw content outlined on the whiteboard and recreate it into compelling slides. It seemed easy enough.

I was unaware of how significant a skill that I was going to have to learn. What happened was like a hazing during hell week. Jesse would review my work then with a red pen, utterly destroy the slides. He nitpicked every single bullet, word, font type, and font size. And he didn't stop there. Once he finished destroying them with the red pen, he would then walk me through what he had done in the most condescending *Why are you such an idiot?* tone of voice. After explaining the changes he was expecting, he physically ripped up the slides in my face. Once he ripped the slides, he would make me put my hand out, and give me the pieces to throw away in the trash. He did this in front of the senior managers in the team room, who seemed unfazed.

The first time he ripped the slides in my face was to this day the most embarrassing moment of my career. While it was brutal, it taught me an invaluable lesson. I began to realize the patterns of feedback. After frustrating moments and painstaking mistakes that first week, I made a decision to take back control of the situation. No one would continue to tear up my deliverables again.

Once I made that decision, I began to approach my work differently. Putting my marketing degree to work, I took massive, massive action. I became obsessed with learning how to create aesthetically sound presentations. I bought books and sought out classes to practice. I researched tools and downloaded presentations that I liked as templates.

By the second week, Jesse had stopped ripping up my slides and handing them to me. He would review my decks and only catch minor mistakes. I tried to create them as perfectly as possible and got pissed when he caught any typos. By the fourth week, Jesse stopped whiteboarding and verbally explained the concepts to me. I would then take his concepts and create slides. By the time I rolled off that project around week six, I was really good at developing aesthetic decks.

The project was a blessing in disguise. To my surprise I was promoted from an analyst to a consultant level at the year's end. From then I built a brand of being able to create polished deliverables, a reputation that has carried me throughout my career. I am so thankful for that opportunity because it instilled a guiding principle that I now come to expect of my teams—without the slide ripping part.

Remember that what is aesthetically acceptable for a deliverable varies depending on the job or situation. So, before you begin working on a deliverable for your client, look at other work that was accepted by your client. Ask the client how they like information presented to them. Or find someone on the client site you trust that will share those insights with you.

It's All about Quality in the Finishing Touches

This last point bears special attention. Go through several complete, front-to-back iterations of a document before submitting for peer or manager reviews. Socialize early and often. The key to nailing each deliverable is to allow the process to take its course.

CONSULTING LEADER INTERVIEW...

Fireside Chat with a Consulting Leader

John Tigh is a principal and leader at the North Highland Company, a global consulting firm. John has served clients in private industry, as an entrepreneur, and in consulting for over twenty years. An active member of the American Society of Inventors and first-generation college graduate, John began consulting to capitalize on his knowledge and experience in print media and publishing by applying publishing fundamentals to modern multichannel and digital product challenges.

In this interview John discusses what he learned about life while working on Wall Street, outlines key consulting techniques, and gives advice to new or aspiring consultants based on his years of experience. He also highlights how he holds his teams accountable to nailing the deliverable each and every time.

Q. Please share how you got into consulting. Has it been everything you expected it to be?

A. The short answer is yes. I started in the industry with degrees in publishing and started in consulting just before the dot-com bubble, literally because of a rocket scientist. A former NASA scientist went out on his own to start a consultancy and got a venture capital firm to back him. I met this scientist through a previous consulting arrangement. I thought the rocket scientist and his team were brilliant, and one day he extended me the opportunity to come and work with him.

At the time there was a lot of consolidation in the publishing market. It seemed to make sense to step away from paper to digital. I got into consulting because of the changing nature of my industry even though I initially had some trepidations about going into consulting. But I took a chance and rolled the dice. I took a role with a boutique content management consulting firm on Wall Street.

I will confess that I didn't really know what I was getting into before I got into it. Turned out that consulting was a fantastic fit for me. Consulting provides the opportunity to be on the cutting edge, to solve complex puzzles, and there's no better place for that than in the business world.

Q. What are your best practices for ramping up on a new project?

A. I like to get to know the people and the company prior to working with them. I do my homework to find areas of commonality. Research such as reviewing financial statements and 10k statements to discover the overall vision and direction of a company—or if there is a lack of vision or direction. I have had experiences where the work the client was doing was not aligned to the strategy. On the people side of things, I've found we may have hobbies or charitable activities in common.

Throughout the years I've discovered everything from a sponsor who had written a children's book to one accused of a human rights violation. The lesson I took from this is always do your research, so you know who you are working with and how best to relate or not to work with. Starting a new project gets me asking a lot of questions. There are the standards project dimensions of scope, duration, requirements, and budget for sure. But there can also be questions of morals, values, empathy, and ethics that must be placed into context and balanced when creating a solution.

One of the unsung benefits to consulting is that you are regularly faced with interesting data and complex nuances, more so than many other professions. That's why I say you have to get to know the people and the company in order to begin to understand the puzzle. For me the most important aspect is having a clear sense of the vision; you have to be able to pull that through the entire project.

After I have performed the research, I ask my team to conduct a similar research exercise. We then do a brainstorming discussion using sticky notes or a whiteboard to help us collectively as a team understand each other, our interpretation of the client's goals, and how we each contribute to meeting those goals. From this we generate a list that helps us all to track those goals and refine our processes toward meeting them.

Everyone hears and sees things very differently. Everyone filters information through their own experiences and desires. This technique puts everyone on the same page. Sharing and addressing clarifying questions up front opens a dialogue in advance, and makes it easier if later something goes amiss and requires a conversation. Uncomfortable situations arise when people think they are at odds, which impact team productivity and dynamics. Through establishing a dialogue in advance, later disruptions through misunderstandings—and their impact on the work—are minimized.

Q. **Share the most significant career experience you've had that shaped your core values and how you operate in business today.**

A. My career in consulting is a bit stilted in some ways because my first experience was on Wall Street during the dot-com bubble. At the time it was fast paced, there was a lot of money everywhere, opportunities everywhere, and there were all sorts of awesome things happening. Being in a bubble is dangerous. It led me to believe or value things that may not have been true at a very young age in my career. Living inside the dot-com bubble taught me that while you may believe you can know and understand everything, there will always be factors that remain out of your control or grasp— the unknown that you need to cultivate respect for and be prepared for.

I was at ground zero on 9/11, and I experienced the anthrax attacks that followed thereafter. Following a good deal of reflection and introspection, the collective experiences shifted my mindset from one of being acquisitive (i.e., me and my ego) to someone more interested in compassion and connection. I began to find mentors, change my thinking, and fundamentally evolve how I do business. I focused on delivering for my people. I began to volunteer, mentor, and coach, which I love. That's when everything clicked, and my career trajectory changed. The collective experiences shifted me toward seeking connections with people. Connection is the best way to obtain the best outcomes.

Q. How do you build rapport with your clients?

A. I spend an extraordinary amount of time thinking about thinking and communicating. I believe that to be a good consultant one should learn how to speak well, be able to tell stories, and demonstrate empathy toward others. I find that appreciating how other people think is the fundamental key to good communication. It helps you to view the world through their eyes and understand their perspective. During my career I became certified in the Hermann Brain Dominance Instrument, a tool to understand an individual's thinking style. It's an invaluable tool in my communications utility belt.

Being fundamentally concerned—understanding where people come from and being able to pick up on their communication cues—is the fastest way to rapport. Finding common ground and understanding how people consume information is critical.

Q. What is sound career advice carried throughout your career that has influenced your experience?

A. I often refer to a piece of advice one of my mentors, Larry Winget, likes to espouse: *Do what you* *say you are going to do, the way you said you are going to do it, and when you said you are going to do it.* I've found when you follow that very simple advice and provide that experience to people, it very quickly builds trust. If there are impediments, which happen sometimes, and you need to adjust to changes, having a rapport and the communication ability when things change, is critical. This is basic blocking and tackling. I don't believe people spend enough time working on communications, but it is a real differentiator in the marketplace. Communications must be both inbound and outbound; you have to consider the messages you are putting out there and how they are received. And if a message is received incorrectly, be compassionate enough to alter the message or admit you were wrong. Put your ego aside and adjust the message to move forward.

Q. How do you currently hold your teams accountable to creating impact for your client's business?

A. I'm pretty direct. That is the way I present information. I like to bookend conversations, experiences, or other information. As I mentioned, when ramping up a team, we talk about everyone's expectations and goals; that's one bookend. As the project progresses, if we are not hitting goals and timelines or if we are chasing other ideas rather than focusing on what we said we were going to do, it's easier to bring that back to center than if you never had that initial conversation. If you set expectations upfront and have everyone agree that is what you are all collectively going to do and have everyone buy-in, it just makes things easier to hold the team accountable. I can't possibly know everything, but having others know that they can approach me and I'll be as open as possible, is critical. Accountability is the nearest neighbor to trust; the more trust you have with your team, the more you hold others accountable.

Q. Knowing what you know now, what advice would you give your younger self about consulting?

A. Leap sooner. I had the opportunity to leap into consulting prior to when I did, but I didn't take it. I would learn everything about business fundamentals—how a business works, what a financial sheet looks like. I think back to when I owned my own company and had to worry about payroll or paying vendors; these are valuable experiences that increase in value over time. Learn what it means to own a business. Take perspectives to see where you are strong and where you might be exposed. Get into selling things. No job is too small.

I'd especially love to tell myself: *Shut up and do the work because the truth is there is a lot to learn, to observe, and figure out.* When you are freshly minted with a degree and you've been assured by your alma mater that you know everything, you really believe that. Break out of that bubble, and recognize how much needs to be evaluated, weighed, and judged to see if it fits for your career.

Don't look for the immediate rewards. You want an objective view that you have done a good job.

If you get into consulting, chances are pretty good that you will do well financially. But if you are looking for the rewards, accolades, the stuff— then you are looking at the wrong thing.

Keep your ego in check; be there to serve.

Try to do one thing every week that will build up stamina and grit. Seek to be where others are not. It's easiest to get noticed that way. You'll begin to see things differently and get invited to other experiences and gain access to situations that you may not have otherwise. I love the ugly jobs because they have always been a great door opener.

Build relationships early on, not just networking. Actually reach out to people and build relationships. Care. There's an amazing ability to reach out to influential people these days because social media has removed all the gatekeepers.

Share your ideas. If you would like a mentor, just reach out and ask. There are no boundaries, only dots to connect. You, me, and others. We are all dots waiting to connect.

Every business is a collection of people and ideas. You have to be able to connect and serve; then you may consult.

13

Take Your Clients Along for the Journey

Customer experience is the next competititive battleground. It's where business is going to be lost or won.

—TOM KNIGHTON

The ability to build and foster client relationships is the bread and butter of a consulting career. Great consultants take time to understand the mindset of a client, establishing relationships to become a trusted advisor, taking clients along the project journey, while dealing with conflict head on. Great consultants seek to build rapport with every interaction to create a sense of comfort and confidence with clients.

> **Client:** the individual or company that hires a vendor, consulting firm, or contractor to help them solve a particular business problem.

Mindset of a Client

Earlier in my career I was concerned with clients perceiving me as a credible consultant. In my mind that meant remaining formal in my client interactions to project credibility. And while clients may have been impressed, I was a good, yet point of sale consultant. I hadn't focused on building the type of rapport to become a trusted advisor. Great consultants operate with a clear understanding of the mindset of a client.

- ◆ Clients are human. Each client has their own motivation, fears, doubts, and dreams. Seek to understand what the client values and how they prioritize those values.
- ◆ Clients want your help. What is keeping them

up at night? Depending on the client's role and company's political climate, seek to understand your client's position and their agenda.

◆ Clients want to be respected and opinions valued. Nobody knows a client's business or industry and environment better than the client themselves. Socialize ideas, suggestions, and initial insights early and often throughout an engagement.

◆ Clients are ambitious. High-performing leaders have an insatiable desire to learn from the best. They want to avoid making some of the same mistakes their competitors or companies in other industries have made.

◆ Clients will ultimately take credit for your work. They take the credit for the solution or recommendations your team comes up with and own the narrative of your hard work. And rightfully so. Position your work to make your client shine.

Establishing Client Relationships, One Interaction at a Time

Great consultants focus on *partnering* with a client by helping them identify key insights to solve extremely complex problems within their organization instead of talking at them. Big Four+ partner Nalika Nanayakkara shared thoughts on the importance of trust. *"When you're with a client, you have to make sure you have their best interest at heart and do the right thing."*

MECE MENTORING MOMENT

❝When I was a young consultant, I was staffed on a large scale implementation, with a bunch of young guns on it. I was the process re-engineering person on the finance team. I was probably twenty-three or twenty-four, working with people that had been at the company for thirty years.

"And here we came in, and it's just that typical demographic of young consultants-old clients. I remember thinking: Oh my God, these people are never going to like me, never going to see my value.

"That became really clear to me early on that it is all about relationship building. Instead of coming in and trying to tell them everything, instead I talk to them about their kids, families, where they live, build the trust first and then the respect comes later, because the respect will come when we start producing work, we start making their lives easier.❞

–Jennifer Maddox, *a transformational consulting leader*

Every single interaction—whether it's in person, over the phone, or via email—either reinforces certainty that your client made the right decision to hire you or creates doubt in their mind of your ability to deliver.

An unwritten rule is to not only deliver the work but to also focus energies on giving your clients the best engagement experience as possible after the contract has been signed, not before. Take time to learn about a client's environment, their challenges, and aspirations. Put yourself in their shoes. Understand the problem you were asked to solve as if you owned the problem. Make sure you focus on solving for the root cause, not the symptoms.

In client meetings, apply the WAIT rule— *why am I talking?* In most client interactions your main job is to listen, observe, and learn.

Use language that is relatable to the way your client communicates. Keep it simple. Create analogies, stories, and narrative to get your message across. When I was a younger consultant, I thought I had to speak with a lot of fancy words, which had the opposite effect. Most clients are not impressed with large vocabulary but rather the impact of your results.In client meetings, apply the WAIT rule—why am I talking? In most client interactions your main job is to listen, observe, and learn.

Become a Trusted Advisor

As mentioned in the book's introduction, one of the main goals of a business consultant is to become a trusted advisor to clients. "Just remember this isn't about you; it's about helping other people," says Craig Berkowitch, partner at a management consulting firm. "Whether it's helping other people grow in other careers

MECE MENTORING MOMENT

❝ *I have real empathy for clients because I have had to sit as a client myself and had to understand the side of the fence where consultants do not have visibility into. Ten years from now when you reflect back on a project, no one will care how good the deliverable was; no one will care about the outcome of the project. The only things people will remember are the interactions and moments you had as a team, including clients. ...*

"If you are transactional based, you are just that. You are one and done. Fundamentally consultants are in the relationship business. Consultants do not know everything; try to learn a lot from your clients just by listening. Senior clients know the answers and do not have the capacity to always think through it. Consultants sometimes make the mistake of thinking that they need to have all of the answers. Consultants need to listen and learn. In those moments, it is based on trust. It is based on trust that people allow you to advise them. ❞

–Greg, *partner at a global consulting firm*

or helping your clients succeed in their business and their organizations."

I highly recommend reading *The Trusted Advisor* by David Maister, a deep dive on the topic of becoming a trusted advisor. In the book the authors share the evolution of the client-advisor relationship continuum. The continuum has four levels, each describing how the client-advisor relationship evolves. It is an excellent book for anyone seeking to become a great consultant.

Be Honorable in Your Interactions with the Client

Don't agree or commit to a deadline, scope, or budget decision you cannot realistically deliver. And if upon discovery you realize that you are committed to an unrealistic scope or deadline, reach out to the client as soon as possible. Clients get upset, organizations are impacted, and consulting teams are fired when consultants do not meet their commitments. It is also unwise to compromise quality to suffer to meet a deadline. This goes back to the guiding principle of having integrity, credibility, and reputation. Great consultants have the courage to relay difficult messages. While clients may not be happy in the short run, being honest creates credibility and trust in the long run.

Include Clients on the Journey

To become a trusted advisor, bring clients along on the journey of co-creating the solution. Consultants cannot go off in the dark and come out on the other side with a solution. Don't try to outsmart or out-articulate your client. Conduct iterative sessions with your clients at crucial junctures to help you make key decisions. Even when clients are expecting that from you, they may not say it explicitly, so be proactive.

Employees at Your Clients' Organizations and Greater Community

Chances are, your client's company will have employees at all levels. Treat all employees at your client's organization with respect, regardless of role. Extend that respect to anyone you meet throughout your travels. This particularly holds true in small towns and cities. The world is small. Relationships, friendships, and alliances may exist that you are unaware of.

Dealing with Difficult Clients

When dealing with a difficult client, seek to first understand their worldview. Actively listen to spoken or unspoken cues. Be empathetic. What has happened or is currently happening to cause the behavior? First, do not take it personally. Second, probe deeper to determine the root cause. Most unhappy clients are the result of a residual unmet need, insecurity, or desire. Try acknowledging the hard work they put into a project or the great ideas they have that go unnoticed. Give them public kudos in front of their leaders or colleagues.

If you are genuine, you can turn a bitter client into a strategic ally. Also accept the fact that you may not be able to change their behavior, no matter what you do. Having proper systems, roles, and responsibility clarity is critical. Document every client interaction, conversation, promises, decisions, and next steps.

CONSULTING LEADER INTERVIEW...

Fireside Chat with a Partner

David Kaufman is the CEO and managing partner

of Acquis Consulting, a global management consulting firm specializing in strategy and implementation, which he started at the age of twenty-eight in 1998. Today Acquis Consulting is a multi-million dollar business that has been recognized five times by *Consulting* magazine as one of the Best Small Firms to Work For. As a co-founder, David is the driving force behind Acquis's extraordinary achievements.

In this interview David highlights how he got started in consulting, shares his breakout story of how he co-launched a consulting firm, highlights how he builds credible relationships with clients, and gives us insights on how he has been a successful consulting leader while building a culture that is aligned with his values.

Q. Please share with us how you decided to go into consulting. What attracted you to the profession that ultimately led you to co-found your own firm?

A. I feel in a lot of ways consulting happened to me. I started as an intern in accounting at Arthur Andersen—a Big Four+ firm at the time—for my junior year in college. The firm contacted me during my senior year and asked if I would be interested in going to the consulting side of the business. I think the firm chose me because I had one extra computer course on my resume. I did 50 percent accounting and 50 percent consulting while at Arthur Andersen, just to stay in the accounting space in order to get my CPA.

I then realized that I began to like the consulting side of the business a lot more than the accounting side. Auditing clients generally didn't want you there whereas the consulting clients wanted to see you on site to partner and help them solve problems. Consulting was more strategic, so I found myself moving more into the consulting direction.

I had always known I wanted to start my own business. I just like the aspect of building something from the ground up. I was open to really any type of business. Since I had an advantage in consulting, it made sense to start a business in consulting. When I left Andersen at twenty-five to go independent, many of my friends thought I was going through a quarter-life crisis. But I knew that I wanted to work for myself. I met my co-founder through business interactions, and we formed Acquis together.

Q. You started your consulting company in 1998 and then 9/11 hit, which impacted the marketplace as a whole. How were you affected? What keeps you going during challenging times in consulting?

A. That was an emotional time for us. Our office was one block away from the World Trade Center. We had large buildings between us, so our building wasn't directly impacted. I was actually in Puerto Rico for a client meeting.

The meeting was at 9:00 a.m., and as one of my colleagues was about to go to that meeting she said, "Why is my cousin calling from California?"

She just ignored the call. We went into the

meeting, and two hours later employees of the company we were visiting came in and interrupted us. They started speaking Spanish. We thought something happened to someone's kid in school. They finally told us and by that time the phones were not working there.

A few things happened. We were first worried about our people. We were small at the time, about twelve people, but our goal was making sure they were okay. Fortunately they were, and some ended up somewhere helping and passing out supplies. Then we focused on getting back to the US, which was an ordeal. One of our clients lost a family member during 9/11, so it was very emotional.

We made it back to the United States but weren't allowed in our office for a few weeks as they feared the building wasn't stable. Afterward, there were a lot of incentives in place to sign a long-term lease downtown, so we were able to build out a great office in Tribeca a few blocks up the road and have been here for the last thirteen years.

We were fortunate not to be too impacted from a business standpoint as a lot of the work we perform is related to cost reduction. We were able to keep our business still going. It was harder times than usual, but we were able to get through it okay.

We always try to give a unique, nice corporate gift. That year we gave out a limited-edition photograph that was taken shortly before 9/11 at the Twin Towers. We made a significant donation to two charities associated with supporting the victims of 9/11.

There are ups and downs in every business. As a consulting firm we always have that balance of trying to get the right utilization. It seems like one day you are too busy and another day you are not busy enough. There's never a perfect stability of utilization, and you are struggling with that. However, we've been fortunate and have been able to grow through the years and keep that utilization relatively steady. We really pride ourselves that we never have any layoffs, treating this place as a family.

I am really proud that in a lot of ways we are less risky than a large firm because we are not beholden to outside investors or a public market where we have to make short-term changes that may not be best for the long run. People perceive a risk when they come to a smaller firm. And we want that risk to pay off for them. I take a lot of pride in getting through those ups and downs.

Q. Share one example of a failure or lessons learned in consulting that has shaped how you do business today.

A. In my first job there were some very difficult clients who were not nice to the consultants, who sometimes lied, or in some cases made people cry. They didn't respect schedules or vacations, and they tried to make the consultants look bad. I was junior at the time and didn't feel empowered to change the situation. That's how you earned your stripes; you just went with it and did the best you could.

But I also noticed even the senior level people didn't feel empowered to do much about it. The clients were paying the bills, and sometimes clients didn't pay the bills. They were trapped in this situation. I realized the ripple effect impact that has on the employees and the culture and wanted to start my own company to feel good about the work we do and to not feel trapped in a disrespectful situation.

Those early experiences have empowered me to sometimes fire clients, even though it has a short-term negative impact. We do it in a way where we support the client with the transition and make it as positive of a situation as possible. It's only happened two or three times, but that's really a big difference to the people on those projects, and to the culture overall because people know we have their back and if the situation is really bad, we are going to come and fight for them and try to make it better. If it's still not better, we are going to take measures to fix it.

Q. What is the craziest experience you have had as a consultant?

A. I have been asked that question before. Fortunately I have generally been able to avoid crazy situations. I think I have a low tolerance on the crazy meter, and if I sense it, I try to stay away. I've certainly seen bad behavior, which you see in all industries, but I don't have a great crazy story for you.

But I do have an interesting travel story. There was one year where I spent a winter in Michigan. I didn't find it the most fun place to spend winter. I was training for a marathon. I had to run outside through the snow in order to train. Our client was six miles away from our hotel, so I would run back to the hotel, and my colleague would take my computer and drive back.

The first time running, I passed an animal shelter. Forty minutes later I saw another animal shelter. I felt it strange that there were a couple of animal shelters in this city. It then hit me that it's the same animal shelter. Somehow I went in a giant circle. On that same run there were people outside who started screaming: *Run, Forest. Run!* I was supposed to run six miles but ended up running fourteen miles because I was running in circles.

Q. What is your top secret to creating credibility with your clients toward being seen as trusted advisor?

A. I think the secret is that you can't fake it. I really love mentoring people, seeing them succeed, watching them grow, and we hire people that have a similar philosophy and want those around them to be successful. Internally, they are supportive of each other. Externally, they want to see their clients succeed, and clients feel that from the first day. We have our mantra: people first. It's the core of every project.

Once clients know that we're there not only to make the project successful, but to make them successful, they very quickly see that difference and trust that, and they want those people around them. I think the reality is we are selling projects on expertise, and that's how clients often make decisions. But with real success the expertise becomes secondary; it's the emotional, the intellect, the empathy, the intelligence, the honesty—those are the things that clients appreciate, and they want to keep working with those types of people.

Q. Knowing what you know now, what advice would you give your younger self?

A. I will start with a story. A few years ago, I was going through a stressful time and decided to make life changes all at once. I got a nutritionist and changed eating habits. I changed the way I worked out. I changed my dating habits. I changed a lot of things. Another thing I changed was actively trying to eliminate negative people from my life.

Sometimes it is difficult to know what was most effective because I made all these changes at the same time. But I really feel that reducing the negativity in my life made a huge difference. Over the years I spent less and less time with negative people and have realized that the negativity brings you down, causes you to make worse decisions, and simply makes life less fun. We just had our annual meeting a couple of weeks ago. We have ninety employees, and I genuinely don't think we have any assholes. I feel that's important to everyone's well-being. It just makes coming to work a lot more enjoyable.

I've learned that people can have different personalities, perspectives, styles, and skills without having that negative energy. If somebody is negative or doesn't make you feel good about yourself, you should stay away. That doesn't mean people should be afraid to give negative feedback, but it should just be done in a supportive and productive way. No negativity—that's probably what I would tell my younger self because it took me a while to figure that out.

Q. Any last remarks on becoming a great consultant?

A. I feel giving back is important for every business, no matter how small. I chair the Manhattan Board of American Cancer Society, and our firm is involved with American Cancer Society and Streetwise Partners. It's always a balance of trying to do things short-term and long-term.

I was one of those people who might have enjoyed helping build a house for those in need but didn't feel I was significantly moving the needle. Now we are getting to a point where we have a lot of people contributing both financially and their time. We created the Acquis social responsibility group to maximize our impact. We just instituted a matching program for employees on contributions they make.

Going back to an earlier question, I would tell my younger self to get involved early and find something you can be passionate about and really make a difference rather than spread yourself too thin on ten different things. We are trying to do that both individually and on a firm level as well.

14

Manage Energy and Bandwidth Remarkably Well

Time has a wonderful way of showing us what matters.

—Unknown

As a consultant you will always feel stretched for time, resources, and knowledge. It's a never-ending challenge of spinning plates, juggling client work, travel, and team relationships. It doesn't stop there. And on top of all that, you must figure out a way to have a personal and family life. The first step to strategically managing energy is to first understand it. Tony Schwartz, CEO of the Energy Project, elaborates on the laws of physics to define energy as the capacity of humans to work in four key dimensions: the body, emotions, mind, and spirit. The key is to identify and assess your energy strategy within each dimension to create shortcuts, life hacks, and mental breaks.

Bandwidth: free or underutilized time; ability to take on additional work or projects.

Devise Shortcuts, Life Hacks, and Intentionally Take Breaks

To manage a demanding consulting career, you have to devise shortcuts, creative solutions, and other means to get things done. Some consultants fall into the trap of thinking they need to do everything, or they need to work all of the time. Working yourself into oblivion is counterproductive.

"Idleness is not just a vacation, an indulgence or a vice; it is as indispensable to the brain as vitamin D is to the body, and deprived of it we suffer a mental affliction

**as disfiguring as rickets.... It is, paradoxically, neces-
sary to getting any work done."** —Tim Kreider

According to Cal Newport in *Deep Work: Rules for Focused Success in a Distracted World,* one evaluates habits and actions in order to structure time for deep work. Deep work is defined as any knowledge work that requires the intense focus and concentration necessary for mastering complex topics more quickly. Consulting deep work varies. Examples are the results of analysis, research summary, project roadmap, or drafting a framework. While it is critical to create the space, it is also easy for obstacles to distract deep work. It is important to balance deep work sessions and mental breaks to allow time to pause and reflect.

Create and Honor Boundaries

Schedule deep work time on your calendar like an important client meeting. I block off a couple of hours five days a week for deep work when I am at my peak state for the day. Several times a year I have deep work marathons where I go off to a secluded place for seventy-two hours of nonstop quiet time.

Strategically Select Extracurricular Activities

Commit to activities that you have a passion for. If you work for a large firm, you may get involved in practice development efforts known as internal initiatives. Although internal initiatives may not be client work, they hold weight when it comes to differentiating your brand at a firm and help create avenues to strengthen relationships. Learn how to manage expectations, particularly when things may change on your project or your availability.

Today I approach taking on internal initiatives with a kill two—or three—birds with one stone approach. I run each internal initiative through what I call the internal initiative sniff test (IIST).

- ◆ I'm going to learn something new in an area that I have always wanted to gain expertise in but did not have an opportunity to.
- ◆ I'm going to refine my executive presence skills.
- ◆ It will help me fulfill a professional development need.
- ◆ I have a genuine interest in the topic.
- ◆ It helps me continue to broaden my network and gain exposure to key stakeholders.

If an internal initiative doesn't meet at least four of the five sniff test criteria, I politely decline the opportunity or recommend another colleague. For example, one of my ongoing internal initiatives is to facilitate my firm's Introduction to Project Management course several times a year to junior consultants. I like teaching this course because I have an opportunity to refine my public speaking skills, while meeting both my firm's and industry certification's continuing professional educational requirements.

Having to prepare for the class keeps me refreshed on key aspects of the methodology and it also helps me connect with other colleagues and key stakeholders. I get to scout out and recruit potential team members for my projects. I also become a resource for younger colleagues on the topic.

CONSULTING LEADER INTERVIEW...

Fireside Chat with a Partner

Kathy is a MBB partner at a top strategy consulting firm. Kathy is a proven leader and executive management professional with over twenty-seven years of experience in the consumer industry. Kathy sits on a number of corporate boards and has decades of executive leadership. In this interview Kathy shares her experiences transitioning into consulting after a storied corporate career, leading practices on running effective meetings, and the importance of inclusiveness in creating a winning team culture.

Q. How did you decide to go into consulting? Is it everything you expected it to be?

A. For well over twenty-five years, I experienced consulting as a client. Then the company I worked at was not only acquired, but operations moved to a different part of the country. I wasn't ready to make that switch, and a friend of mine referred me to my current firm. I've been in management consulting now ten years.

While the work has evolved over those years in terms of what kinds of things I've done and how I've been involved with the firm, it's been a wonderful experience being on the other side of the table and being part of the team that provides consulting. It's been a fun transition.

Q. Has anything surprised you coming into consulting having been on the client side for most of your career?

A. I think the first thing that's totally amazing to me is that as a group consultants are a homogeneous group of super-bright people. These kinds of firms only hire the best and the brightest, and if you're just okay, you don't get in. The consultants I work with bring a perspective to the thought process that is unlike anything I've ever seen since I've been in corporate America.

You're around a lot of smart people, but you're not around 100 percent of people who are brilliant, and that's the case here. I was just astounded by the level of people. Putting that thinking up against a business problem and how they come up with ideas and problem-solving is amazing.

Q. What are leading practices on how to best run a client or team meeting?

A. *Preparation.* It goes without saying that everyone needs to be well-prepared and materials have to be ready in advance. One thing that is grueling is when materials are prepared after midnight or early in the morning before the meeting. It's important to be prepared in advance because you don't get everyone's best thinking at one in the morning.

Conciseness. So many times we don't need a one hundred-page PowerPoint. Know when you need to come in with two pages of key points for discussion.

Facts. Sometimes it's not about your interpretation of the data. This is the data and conclusions from it.

Listening. It's not just about presenting to the client or the team leader presenting to the rest of the team. It's about being iterative and listening, whether from the client or other people on the team that have a different perspective. So often we have our blinders on and fail to listen.

Q. How do you ask for timely, constructive feedback and leverage it to catapult your career?

A. I have been fortunate enough to be both in the corporate world as well as consulting, and both areas really believe in performance evaluations. At my previous organization we did quarterly reviews. I would sit down with my boss at the beginning of the year or a quarter to discuss what I was going to accomplish, what value I bring, and why. I would then go back at the end of that time period to discuss results. This process was very much ingrained in me, and people either took it as a check the box exercise or embraced it. I really embraced it because my performance was in my hands.

I have an old saying: *If it is to be, it is up to me.* It is a quote from Don Beveridge that I memorized from my first job at Hallmark Cards at a sales meeting; it was an ongoing team mantra. So I took it as my career isn't something the company does; it's for me to do. So then I knew what skill sets I needed to pick up. And I think that's important.

Q. What is the best compliment that you have ever received in your career? Why was it so impactful to you?

A. I remember this quote someone said to me a few years back: *You helped me see what I couldn't see.* It was a case where someone who had a lot of potential didn't have the confidence in their potential. I was training this person and giving them opportunities to develop certain skills and a leadership style because I thought she had the skills and just needed to feel more comfortable in them and continue to develop them. She didn't think she had that skill. She's moved on to be very successful, and I've continued to give feedback to her and talk to her.

She said to me, "It's you who helped me see what I couldn't see. I didn't think that I could do that and move on in that leadership role."

I took that as a thank you for mentoring her. It

takes time and effort to mentor someone, but when it's done right, it can be extremely rewarding. This was a case where she didn't see it, and I helped her see it.

Q. What are three pet peeves you see consultants do at a client site or working with their team?

A. The first pet peeve I mostly see with the junior folks: the know-it-all attitude. These are bright and smart people, and they're dealing with big client projects, so there's an ego thing going on. But it doesn't behoove the project and the outcome to have someone who thinks they know it all and who is going to demonstrate that to both the client and to the rest of the team. I'm always looking to provide coaching to say everyone is valued here. Take a breath and give everyone a chance to respond or deal with something.

The second pet peeve is when a team goes through the existing materials of a client and trash it. *Oh, that's junk. They didn't do this right.* You name it, they've trashed it. I've had to take a step back a couple of times and say: *Wait a minute. You basically worked in a retail store for a year and a half before you got your MBA. You're out of school for six months. You're not the expert here. We don't know if that's trash or not. Don't just trash something. There was value for it; we don't know the context.* It bothers me, so my antennas are up when I start hearing that.

Third is, I get particularly aggravated when

the team is interviewing and doesn't have respect for everyone's point of view. The consultant is not really listening in the interview because they've made the decision somehow that this person doesn't have value or that they can't be very smart or whatever barriers they put up. Everyone in an organization that is doing a job has some value, or they wouldn't be in that role. The job for the consultant team is to understand and pull out insights. You've got to respect the client's point of view, why they did it, what they think, etc. You may not agree with it, but you've got to be respectful in that interview.

Q. What is the one thing you do as a leader to create a team culture that makes junior staff want to work for you?

A. I look for quick wins that everyone contributes to. I reward people with positive behavior and reinforce that when they've done something really well. I think that's so critical. I never ask the team to run an analysis or do a project piece or a work stream I don't think is critical to the project. People working for me realize that when I ask for something to be done, it's because it's really needed. It doesn't mean that you have to stay up until two in the morning and I'm going to disregard it when I've seen it for a few seconds the next day. It's going to be a valued input to the team if I've asked for it.

I'm very respectful of everyone's time and

effort and value, but there are times we need stuff, and everyone's going to have to do that. But I don't ask people to do busy work for the sake of research saying, *Wouldn't that be interesting?* There's not enough time to do the interesting stuff; you want to focus on what's important and concise for the client.

Q. What advice would you give your younger self?

A. I would network early on in my career. I got on it later in life only because I didn't have the time to network with friends and colleagues. I chose to spend time with my husband; I should have balanced it all. I really think keeping in contact with folks and helping folks or making connections for folks is important and isn't for later on in your career.

I would seek out alternative points of view earlier in my career. We tend to ask people with similar mindsets their opinions, and they're going to support what we want to hear rather than forcing me to think through what I might choose.

Lastly, there are always three sides to something. Yours, the associates you work with, and the people who are outside of your organization. I focused so much on the internal, myself, what I needed to do. Then I gradually picked up my associates and then eventually the third. I should have started earlier on having all three. It's great to be motivated when you're twenty-five and looking up, but you also need to be thinking around you. I didn't reach out to colleagues, and I didn't reach out once I moved from one place or the other; I didn't keep as close of contact with a lot of people. I wish I had reached out and leveraged those relationships. I was just too busy focusing on what I had to do in the next role.

15

Learn the Art of Influence, Pushback, and Negotiation

Stay strong. Stand up. Have a voice.

—Shawn Johnson

As discussed earlier, great consultants understand the need to navigate organizational politics and how to leverage tactical skills such as influence, pushback, and negotiation. There is a 99.9 percent chance you will have moments throughout your consulting career where you will need to leverage one, two, or all three of these skills to move along interests. Examples of negotiation include a client's expectation of a deliverable or you being extended on an engagement. You might influence leadership decisions to bring on a new team member. It could also mean being *voluntold*. Being voluntold is a phenomenon when you are explicitly volunteered for stretch assignments, special projects,

> **Pushback:** the act of expressing a difference of opinion on a particular topic, concept, or decision.

and internal initiatives designed to help you grow. As with anything, it is not what happens to you; it is about your reaction. Great consultants own the narrative of the situation. A summary of the hundred-plus selected practices, unwritten rules, and habits discussed throughout this book can be found in the appendix.

A summary of the hundred-plus selected practices, unwritten rules, and habits discussed throughout this book can be found in the appendix.

My First Pushback and Negotiation Career Moment

The first time I had to push back at work was on a year-long project I was super excited about rolling off of. I had reached out to my network and was deciding between two equally amazing opportunities. Just as I had scheduled a meeting with my counselor to decide on a project, my resource manager had shocking news. The client wanted to extend me on the project for another six months.

Six months? There went my opportunity to pursue the type of work I wanted to do. I had built up my brand to land any project I wanted. While my current project was a great experience, I was ready to move on. I looked forward to learning something new in subject matter that I was more passionate about. From the time I started my career, I knew that I wanted to do strategy work on the people side. I did not want to become pigeonholed and had heard from colleagues that it was easy to get stuck working on this particular solution.

For the first time in my career, I decided to push back. I remember being very scared and had anxiety for days. Up until that moment I had always done exactly what my employer wanted me to do. But something about this felt different. Luckily, my career counselor and practice leadership were supportive and discussed it with my project leadership. Working with leadership, I brokered a deal to remain on my current engagement for another month while I trained my replacement. Thank goodness I secured a colleague seeking a new project.

I was so thankful and worked my guts out. I must have pulled ninety to one hundred hour weeks for the next month. My goal was not to miss a beat on my new project while making sure that my replacement on the other project was successful. I couldn't skip a beat on either project to prove that I was worthy of those opportunities.

About six weeks later I was able to transition full-time to my dream project. That engagement actually began the trajectory of my current area of expertise. It was exactly that type of consulting work I always wanted to do and a career moment that truly mattered.

Knowing When and How to Push Back and Negotiate Is Key

While the previous story ended well and changed my career, some of my attempts at pushing back were not as successful. I once asked to lead a particular section of a proposal writing effort. I was originally tasked with screening résumés, which is important for an RFP submission but to me was boring. I made sure to do the résumé screening responsibility extremely well while I used up a lot of networking capital to be positioned for a proposal section lead role. Leadership wanted someone with deep experience to play the section lead role I had my eye on. No matter how much I conveyed interest and even wrote up sample abstracts, the senior partner didn't budge. He was adamant about having a certain skill set. What pushing back did do that time was get me out of screening résumés to actually being part of that section lead's team, another great learning opportunity.

You have to know when to hold them, know when

to fold them. There are many times when you may push back, and it doesn't lead you toward your desired goals. That is okay. An unwritten rule is that you must consistently outperform in your current role and stay patient while seeking new opportunities. Great consultants are always on the move because when opportunities open up, they are best positioned to take advantage of them.

Knowing how to gracefully push back is critical. First off, pushback is not always a negative thing perceived as a win-lose situation. If you define pushback in this context, you will burn bridges. Pushback is a series of discussions, explored options, and most of all transparency by socializing ideas with all invested parties. It takes patience and wherewithal to manage the political dynamics of pushing back.

Remember that you always have a choice. It is up to you to decide how to come up with an approach to creatively handle those delicate situations. Unlike most careers where you pretty much follow the beaten path, consulting is a bit different. Large consulting firms cultivate career ownership cultures, where individual consultants own their career. To truly own your career, you have to know the art of pushback and learn how to create win-win situations when doing so.

CONSULTING LEADER INTERVIEW...

Fireside Chat with a Partner

Monica is a partner at a leading management consulting firm. In this interview Monica shares how she got into the profession, the importance of being your authentic self, and shares helpful tips on how to be a trusted advisor.

Q. Why did you choose to go into consulting? Is it everything you expected it to be?

A. I never really decided to go into consulting. I ended up in it. In fact, most of my career was not a result of deliberately planning career moves; they were more opportunities that just arose and were presented based on needs in the organization, coupled with my passion for paving new ground and taking on new challenges. Many roles were brand new ones that hadn't previously even existed. I originally started at Arthur Andersen in audit, and as the office I was in started to do consulting work, they needed people for those projects, but we didn't have an official consulting department. They thought I'd be interested. I was, so I started doing them and essentially just kept doing more and more and more. It was a mix of audit and consulting work but the mix kept on shifting more toward consulting.

Then a big project came up right at the beginning of busy season for audit, and it was going to require full time, and the audit partner said, "If you want to do this consulting project that's full time, it will probably last at least a year. You probably need to shift over to the formal consulting department."

I was in a new office that had a formal consulting group. I thought: *That sounds fun!* So I made the shift, and it was an evolution, and because of the opportunities to do that kind of work, it was getting more and more interesting. I loved my audit background; I loved having all that accounting knowledge but thought it wasn't necessarily something I wanted to do for the rest of my career. I wanted to leverage that foundation, but doing a lot of different kinds of projects for different clients in different industries sounded pretty appealing.

That was in 1991 or 1992 at the height of re-engineering, so that was a pretty fun time to go full steam ahead and dedicate myself to doing consulting work. That first project ended up being life changing—well, at least career changing— because I learned a lot of new skills. During part of it, coincidentally, we had a week's lull in between phases. I was in Ohio, and the engagement team was based in New York. I had the Ohio location, and someone else had a different location.

In New York they said: *Hey, we're piloting some new training at Arthur Andersen. Since we're waiting a week before our next phase starts, why don't you come over and join us for it?*

I said sure, flew to New York, and that week of training was about implementation. People were realizing that re-engineering was not just about wonderful process maps; it was all about change management. That was my first exposure. I came from an audit, CPA background into a training course that was about organizational behavior and change management and communications, something in college I thought was not very technical or very difficult, so I didn't spend much time there.

I developed an unbelievable fascination for and appreciation of it. One of the things we did that week was go through a very simple learning styles instrument, similar to Myers-Briggs. We took our scores and went to the four quadrants of the room, and the sheer realization that people had different learning styles was new to me. I was hugely appreciative because I was still in my twenties learning that, and there were people in the room who were in their fifties who had gone almost their whole career not really knowing that people operate and think and process differently. It explained so much to them after they had muddled through for several decades. That was kind of a life changing and definitely a career changing event that happened to be tied to the project.

Having an appreciation for the people side of change—paired with a lot of technical knowledge I had from process design work plus my whole finance background to make the business case for change—reinforced my desire to focus on large-scale, organizational change.

Then I got an opportunity to do several stints in large-scale corporations over a couple of decades. I thought it would be fun to get back into consulting and did a stint with a boutique customer strategy consultancy. Then I got a call from an old friend to join my current firm.

Q. Has consulting met your expectations given how you fell into it?

A. It's probably more than I expected it to be because of my current firm. We are growing so fast and doing so many new things. With all the technology changes, there's just more to figure out and more solutions to develop at a faster pace than I probably ever would've expected.

Q. What is one skill you perfected that has made all the difference throughout your consulting career?

A. As you can imagine, it's hard to say just one skill. One is the passion and ability and willingness to be adaptable and flexible and learn new skills all the time.

Another one that comes to mind is the insatiable appetite for learning, regardless of whether it's something you need right at the moment. Just learning because it may come in handy someday. So that desire to learn and absorb, whether from clients or colleagues, has probably been another important attribute.

A skill I got much better at was presentation and public speaking. It sounds kind of basic but after taking a class, I realized the power and importance of delivery of content versus just having the content. I was shocked by how much difference delivery can make. That was probably career-changing. I realized it was really about being your full, authentic self.

You need to figure out how you want to come across—typically what your personality is—then make sure that nothing gets in the way of that. In the class I attended, we discussed if you want to be calm or smart or confident or funny or any other list of attributes. Then we were recorded, and I got a chance to watch myself and realized: *Oh, wow! What happened to me? Where did I go?*

That was very interesting. It wasn't just about public speaking; it was about being authentic at work and being yourself. Who do you want to be perceived as? If you are natural then you can actually focus on the content, the technical stuff, and you don't have to worry about all this other stuff that gets in the way.

Q. In your experience what are common themes or decision points of why people leave their firm? What made you stay at those same points in your career?

A. Common themes I've seen is the work-life balance or the intensity of travel. For some younger people, they've come here for a couple of years, and they want to try something new, just because. They're not really thinking of it as being their long-term career necessarily, they simply want some variety.

Other themes are that they weren't planning to leave, but a client or colleague approached them with a phenomenal opportunity at a time when they weren't really sure where they sat at the firm. Uncertainty led them to take other opportunities.

When I first left consulting, I had a bad day. I walked into my friend's office, and he was on the phone with a recruiter. He said: *Hey, so and so is looking for someone. Do you know anyone?* I was like: *Yeah, give them my number.*

So he did. One thing led to another, and I left. I wasn't planning to leave at all at that point. But as the opportunity unfolded, I thought: *I don't know if I'm ready to leave right now, but I'm not sure this is really what I want to do forever.* I wasn't necessarily committed to it as a long-term career. I was probably a second-year manager, and this other job opportunity sounded great. I stay now because it is fun and exhilarating.

Q. What are some of your expectations of the dos and don'ts of client deliverables?

A. Grammar and spelling. Not just from young consultants, seasoned consultants as well. They seem to think that it doesn't have to be right, or they don't know what's right or wrong. They have no idea that the client knows proper English, and it reflects on the content of their work. It sounds pretty boring, but it's necessary.

The other part is clarity of message and simplicity. I sometimes see all sorts of junk on slides that's not simple, but there's also not a clear thought process to begin with. If you ask the person to put the slides away and just talk—*What are you trying to say?*—they can often easily articulate what needs to be put on paper.

My expectations or guidance to young people is think first, get a clear storyline and thought process before you start working on client deliverables.

Q. What actionable steps can younger consultants take to build and master the art of influence toward becoming a trusted advisor to their clients?

A. The things that come to mind are to truly learn and practice active listening. It's hard for younger people. They're just out of school. They want to share what they know. It's really hard to actively listen. But that is a big step toward building a relationship and becoming a trusted advisor.

Another piece would be understanding personality styles to learn how to better relate and connect to different types of people.

The third thing would be to find ways to add value to that client personally and professionally. Work on building credibility and adding value, not trying to make the sale.

Q. How do you advise younger consultants to gracefully push back to help shape their career in a way that creates a win-win for their firm and their career.

A. Encourage younger consultants not to consider pushing back; it implies a negative positioning where someone will win, and someone will lose. It's a pet peeve of mine when I'm in a conversation and hear someone say: *Well, I want to push back on that.* It implies, *Well, I guess we're going to have an argument about that,* instead of, *Oh, that's an interesting perspective that I haven't heard before, I have some thoughts I'd really like to share.* It opens up a completely different conversation.

Usually the person on the receiving end of the discussion is probably going to be more than willing to help when you bring them into the discussion. Crafting the message properly quickly turns the conversation into more of a teaming discussion of *How can you help me achieve this?* versus *I don't want to be in your practice or your project anymore.*

It's like coaching, consultation, and guidance—be upfront, have that conversation. The other part of it is to network with people on other projects that you think you want to be working with—especially if it's a different area—and ask if there are things you can work on for them to get to know them and get to know that area better.

If you want to roll off a long-term engagement, the earlier the better to minimize disruptions. If it looks like a win-win, it's much easier for that person running an engagement or a person in a practice to ask for you.

Q. What is your secret travel tip to help create a sense of work-life balance while you're on the road?

A. Trying to see if there's something non-work related

to add to the trip. In New York for example, going shopping or going to a concert or a Broadway show or a different type of cultural restaurant. Or finding a friend or relative in the city that you can see on that trip, often by just adding a day. So maximizing the trip by doing something that's not work-related is important.

Q. Any last remarks on becoming a great consultant?

A. When I was in school, an alumnus had opened a small business and came back to the school to give a lecture on his experiences. On the blackboard in our big accounting classroom, he wrote in huge letters LOVE. The point being do what you love to do. Do what you love. Know there will be good days and bad days, but if on average you're not loving what you're doing and wanting to show up at work every day, then something has to change.

As Joseph Campbell stated in the *Power of Myth*, which relates to authenticity: *follow your bliss.* Another quote I like says: *If you follow the path that's been laid out for you or that everyone else follows, it's not your own.* If you're just trying to replicate every step that someone else has done, then it's not your own path.

16

Roll Off with Grace

If you want something new, you have to stop doing something old.

—PETER DRUCKER

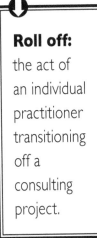

Transitional periods in your consulting career are critical junctures. What goes up, must come down. It's the same concept in consulting. Projects you roll onto, you will roll off of. One main advantage of a consulting career is that you know there is always a beginning and an end to a project. In traditional corporate roles, you may drone on and on in a never-ending cycle with work. I have always loved consulting because if I do not like a project, I rely on the fact that it will end at some point.

Roll off: the act of an individual practitioner transitioning off a consulting project.

The concept of rolling off also speaks to general transitions in your career. Rolling off techniques are used whether transferring out of a practice, moving to a new office in another region or country, or resigning to go to another firm or back to school. Rolling off should be a graceful act. Seek to roll off a project, job, or firm on a high note. Before attempting to roll off if you're on a project you don't like, figure out why.

You are walking away after having built relationships and gained experiences. Great consultants are always remembered when they roll off. Are you going to be memorable when you leave?

Rolling off should be a graceful act. Seek to roll off a project, job, or firm on a high note. Before attempting to roll off if you're on a project you don't like, figure out why.

Selected Practices of a Graceful Roll Off

- ◆ End the project as strong as you began. Roll off with the same level of enthusiasm and professionalism as you had when you obtained the opportunity in the first place.
- ◆ Think through the entire lifecycle of your time on an engagement then script out what you would like to have happen on a project before it starts. Plan your roll off months ahead.
- ◆ Structure project folders to easily transfer knowledge to someone taking over your role or shutting the project down.

Keep Relationships Intact during Roll Off

Rolling off a project is to be handled delicately and gracefully. I see many consultants become really careless when it comes to rolling off a project. Imagine all the hard work you have done toiling on a project. You worked hard to build a reputation. Teams come to count on you. Both clients and leaders like and trust you. Mishandling a project roll-off translates to lost trust and credibility.

The trust, reliability, and likeability you spent time building can evaporate within minutes. Remember the saying: *People may not remember what you said, but they remember how you made them feel.* Great consultants exit gracefully to leverage those network connections in the future. Sometimes consultants develop tunnel vision and do not take the time to understand how actions impact the bigger picture of a career. Great consultants also keep in touch with their clients and former team members.

CONSULTING LEADER INTERVIEW...

Fireside Chat with a Partner

Ellen Zimiles, named one of the Top 25 Consultants in 2016 by *Consulting* magazine, is a partner and head of investigations and global compliance at Navigant Consulting, a publicly-traded global professional services firm. She oversees a growing revenue segment with three hundred consultants at Navigant. Under her leadership, Navigant has become a trusted advisor and go-to resource for global banks confronting the post-Dodd-Frank regulatory environment as well as a partner to governments seeking monitors to ensure compliance with consent decrees.

A former prosecutor for the US Attorney, Ellen discusses how she started in consulting then started her own company that was bought out by a publicly-traded consulting firm. In this interview she also shares her career journey, her biggest lessons learned, and guidance on the most impactful ways to become a great consultant.

Q. Please share how you got started in consulting. Is it everything you expected it to be?

A. I was a federal prosecutor before going into consulting. I was chief of the forfeiture unit at the US Attorney's Office for the Southern District of New York. In this role, we took over a lot of companies and buildings, and I really liked learning how companies worked. When I was going to leave this type of work, I decided to go to a consulting firm where I dealt with how companies operate versus just the legal aspect.

That's how I got into consulting. I worked for KPMG for almost a decade. When I first started consulting, I had to learn quite a bit. When you're a prosecutor you look mainly at the negative; you want to see if there's been a violation. When you are a consultant, you look not just for the negatives; you also look for what works well. You want to get the bigger balance of the organization. If somebody murders someone or shoots somebody, you don't say: *Yes, that they did, but then they went to church on Sunday.* You just look at the act itself. When you're a consultant, it's looking more at the big picture. And I did have to learn that lesson.

I had to do a review with a client, and I had thirteen things they did wrong, and the client said to me, "Didn't I do anything right? You know my bosses are going to see this, with the things I did right, can you include that?"

I said, "You know what? You're totally right; let's do that."

That was a very good lesson. There are things I didn't appreciate until I started doing it. I learned a lot about how business operates. Not just the business we consult for but also the business I was operating in, how firms make money, how they don't.

When I started my own firm, with private equity funds backing me, I learned how to operate a company and how to make it successful, what works well, what doesn't work well. The importance of treating people right, the importance of being direct and honest even though it's not always fun. How to deliver that message with humanity and empathy.

I learned a lot about managing people and managing a company through that. I then sold that company to Navigant in 2010 and have been with Navigant since. And even with Navigant, even though it wasn't always smooth, I figured out how to work here, and I think it's actually worked out quite well.

It took time to go from having your own company to then coming into a publicly-traded company. Client work has been fairly consistent, but I've developed as a consultant in terms of looking at the big picture of going out and trying to understand and prioritize different issues. I have been very fortunate, and it was worth coming over to consulting; I've really gotten to have a great career that's very broad but deep.

Q. In your experience, what are common themes or decision points of why colleagues, members of your team, etc., leave their firm? What made you stay at those same points in your career?

A. Not being respected. Sometimes it's money. But if you feel like you're respected, like your voice is being heard, that you get to do interesting work that you can see a career path, then you shouldn't leave. If you don't see those things, then it's not a good place.

As I have developed over time, I stay because I believe I have received those things, and I also believe I have an obligation to the people I have brought in and who I work with to try to make this the best place they can be and to give them a career path. I feel like I've had a really great career and I want to give other people great careers. I think if people in general feel they are respected and their voices are heard, they do meaningful work, and they're compensated appropriately.

Q. What advice would you give consultants seeking to get staffed on a certain project or join a specific competency or sector, particularly those seeking glamorous projects?

A. It's always fun to work on something glamorous although the work isn't always glamorous. The engagement might seem exciting because of who the client is, but sometimes the work is pretty dreadful. You want to work with the right team and get the right kind of work. You want your experience to develop you; I often see people who get promoted too early and don't know enough about the work they do, then they become a manager and they're managing people but don't really know how to do that work well.

Also, managing people is not necessarily natural to people, and you have to learn how to manage and learn how to get someone to do something they wouldn't do otherwise. How do you get someone to reveal the best part of their world? Not everybody can do the same things. Everyone is different, their strengths and weaknesses, and you have to be thoughtful about that as well.

Q. In your opinion, what are three impactful, quick wins that an individual should consider doing to become a great consultant?

A. One is to pick a topic that they have some passion about and write about it. Have other people read it and say: *Does this make sense?* And listen to others' feedback on that. And then put that out there. When you have to write something, challenge yourself to write it, and make it accessible to someone who doesn't know about it.

Work on writing because at the end of the day, all the client is left with is your written product. If you're not a good writer that will always hold you back. You can have a great meeting with somebody, but those meetings don't necessarily carry the day because the product may be looked at two years later.

You have to work on your written product, work on your knowledge base and your ability to speak about a topic. If you really are interested in it and have enthusiasm about it, that goes so far. People will understand and believe what you say and will know that you really understand that particular subject matter area.

Q. How often do you celebrate successes in consulting with your colleagues or team? What are ways that you do?

A. We do it in multiple ways; there is no one way to do it because some things require more, others require less. One example is that I had a big event at my house for female millennials that had an issue with something they wanted to discuss. With over fifty people in attendance, they appreciated that they could speak to me and the CEO of the firm to discuss the issues they had, how to address them, and how to communicate better. It was great, and I think they appreciated having themselves heard and having very high-level people respond to them.

Q. Knowing what you know now in consulting, what advice would you give your younger self?

A. Don't get frustrated with people who are at the firm who may have their own agendas. And sometimes you get into turf battles with people. Don't worry about them. If someone doesn't treat you the right way, just like Michelle Obama says: *When they go low, you go high.* As my younger self I would have gotten more upset if I didn't think somebody was acting properly; I get much less worried about that stuff now.

REFLECTIONS OF A CONSULTING CAREER

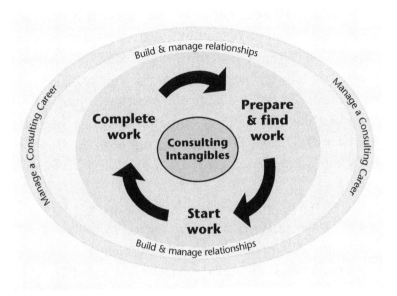

FIGURE 15. Managing Your Consulting Career Puts It All Together

The same way great consultants use a systematic approach to work, they also have a method of pausing, reflecting, and making critical career decisions. In order to do this well, consultants make strategic decisions based on facts, not fiction. Avoid making decisions based on raw emotions. Create a personal board of directors comprised of mentors, advisors, and sponsors to help you make career decisions. Gather information, conduct analysis, and consult trusted sources to make informed career decisions.

Seek to have harmony in your career but also have contingency career plans. Sometimes we go through challenges or obstacles in life that steer us toward our true path. Follow your head and your heart. We each inherently know when something is good for us or if a situation is toxic.

Consulting does not have to be a one dimensional, linear career path of self-imposed rules and boundaries. Consulting is like tofu; it can take on whatever "taste" or "flavor" you choose to for your career. Great consultants do not live a life of limitation or judge those around them for making empowered decisions. Live your truth. Do not fall into the trap of making career decisions solely based on the approval or judgment of others.

I've been at a colleague's going away party and heard: *Wow, Billy is so lucky. He's getting out of this prison and going to work for a startup. How cool is that?*

I glance over and think: *Prison? Is this really coming from a twenty-nine-year-old MBA graduate making over $100K a year in a career they chose?*

Don't become that type of consultant, spewing hate and divisive judgment yet envious of those making bold career moves. If you have anxiety on Sunday (Sunday Scaries), hate Mondays, get hope on hump day Wednesdays, or bursting with a sigh of relief on Friday (or your travel day), seriously think if a consulting career is really for you. If consulting is not for you, try something else. If you do not like your project, practice, or firm, then try something else. I've also witnessed miserable, POS or role-player consultants act superior and ridiculously judge colleagues or peers based on frivolous non-factors such as working for a smaller firm, being an experienced hire from industry, or coming in from a firm acquisition, graduating from a small college, or even servicing certain types of clients. Don't become that type of consultant either.

As a consultant, you will feel like you are constantly at a crossroads due to the temporary nature of our work. Discussions about exit opportunities outside of consulting is a topic consultants never get tired of. Great consultants are not afraid to use lily pads and ladders in their careers, a concept I adapted from Adam Poswolsky's book *The Quarter-Life Breakthrough*, which offers tactics to consider when you feel stuck. Like a frog, use lily pads to make leaps from one area to another at the same level that offers opportunities to gain a breadth of exposure to a host of new skills and experiences. Even if that means making less money or slowing down the speed of promotions. Other times it makes better sense to move full steam ahead up a ladder to gain experience of new levels of responsibilities and challenges.

Deciding when to leverage which path depends on where you are in life. Do not let anyone define when you use which approach. Great consultants are found working at consulting firms, working for themselves, starting their own consulting firm, or employed as internal consultants within an organization. What is amazing about consulting is the flexibility. You have the power to decide when and how you use a lily pad or ladder. Do not let anyone take that power away from you.

Great consultants have purpose. While they may not have a five- to ten-year career plan mapped out, they are willing to try new things.

"I would just reinforce that when planning careers find something really enjoyable," says Monica, a partner at a leading management consulting firm.

Own the narrative of your experiences and career. Deciding how to manage a sustainable career is knowing your options and not being afraid to forge into the unknown. You will realize how blessed you are and how magical your consulting career will become.

17

Shape Your Consulting Experience

A mind that is stretched by a new experience can never go back to its old dimensions.

—OLIVER WENDELL HOLMES

The key to a successful consulting career is not working at the biggest or most prestigious consulting firm, although that offers amazing opportunities. It's not graduating from a top Ivy League school, although that is impressive and commendable. It's not growing up in a wealthy family with knowledge, resources, and connections although that is a lucky set of circumstances. Pedigree does create a competitive edge. They pale in comparison to what really matters in consulting: experience.

Experiences Defined

Experiences are a summary of different clients, challenges, business problems, and teams. Experiences offer the opportunity to build skills, knowledge, and expertise. Clients pay for experience and expertise. The more experience you obtain is a surefire way to begin building your tool kit of knowledge.

Embrace the Journey of Experiences

At the beginning of your career, say yes to any and every type of experience that you have the bandwidth to take on. Do not worry about whether you think you will like it or not. Sometimes you know exactly what you want to focus on as I did. Even so, the goal is to learn as much as possible. Chances are if you are just getting started, your career interests are not completely defined. That's okay. Great consultants have an open mind and stay receptive to a wide variety of experiences. They under-

WAYS TO GAIN EXPERIENCES IN A CONSULTING CAREER

Type of Consulting Experience	Description
Market-facing (external) consultant at a boutique, medium sized, or large consulting firm.	Most traditional consulting career path. Offers you the ability to gain exposure to a breadth and depth of varied business experiences with clients in a short amount of time with the backing of a firm network and infrastructure.
In-house (internal) consultant within an organization.	With more schedule stability and less travel, internal consulting allows you an opportunity to build influential skills, have visibility to the leadership, and shape the strategic agenda while understanding the needs and mindset of a client and gaining firsthand experience on executing strategic recommendations.
Independent consultant or boutique firm owner.	Offers ultimate flexibility and career ownership in consulting. Ideal if you have an entrepreneurial spirit, strong network, and solid expertise in targeted areas.

stand that this will help them develop and refine core consulting skills.

The best way to gain experience is to step up and ask. Do the work that no one else wants to do. Those are the golden opportunities. It's usually in the least sexy or in the hardest work that you learn the most. The nuggets you learn will lead to more exciting opportunities over time.

Embrace the grunt work. It is in the repetition where you build the skills, habits, and stamina of the business. In the future, advanced technologies will replace some of the tedious work that has to be done on engagements. But until then, consultants have to do it. Instead of complaining, enjoy those moments. There is something to be said about building fundamental basic skills.

Consultants tend to always complain about being on the same project for years. What they fail to realize is that during this time frame there is an opportunity to create meaningful and deep relationships.

Embrace when you do not get that performance rating, bonus, or promotion you think you deserved. It's in those moments you learn how to deal with disappointment. Your attitude about those moments determines your altitude. Accept that sometimes decisions are within your span of control and sometimes they are not.

Embrace the moments when you feel that someone asked you to do something that you deemed beneath your talents. You didn't get that fancy MBA to collate folders and make copies for a presentation, right?

Once you have certain experiences under your belt, take control of your career by having a clear end goal in mind for each experience.

I have gained the most experience in stretch roles. Some stretch roles were a smashing success, others not so much. I am so thankful for these experiences because it helped me sharpen my leadership skills. Now

I gauge where I am on the learning curve and adjust as needed. In my younger days, it was more of a *let me try this and see if it sticks*. I wouldn't advise going through the motions without support; do not be an island of one. Reach out to peers, managers, and leadership for the support you need.

Moving onto New Projects vs. Extensions

Consultants are brought onto a project for a temporary endeavor, and due to the volatile, ever-evolving nature of client environment, there is always a likelihood of being extended or work being cut short due to budget cuts.

Many times when a consultant doesn't like a project, it's because:

- They don't like or understand their individual role; have a fear of being pigeonholed.
- They don't like how the project is being managed.
- The work was not what they expected it to be.
- They don't fit into the team culture.

What's Next in Your Career?

People decide on a career in consulting for many reasons. Some stay longer than they expected in the career, while others spend a couple of years and move on. If you are not sure what your long-term career goals are, start giving it some thought. Be honest with yourself in answering the questions. Separate fact from fiction and clarify how you are feeling. Ignoring your feelings will only prevent you from performing your best. Clarity is powerful.

Once you have made a decision, stick to it. Constant symptoms of FOMO—fear of missing out—or imposter syndrome is a career destabilizer. When you live in doubt and uncertainty of a decision, that energy flows into your daily habits and practices. You don't give it your best. Be great! No regrets, no looking back. Keep moving forward!

CONSULTING LEADER INTERVIEW...

Fireside Chat with a Partner

Diane is a partner and practice leader of a large global consulting firm. With over twenty plus years of experience, Diane shares how she got started in consulting, the best career advice she's ever received, and an experience that helped shape how she does business today.

Q. Share how you decided to go into consulting? Is it everything you expected it to be?

A. I am a problem-solver by nature. Upon graduation, it wasn't clear, though, how to apply my love of solving problems with my need to support myself! I settled on consulting after finding a graduate program that fed my curiosity about the intersection between strategy, psychology, and organization. I was thrilled to find an entire career called Human Performance Design (now Human Capital, Change Management, People Analytics) where I could solve problems every day that would make a difference to individual people. Consulting "called me" initially because of the opportunity to be exposed to different companies, industries, business issues; it has "kept me" given both my riad experiences and amazingly bright colleagues and clients passionate about making the people experience a great one.

As for consulting being everything I expected it to be? I never had an expectation going in, so I would say it has been a learning experience personally and professionally. On the one hand, I've traveled the world, solved some amazingly important business issues with clients, and continued to stay relevant in a very fast-paced environment. On the other hand, I've made personal sacrifices given the lifestyle, and sometimes I leave a client thinking "I'd like to stick around to see how this turns out!" I think what's most important for me as I reflect on my 20+ year career is this: I've made it what I wanted and needed it to be at every stage of my career. I consciously chose to be where I was, doing what I was doing, through the good and bad.

Q. Share the best career advice you received from an unlikely source.

A. I've been incredibly fortunate to have mentors along my consulting journey. I live by the following pieces of advice many have shared through the years:

  1. Challenge yourself every day. Wake up asking "how am I relevant today?" Find ways to stay relevant.

2. Build and nurture relationships. Every week nurture an existing relationship and make a new one. Your clients are your network.

3. Failure is critical to your growth. Celebrate the tough times. It's too easy to jump ship. You learn more when things aren't going well.

4. Know yourself and manage your energy. Consulting is a lifestyle, not just a job. It's tough on relationships, physical and mental health. Always know your boundaries and actively nurture your well-being.

Q. Describe the one career experience that has shaped your values and how you do business today.

A. My values and how I do business today are shaped by my upbringing, professional and personal experiences. One professional experience stands out for me over the years. I was a young manager working for a seasoned director. We were in a working session with a team of engineers who were very unhappy that they would be required to use a CAD tool that they hadn't chosen or felt was the leading tool at the time. I watched as my boss expertly used humor and storytelling to bring the engineers into the discussion and through a very difficult training session. It was at that moment when I saw the power of humor and storytelling to diffuse a tough situation.

Q. How do you balance the art of negotiation and influence when you push back from a client, peers, or your firm?

A. Listen carefully. I think a lot of times we rush to a solution or an answer and in the process, alienate different stakeholders. If you spend time listening to individual stakeholder viewpoints, then consider options that can be a starting point for a negotiation, you are more likely to bring people willingly to the table.

Q. Any last remarks on becoming a great consultant?

A. Spend time in your client's shoes so you really understand what it takes to make change stick in an organization.

18

Follow the Traditional Consulting Path

It's a beautiful thing when a career and passion come together.

—AUTHOR UNKNOWN

There are specific keys and milestones to success as you consider each level of your career. Traditional career milestones in a consulting career are typically pre-packaged as an "up-or-out" partner career model at the top consulting firms. Great consultants proactively plan their career trajectory on a traditional path as early on as possible.

> **Traditional partner path:** the time-based career path at most large consulting firms; while the actual rank title may change from firm to firm, career progression milestones used to quantify the experience level of a consultant.

Variables to a Promotion in Consulting

A commonly asked question by new consultants: *How do I create a career path to move up the ladder as quickly as possible?* Guess what? There is no exact method toward a faster promotion. Upward mobility at higher levels is a combination of seven variables:

- ◆ skillset needs versus timing of need/demand in the market
- ◆ financial health of your firm/practice/region to afford your promotion
- ◆ economic outlook and trends of the market
- ◆ proximity of access and visibility to leadership
- ◆ strength of your network, client relationships, and ability to influence

- strength of your mentorship/sponsorship/circle of trust
- current capacity to operate at the next level

I strongly advise against early promotions to the next level until you are operationally ready. What does operationally ready mean? You are operating comfortably at the next level for at least 1–2 years. Comfortably means that you deliver day in and day out with certainty, confidence, and capabilities at the next career level. It also means you have the right experiences, rela-

Sometimes career success on a traditional partner path is as simple as good timing and sheer luck.

tionships, mentorship support, skills, and capacity to tackle the challenging expectations of the next role. Sometimes career success on a traditional partner path is as simple as good timing and sheer luck.

Once promoted to the next career level, leadership immediately starts expecting more from you, which could have lasting impact on your personal brand or reputation if you cannot deliver.

The Long-Distance Run to Partner

Newer consultants are always on a mad dash to what is intended to be a career-long journey. Many consultants work themselves to death in pursuit of perfection, prestige, and promotions. Stay the course and enjoy the journey. A long-term career is a marathon, not a sprint. Once I accepted that consulting could be whatever I define the career to be for me personally and not based on the approval of others, everything changed.

- Treat constructive feedback as a performance and career booster shot. Instead of wallowing or being defensive, embrace it. Feedback gives you a glimpse of actions to take your performance to the next level.

- Do not refuse a project because you don't think the client or work is not glamorous enough. Those are the diamonds in the rough that provide the opportunity to position yourself to do extremely well. Instead, refuse projects that will rob you of a supportive, coaching environment. Stay clear of vindictive, toxic team cultures.

- Do not limit yourself solely to tried-and-true career paths.

CONSULTING LEADER INTERVIEW...

Fireside Chat with a Partner

Udanda is a recently promoted partner at a leading management consulting firm with over sixteen years of experience in the financial technology sector. A University of North Carolina graduate, Udanda spent her entire career at one firm, moving up through the ranks from intern to partner. In this interview Udanda highlights recent experiences in her transition to the partnership while moving to a new city to lead up a new practice, shares thoughts on her experiences as an African-American woman partner, and describes how she made the decision to become a partner.

Q. How did you decide to go into consulting?

A. Growing up I wanted to be a doctor and went to the UNC Chapel Hill. I worked in the hospital all four years. During my second year in college, I decided that's not the place I wanted to be and spend the next four years of my life after college. While I love taking care of people in need, I didn't like being around sick people. At that time, I was also trying to figure out: *Okay I'm interested in biology, but I'm not really learning about practical things about what's really moving the world.* I didn't feel glued or tied to the sciences.

I decided to take an accounting course as one of my electives because it was one of the most popular classes on campus. I surprisingly enjoyed it. I thought: *Well, that's weird.* At the time it was too late to get into the business school, so I decided to finish my biology degree. I pursued a master's in accounting because it seemed to be a better fit for me. The plan was to have two years of experience at my consulting firm and then go to medical school.

As I started working, the tables really turned in year two. I started getting all types of global experience and exposure. I thought: *Maybe you need this opportunity. Let me try it.* And, that's pretty much the story of my career. Fast forward a decade later, I started thinking that maybe I needed to go back to my childhood dream because that's kind of what I wanted to do.

My husband said to me, "Udanda, you're

enjoying what you're doing. The only reason you're struggling with this, quite frankly, is because it doesn't reconcile to what you thought."

I realized that I had to let go of my childhood dreams that had envisioned what I would like as an adult. My career had me going places, experiencing things, and I felt like I was getting something out of it. So four years ago I released the childhood dream in exchange for the reality of how I feel now. And I think that that has worked well for me. I've gotten comfortable in my skin and truly began to embrace my career.

And that leads me to today. I got promoted in 2016. It took a long time for me, but I wasn't ready. And in some cases, I felt like maybe if I didn't move from Chicago, I would've gotten promoted earlier; maybe if I didn't have a kid, I would've gotten promoted earlier. And what I realized was to let things ride and enjoy the rodeo. Enjoy what you're doing, and then everything else will surface as it needs to. And if it doesn't happen, it means it wasn't meant to be. The one critical point I've always said is stay focused and do the best you can.

Our younger folks, they're like: *Oh, I don't know if I'm a lifer. I don't know if I want to be a partner.* I didn't know that either. I didn't even know it twelve years in. I was still struggling. But what I knew was that I wanted to do the best that I can. Maximize the potential into reality versus theory, and that's how I've approached the career.

Today I lead a Fintech assurance practice in

the West that I am focused on building out. I think it's important to stretch and allow stretching to happen in your career. Because those are the moments that you really grow the steepest.

Q. Looking back, has consulting been everything you expected it to be?

A. It is evolving. I am still learning. As a person that has ownership in leading a practice, a person who's a newly promoted partner, I don't feel quite like an intern, and I don't feel like I'm a staff one, but pretty close to the rising staff two. That's what I felt like in this past year. There is this research that the firm puts out about someone when they are promoted to partnership or they go into a new position. It's called the smile effect. You go through a high, then over a certain period of time you dip, and then you come back up.

Mine hasn't been quite the smile. Mine has been what I call a little jack-o'-lantern face moving up and down, up and down, up and down because everything is new. I am in a new office, I am in a new city, I have new colleagues, different culture. And I have moments where I get my groove then something else happens.

In hindsight, I am in the right place. What I learned is that people see things that you don't see in yourself. And so the reality is that people are confident in me, and I need to have that same confidence in myself. I will grow into this role, and it's exciting.

One person told me, "You know, there are a lot of black consultants that are looking to you. They are so excited to see an African-American, a black person—female, at that—in our office."

Wow. really? And I said "Well, come to my door, call me, email me, can you tell whoever is watching me, don't just watch me, come talk to me. I'm happy to sit down with the group and have a whole conversation."

I tell people: Don't get stuck on color. I look at my internal board of directors, and there are not a lot of those that are black women. There are quite a few that are women, but there are also quite a few that are white males. I feel like at my firm it's less about your color, more about your service delivery and your technical competencies to the firm. If your service delivery, your teaming, and technical competency are on point, then they don't really care what you look like. They'll remember you for you.

Q. How do you ask for timely, constructive feedback and leverage it to catapult your career?

A. One of my mentors, Malcolm, says it nicely: "Don't spend 80 percent of our time talking about what I can see; spend 80 percent of the time discussing feedback that I don't see."

What would you have liked for me to have done better? Then I go talk to other partners or other people who are outside of the specific engagement and ask: *What did you hear?* I try to seek feedback from people I am comfortable with or people who are straight shooters. They're just going to tell you what they have heard.

One time I got feedback: *Well done. But it takes a long time for her to close things out.* I was like: *What? Really?* Well, there was a perception I can't close things out. Let me show you how I close out, and it's like how are you communicating where you are in the process. So that was a pivotal feedback.

Q. What is the best compliment that you have ever received in your career? Why was it so impactful to you?

A. I never realized who was watching me. I wasn't very conscious of that until a young black woman said: "You know we are all watching you and we are silently cheering."

She told me that two years ago before I made partner.

"We didn't see your name on the list, but we are silently cheering you. When we see it, it's going to be a great day."

I realized it wasn't about me. I never saw myself as a trailblazer, but working with our young folks and letting them see that they have a voice and that they too belong. You may not feel like you belong right now, but stay the course in what you are doing and it would evolve.

Another compliment came from my late father-in-law. He had a nickname for me that I just learned. He called me the little drill sergeant. At first, I was kind of offended, but then with his passing and the role that I played naturally in the family, it's like: *Oh, he's right; I am a little drill sergeant.* It's now the best nickname; I wish he could have said it to my face, but he never did. I don't think he felt comfortable, but he always said it to his sons. And one of them, my brother-in-law, sent me a message that said: *You are truly the name my father gave you. Thank you because we needed that during this time.* That's probably personally the second-best compliment.

Q. Do you recall the very moment you decided that you were going to become a partner? What influenced or informed your decision?

A. It was four years ago I made the decision, and a couple of things influenced it. Hearing from leadership who felt that way and said: *You have what it takes. You can and will do this if you do XYZ.* Once I heard it from others, it helped me frame up what I was going to do. Stay the course. Talk about your canvas.

I made the decision either you stay or you leave, and if you're leaving start looking at what you're interested in. And every time I looked I got stuck. I realized, and what I tell people all the time who are leaving, I say: *Okay, tell me why you are leaving.* And they give me all the things of why they're leaving but what I want to know is: *What are you going to?* I just started communicating it.

I realized I wanted to make sure that if I left consulting I was leaving because I was going toward something else that I wanted, not leaving because of X, Y, and Z. A lot of people leave because of the hours, clients, because they don't get the exposure, because they are bored. I'm like: *What are you going to do? How is it going to improve for what you need? What would be that agent of change for you in a new position?*

And I wasn't really finding that for myself, so that's when I decided: *Okay, twelve years I'm in. Keep going. Let's rock and see what happens.* And it was just an automatic decision that was made. *Okay, you want to be a partner. You need to start talking about it and how you are going to create the steps for a promotion.*

You've got to create a buzz about yourself.

Q. What are three pet peeves you have that you see consultants do at a client site or working with their team?

A. Communicating electronically. Get off the phone. Talk in person. Talk to your team in person, not through chat.

Over-promising, under-delivering. If you have ten other things going on, talk to me about your ten other things and how what I'm asking you fits into it or it doesn't. And it's okay to say it doesn't. But when you say yes and then it just drags on, it has a ripple effect. It means something down the road.

Consultants that are not good at giving honest feedback and helping coach someone. Which is odd because we are consulting, we are helping engagements, or we're helping companies with a particular issue. But we don't do well trying to coach and mold our people. And part of it is, if you have it, you have it. And if you don't, you cut your losses. But some cultures are more up or out, and other cultures give people the benefit of the doubt. And then they go through this progressive cycle, and in a year or so the person leaves or gets severed.

Q. What advice would you give your younger self?

A. Try to find time to read more about things that interest me. Take time for myself, and make sure that I stay healthy as possible because I think your diet and exercise are key to the energy you have. Whereas I tend to go on adrenaline. As I have gotten older, I've realized in the last busy seasons when I have changed my diet drastically to a much healthier way, I felt better. I thought clearer, I worked harder—not necessarily in time but in productivity.

Be comfortable saying: *I don't really know what you're talking about. I don't understand. Help me work through this.* And don't shy away from some of the challenges; you may not know what to do, but somebody will help you figure it out.

Q. Any last remarks on becoming a great consultant?

A. Emphasize your competencies. Have a *yes, I can,* and *yes, I will* attitude. Being very eager to help goes a long way.

A lot of people who are very smart and went to great schools but then get into consulting and think: *Why am I doing this? This is below who I am. I didn't come to get paid to do this. I'm getting paid to do something great, and you are having me do this.* I would tell people to look at what makes an engagement. Look at the pricing skill and the economics. If it is going to take the partner thirty seconds to do it and take a staff two hours to do the same work, it might make sense for the partner to do it. But if it's low risk, you are going to have the staff involved in it. People sometimes forget that piece of the apprenticeship model. When they start as young consultants, they have to spend time coaching new consultants.

19

Explore Nontraditional Consulting Careers

Life isn't a matter of milestones, but of moments.
—Rose Kennedy

Over time you will realize what you like and don't like in the consulting space as you progress in your career. Non-traditional consulting career tracks will accelerate as a result of disruptive technologies. We will continue to see a rise of subject matter expert consultants, gig consultants, and consulting entrepreneurs.

Subject matter expert (SME): practitioners with deep expertise and knowledge in a specific function, domain, technology, or industry.

Specialist and SME

If you crave the ideation phases of consulting, becoming a specialist is a great option. Specialists prefer the service delivery side such as creation of frameworks and methodologies. Subject matter experts also conduct research and author thought leadership books or articles. Experts focus on influencing emerging trends and advising clients more so than the practice operations, sales, and team-building.

Internal Consultants

Internal consultants are essentially in-house expertise. They consult internally for an organization instead of being billed out. Many companies decide the tremendous cost-savings is more beneficial than hiring contracted help. Internal consulting is a great avenue if you want to gain experience in creating and actually owning the implementation and sustainment of your recommendations. Internal consulting also helps you hone in on your ability to build long-term relationships and influence within an organization.

Gig Consultants, Freelancers, Independent Consultants, and Solopreneurs

If you are a seasoned professional with significant experience and a strong network, becoming an independent consultant is worth exploring. An increasing number of organizations are leveraging this resource model to keep costs down and scale capabilities based on demand to maintain profitable growth. Going independent is one of most flexible in the career track models, but also high risk due to the need for ongoing business development activities to sustain a healthy pipeline of future work.

Firms love the gig model because they scale resource needs without carrying a bench. Individuals love the gig model because of the autonomy. They have an opportunity to gain experiences without committing long-term to one employer.

Boutique Consulting Firm Owners

In today's marketplace with advanced technology, boutique firms can compete with the larger consulting houses. One such example is GovStrive, an eighteen-person boutique HR consulting firm with two locations founded by one of my former counselors, James Sasser.

According to GovStrive's website, the company "is

MECE MENTORING MOMENT

❝Even a challenging day in my company is better than a stable day at a big company. Now, my personal DNA is embedded in every decision in my company; I own every decision and see the impact of those decisions immediately throughout my company. That level of accountability is a fulfilling and exciting motivator.❞

–Paige Arnoff-Fenn, *CEO of Mavens & Moguls*

a professional services firm focused on delivering best-value, results-driven services and solutions to support our clients' most critical mission-related transactional needs within Federal Human Resources (HR) organizations."

When asked about what he has learned about running his own firm versus working in a large company for those that may be considering this path, James says, "Successful careers in big consulting offer lots of client experiences, training and lessons learned. As a small business owner, the best advice that I can give—as simple as it might sound—is always plan your work and work your plan."

If you are entrepreneurial with a solid network, creating a consulting firm may be the right choice for you if you are willing to take the risks.

David Kaufman, the co-founder of Acquis Consulting, took a big risk that paid off. "When I left Arthur Andersen, the partner there tried to convince me not to leave. She said: *You're really taking a big risk. Arthur Andersen will be around forever, and who knows what will happen if you go on your own.*"

CONSULTING LEADER INTERVIEW...

Fireside Chat with a Consulting Leader

Amy Munichiello is a director at a global management consulting firm where she leads an internal consulting practice focused on designing solutions to retain and develop leaders, enable the highest performing teams, build an inclusive culture, and drive employee engagement.

An active Skidmore College alum, Amy began her career as a change management consultant providing solutions to Fortune 500 clients at both a boutique and Big Four+ consulting firm.

In this interview Amy discusses how she transitioned from market facing to internal consulting work and provides sage advice to young women seeking a fulfilling career in the consulting profession.

Q. Why did you choose to go into consulting? Is it everything you expected it to be?

A. When I went to Skidmore, I went thinking that I would go into law. I ultimately wanted to become a US senator and knew I needed to aim for law school as a next step. I had a passion for politics and a desire for impacting social policy and felt that was probably the right career move for me. When I went to college, my whole world opened up. I was pretty shocked at the vast opportunities that were available to me and started to take classes in lots of different areas.

I would call home once a month telling my parents that I was changing my major or doubling or tripling. If I could have quadrupled my major, I would have. I just soaked it all in. I was not as hooked on the political science area as I thought, even though I did finish my political science major—along with a business major ultimately.

During my junior year, I decided to take a very popular experiential business course modeled after a Harvard Business School business case class. I wanted to see what the hype was all about. I was very late to the game, taking this course late in my college career. This introductory course was a major semester course in which students were given a real business case, put into teams to solve the business problem, and presented to a panel of real-life executives at the end of the year. It just sounded really dynamic and challenging. It was during this experience that a light bulb went off for me, igniting a spark in me around business. I decided to double-major and began taking as many business classes as humanly possible. While I was good at accounting and finance, it was not exciting for me.

I knew there was something else out there, but couldn't figure it out. I took my first organizational behavior class with a professor who was not only interesting and a skilled organizational consultant outside of being a professor, but she was a role model for me. She was a champion of women's advancement, and it was a whole new world that opened up for me through her class. I fell in love with the organizational behavior side of business. I started taking psychology and social work classes in order to figure out how I could translate that passion for human behavior into a career. I went to a panel of alumni that were talking about what they did for a living, and there was a woman there who worked for one of the large, Big Four+ consulting firms at the time as a change management consultant. The fire was lit!

Consulting for me evolved over time; in different stages of my life, it meant different things. When I was younger and single, being a road warrior was something I thrived in. As I had a family that needed to change. I was able to still focus on building my consulting skills set, being surrounded by really smart people, and challenging myself mentally but doing it in a way that enabled me to have the life I wanted to have outside of work.

Somebody recently said something to me like: Well, when you were in consulting ... And I said: *I AM in consulting!* Just because I'm non-chargeable doesn't mean I'm still not a consultant. I still use those tools, methodologies, and that mindset when servicing my clients. I'm just non-chargeable.

Q. What is a common, career-limiting blind spot you have seen from younger consultants?

A. I see a few that come to mind, and I actually lived this myself. I opted out of consulting because I was concerned about how I was going to be able to find a partner in my life and have the kind of family that I wanted to have when I was on the road so much. And I think, looking back, I was a little bit shortsighted. I didn't have the people in my life that were pushing back on me the way that I needed in order to see the bigger picture. I also continue to hear the same exact thing nowadays. We do a better job of being more transparent, and certainly it has been much more mainstream than it was in the '90s seeing both women and men wanting to have a family and live the consulting lifestyle. It has been a big focus of my career, going forward.

I still see that same challenge with younger consultants who are trying to plan ahead so much, as opposed to just trying it. And I remember very, very vividly, many years later sitting in a women's forum at my current firm, a panel of executives were talking about their experiences, and there was a woman that spoke about "just going for it."

She said, "Listen, you've all made it. Look at what you've accomplished, where you've come from. Did you ever think that you would be doing what you're doing currently? And why are you already thinking that you can't do it; why are you opting out before you try things?"

For me, that was a giant *aha* moment.

The other piece that resonates for me in myself,

and I see it in other less seasoned consultants, is impatience. Wanting to advance at a faster rate than maybe what should be and more importantly, not necessarily appreciating the journey along the way. Not realizing that the journey is really critical and each journey you take all connect with each other. They build on each other, and they do really make you and take you to that next level. As opposed to just advancement in rank or advancement in compensation or advancement in title, prestige.

Q. In your experience, what are common themes and decision points of why people leave their firm? What made you stay at those same points in your career?

A. You probably heard them already: being able to have a fulfilling life in the way that we want to have it, having more predictability over our time, and juggling that with a really fulfilling career. I think work-life balance is still elusive, certainly especially in high travel environments. That being said, I do think that oftentimes people think the grass is always greener.

I do see people also leaving for great career opportunities. You know we surround ourselves with really intelligent people, and sometimes they just have great career opportunities that then afford them to have a broader reach, bigger impact, leadership opportunities as well as maybe more predictable schedules as well.

What has made me stay? I think it's the same theme. I mean, why have I stayed at my current firm for seventeen years? I think as my skills have evolved and as my leadership needs have evolved, I have been very fortunate to be in an organization that has provided me with opportunities to take advantage of, to fulfill my personal needs, my professional needs, and to be challenged. I'm not bored, everything's always changing, it's very fast paced, and I thrive in that kind of environment. So to be able to continue to grow a really significant career in that kind of environment has been important. The other undervalued success factor to "how I do it" is that I have a partner who is just as vested in my success as I am—he enables me, supports me, and cheers me on in all that I do.

Q. What are some of your expectations of dos and don'ts of client deliverables?

A. It's really important to ask a lot of questions before you get to the point where you produce deliverables. Oftentimes we are too quick to execute and check off a to-do as opposed to making sure that the deliverable is truly what the need is. Asking really strong, powerful, consultative questions is key to get there. I am a type-A person, so I think for me at first glance, really high-quality deliverables are important— things like spelling, making sure that there's a story to tell, making sure that your deliverables are thought out and strategic.

And I think the other piece that's really critical is using that 80:20 rule, making sure that you don't have to have everything 100 percent thought out and perfect because I think we're all very detail-oriented people, and that would just mean that we're probably spinning our wheels a bit too much.

Q. Describe your most significant accomplishment as well as your biggest career setback. What did you learn from both experiences?

A. Having a robust career in this industry overall has been a significant accomplishment. I didn't have women in my life that were working outside of the home in that way. I have always felt that I've been a little bit on my own in charting my own course. That being said, I learned to surround myself with really amazing people who provided me with a diverse view, and that certainly included people in my family as well.

I've picked and pulled different things from the people that surround me to help guide me in the journey. I have continued to have a really fulfilling career in a professional service environment, which is very demanding. I've also been very involved in external boards, which has been important for me from a career growth and community involvement perspective. All the while still being true to my most important priority, which is my family, and learning how to be comfortable with the choices I make and being comfortable with the mother I am, the wife I am, the sister, the daughter, and the leader I am has been important to me, and I'm very proud of it.

In terms of career setbacks, I was very shortsighted to leave client service when I did. That being said, I wouldn't change what I've done. I didn't fully appreciate the choice I was making because I was a high performer; I should have spent a little bit more time and should have thought a little bit more about when I was leaving and why I was leaving. I don't know if it was a setback; it was just a change in the trajectory, and I think it was a significant one for me.

The other thing is the opportunities I've turned down have definitely been inflection points in my life. I do remember being about nine months pregnant with my first child, and the role that I was in was no longer available due to a firm reorganization. I was offered another role, and it was a great leadership opportunity, but unfortunately I was nine months pregnant. The majority of the role was based in New York City, which would have meant a significant amount of travel. That was a really gut-wrenching decision because it was a really great opportunity, and the decision was really hard. It was the first time that I had to think about somebody other than myself. I wouldn't consider it a setback, but it was an inflection point in my career that was a big one for me.

Q. How do you advise younger consultants to gracefully push back to help shape their career?

A. I was at a recent board meeting and had lunch with a bunch of younger women who were interested in going into business and in consulting. I spent a lot of time giving them my advice and a couple of things that I spoke to them about was surrounding themselves with a diverse set of people to challenge their thinking and help guide them. For many years I surrounded myself with people like myself, and people that made me feel good about myself, and oftentimes when I did have challenges, they were just feeding back what I wanted to hear, and that wasn't taking me to the next level.

I was explaining to them: *You know, it's so important to surround yourself with people who have different styles and experiences and perspectives because it will help you grow as a leader. It has helped me tremendously; look at life through a different lens, and look at the situations and look at experiences and opportunities through a very different lens.* For me this has been an important learning that I impart on younger consultants.

Q. Describe the one experience, personal or professional, that has shaped your values and how you do business today.

A. Nine years ago I was tasked with designing an experience for a large women's leadership conference. I had a blank piece of paper and knew there'd be about between nine hundred and one thousand attendees. I knew that the firm was at a point where we were a little bit tired of the conversation around gender; it was still feeling very polarized. I was basically given a blank piece of paper to think about how we were going to shift the culture from a gender equity standpoint. I had the opportunity to spend the next year designing a lot of the foundation of our work around unconscious bias. That experience has rocked my world; it fundamentally changed who I am as a person, it changed how I look at the world, it changed who I am as a leader, it changed who I am as a contributor in this world, and it certainly changed me as a mother as well because I learned so much about myself in the process.

Q. Knowing what you know now, what advice would you give your younger self?

A. Don't worry so much about the future. Enjoy the present, think about the future, plan for the future, but don't overanalyze the path to the future. Be confident in who you are and what you bring to the table, and be proud of that because it's your journey.

Q. What is your secret travel tip to help create a sense of work-life balance while you are on the road?

A. I purposefully take the train to New York instead of flying out of Boston. One reason is that I like to sit on the train side aligned to the coast, so that I see the sunrise and if I'm lucky the sunset. It is my way of taking a break and looking out at the world as I'm traveling. Another reason is because the train ride gives me three-and-a-half hours of dedicated time each way. I can strategically go through email and postal mail. I bring magazines and articles and any reading that I have accumulated. And it enables me to really get on top of my life professionally. When I arrive home, when I get back, I'm much more organized and can focus on my husband and children in a different way. That has been very important for me.

Two other things that I've done over the years. I dedicate one night a week to work late, and that's my way of being able to stay on top of things. Making sure that I'm staying on top of important projects, emails, articles, things outside of day-to-day meetings in order to enable me to be more flexible throughout the week. Another thing that I've really tried very hard to do is work from home on Fridays. It has also been a way for me to pick up my kids from school, drop them off, and feel like I'm a little bit more human and also don't have to commute anywhere.

Lastly, my husband and I actually make it a point to sit down—over a bottle of wine of course—usually twice a year to discuss how things are working as a family, how we feel about the way we're operating our home and our marriage. And to see if it's working for each of us and our kids. It has been really important for us to have that dedicated time to do a check-in. And we have made changes to how we are teaming together over the years as well.

Q. Any last remarks on becoming a great consultant?

A. After I had my kids, I had a really hard time personally understanding the concept of ambition and what that meant or didn't mean as I had this new role as mother. It was heartrending for me to figure out what does ambition mean. What I came to learn and embrace took a long time; I realized that I can be a mother and still be ambitious, and they're not two separate entities. Linking them with an *and* was critical and also monumental.

That was a journey for me that I also try to impart to my daughter and my son as well as to younger women who are starting their families too. In the consulting environment you know we're really smart, driven, and we want other things. Ambition shouldn't be a dirty word. And I think for a long time for women, ambition has always been in question. I have to really attribute my part of my journey, my *aha* journey is from the people that I've interacted with, that I surround myself with, that think differently than me, and who help me get there. I think that's important.

20

Make Consulting Career Decisions That Matter

The grass isn't greener on the other side; the grass is green where you water it.

—UNKNOWN

If you are reading this book, chances are you might be thinking about going into consulting or deciding whether to stay in consulting and refine your skills or move on. There are a number of options to choose from.

> **Experienced hires:** new hires into consulting that have previous work or industry experience.

Exit Opportunities to Other Consulting Firms

As discussed in Chapter Seven, determine key differences and nuances between consulting firms. Leave a consulting firm for reasons such as culture or experience fit. Don't allow bad days to dictate your consulting career decisions; weigh the pros and cons of both long and short term exit opportunities. Don't jump consulting firms because of a jerk manager, a difficult client, or an extra $10k bump in salary. Factor in the value of the relationships you have built at the firm. Remember everything in business is personal; you run the risk of alienating your current relationships if you jump to a direct competitor. While leaping consulting firms sometimes translates to progressing up to the next rank, make sure you are ready for the ramp up. Have a game plan to hit the ground running. You will be expected to deliver at the same level and pace as your peers if you are going to a similar consulting firm.

In a new firm, your priority is to *quickly* build your credibility. Most firms have a supportive career construct for campus hires but struggle with the caring

If you do decide to leave for the greener grass of another consulting firm, be ready to run like a gazelle for the first year.

and feeding of the career journey of an experienced hire. When you join a new firm, remember you are essentially starting over. It usually takes about two to three full years to rebuild a network, brand, and client relationships. If you do decide to leave for the greener grass of another consulting firm, be ready to run like a gazelle for the first year.

Exit Opportunities to Industry

If you are already in consulting and think it is time to move on, there are thousands of companies seeking to leverage the knowledge you have amassed. Exit opportunities are lucrative and abundant if timed well with the needs of the marketplace and your area of expertise. The longer your consulting tenure is, the more lucrative industry opportunities can become. Switching from consulting to an industry role can be a culture shock, but will give you an opportunity to build deeper expertise in a desired industry.

Exit Opportunities to Higher Education

If you are planning to leave consulting to obtain professional degrees such as a Masters of Business Administration (MBA), or doctorate, focus on building an ironclad network to leave with an impeccable personal brand. Cultivating those relationships during your time in school will pay off dividends in the future.

Exit Opportunities to Entrepreneurial Ventures

Many former consultants decide to cut their teeth as an entrepreneur since consulting provides a valuable training ground for starting a company or going independent. Almost all skills and experiences obtained as a consultant are transferable when running your own company.

Exit Opportunities to Non-Profit

Many consultants decide to pursue meaningful work in the non-profit space. Like industry, consultants going into non-profit are in high demand.

Industry Hires into Consulting

Individuals from industry come in for various reasons. Some seek consulting experiences, while others joined the profession through a strategic acquisition. Becoming a consultant after obtaining industry experience puts you at a distinct advantage. Your perspectives will be a breath of fresh air on engagements with career consultants and campus hires. When seeking a firm, look for your tribe. Industry hires that bring their authenticity and uniqueness to the table become great consultants and leaders.

CONSULTING LEADER INTERVIEW...

Fireside Chat with a Consulting Leader

Steve Thomas is an executive director specializing

in business performance improvement programs. Steve has significant leadership experience in information technology and global business transformation service delivery at a leading management consulting firm.

A University of Hawaii and Pepperdine University graduate, Steve is an experienced hire that successfully transitioned back and forth between industry and consulting several times throughout his career. In this interview Steve discusses how he went from being an aerospace programmer to becoming a consultant, how humor has helped him succeed, and his secret travel tip.

Q. Why did you choose to go into consulting?

A. I started out of college as a programmer, progressing over a number of years through the programming ranks and into systems analyst and project manager type positions. At the time I was working on a large aerospace and defense program, and we happened to have one of the Big Four+ consulting firms working with us in our manufacturing area. I found it interesting working with them; I observed how they work, and I thought to myself: *I can do what they are doing.* In fact, they were just repeating what I was telling them should be done. They were just pirating all the good ideas I had, regurgitating up to leadership. Leadership was thinking: *Wow, that's great.*

Fast forward two years later; we were working with another Big Four+ consulting firm, and I saw similar activity but with a different part of the business. While they were smart individuals that I got along well with, a lot of the things that I was saying the consultants were reusing. In both cases, both consulting firms added some experiences from elsewhere, but for the most part they took our recommendations and were able to effectively convince management to spend money on implementing our recommendations, which I thought was kind of fascinating.

Long story short, the company I was working for was moving my role across the country to Atlanta, GA. I was living in LA at the time.

My wife said, "We're not moving."

I basically said, "Okay. I guess I gotta go find a new job."

So the first thing I did was call both of the partners I worked with at the consulting firms. I spoke to both sets of leadership to see if they had an opportunity because I had very good relationships with them; both firms held me in high regard.

During the interview process, both firms asked me: *Why do you think you would be a good consultant?*

And my response to that was, "Well, I've actually been doing that internally for the past six years in my industry job. Being an internal consultant to all of my customers, understanding their requirements, understanding their needs, coming up with good solutions and then, building, deploying, and managing projects."

To me consultant was just another extension of what I do anyway. It wasn't that I was becoming a consultant, I am a consultant. I just was not working for one of the management consulting firms. That's really how I got into consulting. It was more of a necessity to change employers. I picked the firm that was more of a cultural fit for me.

The work I do parallels becoming a physician who helps patients feel better, get better, do better by diagnosing the illness, and coming up with a treatment. If you think of what consultants do on a day-to-day basis, we're just physicians of companies and organizations. We come in, look at the symptoms, diagnose, and come out with recommendations on how to make it better. Turns out this is what happened to become my practice.

And what was interesting is the correlation wasn't something that I figured out right away. It took fifteen to twenty years into my career before it dawned on me why I love this work.

Q. What was the one skill you perfected that made all the difference throughout your consulting career.

A. I have nicknames for people, which I don't always share, and I don't have nicknames for everybody. I'm only average or maybe a little bit below average in remembering people's names. I remember people's faces all the time. As part of trying to remember people's names, I've come up with mnemonics that become personal nicknames for people. An example is a person's last name is Cunningham I would call *sly pig*. Once in a while they slip out—in this case it did, and the person liked it.

Being able to find humor in things and to keep tensions down. The second thing is understanding the business from the other side of the table. That comes from having worked on the other side of the desk. I've gone back and forth between industry and consulting; I left my current firm three times.

I started my career in industry then went to consulting. Then I had an opportunity to go run an IT organization, which I did in application development. When I completed a large transformation, I got bored running the organization and then came back to the firm the first time. I left with the divestiture to another consulting firm and stayed there for eight years. Then came back to my current firm leaving in about three years because I had an amazing executive leadership opportunity for a period of time. I ended up coming back to my current firm and have been here since.

When I came back the first time, I was working with a senior manager on a proposal. He says, "I don't know what you're capable of, but let's go visit the client."

So we went and visited the client, had the discussions, put together the proposal within three or four days, submitted it, and he just said, "Wow, if I hadn't known better I would have thought that you've been with us all the time, that you never left."

I said, "Well, it's like riding a bicycle."

Another key strength was really understanding how businesses work and basically understanding processes. I'm very good at unraveling processes into their component parts so I can understand each component and look for ways to improve them.

Overall it is my ability to find humor even in the most difficult situations while keeping tensions down that has been a survival skill for me.

Q. What was the best compliment you ever received in your career?

A. The best compliment I've ever gotten in my career was sitting in a room of aeronautical and space engineers working on a very complex program, contributing to the discussions, and the vice president of the program was standing there and looked up all of a sudden and says, "Where's my IT representative?"

I raised my hand, and he goes, "Oh, I thought you were one of us."

To me that's always been one of the best compliments I've ever had in my career, about understanding and learning the way the business works and what the business is so that you are recognized as a contributor to the team. So the fact that he didn't even recognize an IT guy, an outsider basically, was probably the best compliment I could have gotten.

Q. In your experience, what are common themes

or decision points of why people leave their firm? What made you stay at those same points in your career?

A. Back to my point about being a physician to companies and helping people and organizations fix themselves. You have to ask yourself: *Okay, what is my personal purpose?*

Consultants need to understand their purpose. Why did you join the firm in the first place, right? Is it only because it was the best offer, best job, career path? There had to have been something more than just money that attracted you to an organization.

My first job out of college was with a large aerospace manufacturer. I loved airplanes, still do, and the fact that I got to work for a company that built some of the leading state-of-the-art type aircraft and everything, that was a passion for me. One of the primary reasons I left there was the new employer paid for 100 percent of my MBA. I actually went back to the company later prior to joining the consulting firm. So I had a distinct purpose, and when you do change you never think you're going back. I never thought I would come back to any of the firms that I left. It just so happened that the companies were always looking for someone with my skills. I was always in a position of advantage. My career changes always met a specific purpose for me.

Young consultants really have to look at it from the standpoint of why are they doing this and if they look at moving to another organization, what's the purpose of that move? Is it money? Career advancement? If it's either one of those, why couldn't you get it at the place you are at? That's the question. It was always faster to progress by jumping, but that shouldn't be the primary reason for jumping. The reason should be for more skills, professional growth, or pursuing a passion.

I've looked at resumes of people who have changed jobs a lot, and I have a tendency not to hire them because I don't want to make the investment of a couple of years improving their skill sets or their capabilities only to have them leave for someone else. You don't want to be jumping all the time because that is not something that is looked on favorably by future employers. Each move needs to fulfill a purpose.

Q. How do you suggest consultants seek out career mentors and sponsors?

A. When you get on a project, do the best job you can. Look for and ask for opportunities to do more. What'll happen is, if someone sees your ambition, and not in a negative way but in a positive way, chances are they will follow your career and help you throughout.

There was one individual I was working with when he got staffed on his first engagement ever. He was on the beach for three or four months and wondering if he was going to lose his job. They assigned him to work with me, and I mentored him, took an interest in his career development. From there his career has soared. As a mentor, the key is helping young people; as a young person the key is doing a great job. The more senior members of your organization you impress, the more will help you succeed.

That's how a natural mentor comes out, as opposed to in a format where you get assigned somebody formally. While those are good, they generally don't have a vested interest in your success from the start of the relationship, whereas in a true mentor relationship, that mentor has a vested interest because they believe in you. And you may not always have contact with them or constant contact, but I can guarantee you they are always available.

I've had some people that I've told: *Yeah, feel free to call*, and they will two years down the road or whatever. Whether it's just to say hi or it's: *Hey, I've got this situation, what do you think?* And mentoring to me is really more informal than formal. So look for mentors. And then always do the best you can and don't be afraid to ask for more.

Q. Describe the one experience that has shaped your values and how you do business today.

A. During my promotion process, we discussed a series of key projects/contributions I made to the practice from my sponsor. I had never thought of them as seminal moments for me or the firm. I was asked to join a new practice, and the first assignment was to assess a struggling engagement.

One of the senior partners called up our practice lead and said, "We've got some problems out there. I need you to go out there and fix it."

I didn't realize at the time how important that was to the bigger picture. In fact, I didn't know about it until I was talking to my practice leader about my promotion and he said, "Remember I asked you to come out and spend a few weeks out there to dig into it and figure out what was going on? After about three days on site, I had to leave due to some family issues that I had to go take care of, and I asked you to take this on by yourself, including readouts to the senior partners. Do you realize that was a critical moment for the competency because you gave credibility to what we were doing?"

I said, "I didn't realize that, but thank you."

Then he goes, "And you realize that I wasn't even there. You did it all by yourself. And you realize that once you gave all the recommendations and they agreed to it, we had you go fix it?"

So one of the things I learned was if you do an assessment and they like the result, they're going to ask you to actually deliver on it. So I did. My work on that engagement became one of the cornerstone solutions, methods, and processes of the practice today. This example and many others were big experiences that really shaped how I do business. I became very good at handling very challenging and difficult clients.

Q. What is your secret travel tip to help create a sense of work-life balance while you are on the road?

A. I actually unpack my suitcase when I'm going to be in a town for more than a couple of nights. Two reasons, actually. It's more of a safety thing than anything else. If I unpack the suitcase, I can see what I have and don't have. So in some respect it's not that I want to make the road a home or the hotel room a home, but by unpacking I know what I need to prepare for.

For example, I flew over to Tokyo, unpacked, and I'd forgotten my ties at home. This was at a time in business when we had to wear ties. Turns out it was a Sunday afternoon when I landed, and I literally had to go find someplace to buy at least two ties. Had I not unpacked everything, I probably wouldn't have noticed it until it was too late and that would have been embarrassing to show up to the client without a tie on.

Another travel tip is making time to go and work out. If you can do self-improvement things while you're out on the road, that's the thing to do. I usually do a lot of books on tape and other self-improvement types of activities. But the most important tip is to unpack your suitcase.

Q. Any last remarks on becoming a great consultant?

A. Don't be afraid of requests to do something that may be outside of your comfort zone. There are a number of times I have been asked to do stuff that I didn't really know too much about, but I was interested in it. Be a sponge on everything, look at everything as an opportunity to learn and grow. When somebody asks you to do something, it's because they either (1) believe you can do it, (2) think you need to do it from a growth perspective, or (3) are challenging you because they want to see whether or not you're a future leader. If you are given an assignment that you don't think you're capable of doing, give it a shot because you may stretch yourself and have a person that continually will support you in your growth. You will then gain confidence as well.

21

Prepare for Consulting of the Future

The best way to predict the future is to create it.

—Abraham Lincoln

The consulting profession has entered an unprecedented time in history and will radically shift in the next ten to twenty years. Consulting business models have remained relatively the same for more than one hundred years since the profession was first created by Arthur D. Little—until now. According to an article in the *Harvard Business Review*, artificial intelligence is in beginning stages to help organizations make more complex decisions in key areas such as human resources, budgeting, marketing, capital allocation, and corporate strategy, which could potentially evolve the role of a management consultant from analysis to judgment. Quant consultants—or "robo" advisors as this artificial intelligence technology is also called—offer faster, better, and more profound insights at a fraction of the cost and time of today's consulting firms and other specialized workers. This type of technological disruption is still very much in its infancy. It will be interesting to see marketplace shifts take place in consulting as disruptive AI technologies scale and its adoption not only accelerates, but is normalized.

Consulting of the future: emerging trends in the consulting profession.

The Role of Artificial Intelligence (AI) in Consulting

According to Moore's Law—an observation made by Intel co-founder Gordon Moore in 1965—computer chip capability doubles approximately every two years. Computers, machines that run on computers, and computing power all become smaller and faster with time. In *Rise of the Robots*, author Martin Ford discusses two key concepts to consider on how AI will permeate consulting: exponential growth capability in AI and genetic programming. Ford applies Moore's Law to the exponential growth trends we are seeing take shape in AI. This increased speed of capacity will bring rise to emerging industries such as 3-D printing produces food, or mass produced self-driving cars.

Another AI concept that Ford discusses is genetic programming. Genetic programming allows AI to improve upon itself in an adaptive fashion. Similar to Darwinian methods that mammals use to evolve, only the best changes to code survive. Most of the research on the future written today appears to paint a pretty grim picture for mankind.

In the book *Humans Need Not Apply* by Jerry Kaplan, unprecedented automation will create massive unemployment. This acceleration of automation will render most knowledge skills obsolete. Theoretical concepts written today are based on the mental map and paradigms of today's macroeconomic scarcity models, which have continued to fail when we think about the rise of tech companies like Amazon, Uber, etc.

In turn this will make way for what Kaplan calls synthetic intellects or artificial intelligent laborers. The book also explores ideas of AI machines seeking to obtain legal status as people and sophisticated iterations that will manage real people—the stuff of science fiction.

Putting It All Together

I do not think consulting as a profession will go away, but I do believe the traditional consulting operating models, organizational structures, and go to market strategies will fundamentally change. The work of consultants will continue to fuel client transformations into the new economy.

Leverage practices and unwritten rules to unconsciously build habits of a great consultant. The complexity of the human experience will be the hardest to replicate. Become a trusted advisor who seeks to maintain connectivity to all types of people. Stay informed on the latest trends in the various industries. Develop a niche or unique skill set within your profession.

If you are new to the profession, start researching, following, and understanding emerging trends in key topics. As of this writing the hotbed consulting areas are in digitalization, the future of work, robotics, and cybersecurity.

If you are already in consulting, think about how you will reinvent yourself to stay ahead of market demands because it is all about positioning, as discussed in the introductory chapter. Chances are if you have been in consulting for at least five to ten years, you have lived through a number of reinventions. Accelerating ideas, technologies, and capabilities make you question the very existence of the profession as you currently know it.

While none of us are able to accurately predict what is ahead, great consultants are influencers and creators of the future. And there is nothing more exciting than being an active player on the brink of the greatest transition of the human journey.

CONSULTING LEADER INTERVIEW...

Fireside Chat with a Partner

Siva K. is a technology partner and a travel, transportation, and hospitality services sector leader at a Big Four+ management consulting firm. A graduate of the Indian Institute of Technology, one of India's leading universities, Siva is well regarded as a technological genius on developing and executing digitally enabled industry strategies and solutions. Siva is not only a consulting partner but also an IBM Distinguished Engineer, a rare combination.

In this interview Siva shares his thoughts on the future of consulting, how he got started in the profession, and how he ended up accidentally receiving the best career advice from the head of NASA.

Q. Share how you decided to go into consulting. Is it everything you expected it to be?

A. My entry into consulting was somewhat opportunistic. When I was in India, I used to be a civil service officer in the Indian government and actually started consulting services for a railroad company in a firm focused on civil engineering management for developing countries. During my time with this firm, I advised client countries such as Mexico, Iraq, Libya, Nigeria, and Ethiopia.

Essentially, it is an external focusing consulting company.

So I thought: *It's a change. So let me go into consulting and see what life is like.*

At the time I did not know that consultants mainly travel. I was able to travel every Monday to Friday, which was not something I was expecting. The experience gave me an opportunity to use my analytical and creative thinking in helping customers. What was interesting is that while I was a civil servant, I was on the other side of the table. I was listening to people who were trying to sell me. That gave me a perspective and helped me build empathy.

If you put yourself in another person's shoes, what would you do? And what advice would you give? And what advice would you seek? That gave me a very good opportunity to utilize the importance of patience and made me a successful consultant. That is how I entered into consulting. Along the way I came to the United States and worked at a technology company that provided consulting for all the airlines. From there I then went to a global consulting organization and led work in travel, hospitality, transportation until I transitioned to my current firm.

In hindsight, I never even heard of consulting, and I entered it.

The second question, is it everything you expected it to be? The answer is yes and no. It gave me an opportunity to keep my brain sharp and come across different kinds of cultures, different kinds of challenging problems. And at the end of the day, when you solve the problems you feel very good. And most importantly, you help some customers achieve their goal. You are enabling customers to succeed, which is a very good feeling.

But sometimes you also feel frustrated because as a consultant you also encounter some political upheavals, battles that you need to play in, and very unpleasant situations. As with any career, you get frustrated at times with certain dynamics. But for the most part I enjoy consulting.

Q. Siva, in my previous experience working with you, I will always remember your steadfastness in the face of challenges and have always sought to model that behavior myself. What are other key traits you believe consulting leaders should seek to model regularly with younger consultants?

A. Thank you. I pride myself for the steadfastness no matter the circumstances or stress level. You will have ups and downs; everybody does, but you need to speak to your mission and approach, not to be wayward unless external situations warrant you to change your actions beyond your control. For example, if one is working on a life sciences project and all of a sudden a new regulation comes out, it may alter your product. So that is number one.

Steadfastness and loyalty. I'm always loyal to my people. You are as good as your leader. With your folks moving up their success is actually your success as well. A good leader will take the entire team with him or her, that's number two.

Number three is good leaders are always good listeners and have empathy for others. What would the other person be thinking if you were in his or her shoes? If you have empathy, that will make you a better leader.

Q. Share the best career advice you received from an unlikely source.

A. I was at the airport in Virginia headed to Dallas and the flight was delayed by more than four hours. I happened to be sitting right next to a gentleman, and we started talking our shared interest in space and astronomy. We sat there for hours talking, having a very detailed and deep astronomical talk.

At the end of the conversation, he said, "Why don't you join us as astronomy scientist?"

And I asked, "Who do you work for?"

While I am not a scientist, I was really honored that he thought so highly of me to be qualified enough to become one.

He said, "I like the way you talk and under any circumstances don't try to be somebody else than what you are. Even if people may not appreciate it. But that's what takes you to the next level—your forthrightness and your honesty. Do what is right without second-guessing yourself."

I took that advice seriously and being authentic has always worked out for me in the long run. Turns out the gentlemen I was speaking to was the head of NASA at the time.

Q. Describe the one career experience that has shaped your values and how you do business today.

A. Prior to joining consulting when I was a civil engineer, we were trying to repair a tunnel that connected two cities in India. The tunnel was leaking like crazy, and nobody knew why. Tunnels don't leak because there is nothing there. We tried everything. Finally it occurred to me that water must be coming up from a very high elevation. I asked the Indian Army to provide me with a helicopter so I could actually go and see. The Army advised me against that. Flying over the tunnel in a helicopter is not a good thing and very risky. But being young, I said in my head: *Let's go*. We actually went to a very high altitude, found out there was a lake there, and the lake was the reason why it is leaking. Once we knew the source, we could control the water leakage.

That experience taught me a couple of things. Do not give up on yourself because there is always a light at the end of the tunnel. It may be skewed, it may test your patience—in this case it truly tested me for fourteen days—but you give a 110 percent effort. Sometimes you get discouraged, but persistence always pays off.

That's what I normally do, even today. I am very persistent; I am not going to give up so easily. I have a few failures, but I learned a lot from the failures as well. That tenacity taught me that you have to be persistent and it will lead to success down the road. You will face obstacles, but understand the obstacles you face are there to help you learn and overcome.

Q. Share your most significant accomplishment to date in consulting that you are the proudest of.

A. Becoming both a partner as well as an IBM distinguished engineer—which only three people ever achieved in history—is my best accomplishment in consulting.

Q. What do you think the future trends of the consulting profession look like in the next ten to twenty years?

A. It's tough to accurately predict the future. Given current trends, I can see something like a fractional consulting model, almost like Uber for consulting. For example, if there is a project, clients can fraction the work and people all over the world would collaborate and consult clients collectively. That is quite possible given the advent of social media; independent consultants from all over the world could form temporary coalitions for a given amount of work which was probably unheard of previously. Today it is possible.

As a fractional, independent consultant, in a given day you may be working a couple of hours for one coalition. You may form a coalition of like-minded people to actually work on a project someone puts out on the marketplace. There could very well be a consortium of independent consultants as well, not affiliated with any other consulting company. That is something that could come in the next ten to twelve years.

The second one is disruption from machine automation, machine learning. Cognitive computing could actually eliminate a majority of the consulting positions that we see today. For example, in the medical field Watson has an effective cardiologist; he can give you better advice in the interaction. That could come in consulting too because part of consulting is that you give advice based on the duration or problem. If you have this kind of machine learning and inordinate amounts of data that the system can actually leverage and give you advice, then that could be a threat to the consulting. Then, consulting will be how do you manage and configure these advanced systems? So your consulting will elevate and morph into another level to manage this advanced, sophisticated system.

In short, people will still do consulting; the human capital or organization development work will be there, but the organizational development strategies that you do will change because the companies will become exponential companies. Right now most companies only do linear growth. For example, next quarter a company may report 5 percent growth; whereas exponential organizations like Uber can experience sky-rocketing growth.

Uber started with one car less than nine years ago. Today Uber has over one million drivers, rivaling some of the largest employers in the world. That is exponential organization growth. Do you think the organizational structure that we normally use will be applicable for Uber? I don't think so. Consulting will change dramatically because organizations are changing.

I think the playing field will be leveled; there will be much more global collaboration, consulting will never be geographic boundaries. For a project we might actually have to collaborate round-the-clock between countries, so collaboration will grow much more diverse. Think of it something like Consultants without Boundaries.

Technology and the consulting environment is changing at a fast pace. The ecosystem in general is just mind-boggling.

Q. How do you balance the art of negotiation and influence when you push back from a client, peers, or your firm?

A. If the relationship is a value for money con-versation, I think you negotiate with a mutual value. Many times when you think negotiation, people think like a used car salesman. I got $20,000, you save $10,000.

In reality that is not a value-driven conversation; it is just a pure transactional conversation. When you listen to someone's request for negotiation, it's about value. You just can't give something away without getting something in return.

The number one advice is to have fact-based conversations, take emotions out. I know it is hard, even for me, but that is what you need to do. That is when you need to push back, whether it is to the clients, to your peers, or at home. You cannot take something that is unreasonable, and you cannot deliver it because you're setting up for failure, which does not bode well for you in the long run.

Q. Share your tips and best practices of how you ramp up on a new project or at a new firm?

A. It is very easy. Right now I am in a new firm. Only one and a half years. So the best practice is know your role, learn what expectations are being put upon you from your management and peers, and also try to understand the culture in the organization. If you are going into a new firm, know the culture.

And more importantly network, network, network. The bigger your network, the more visibility you have, the more people know what you are known for, from an eminence perspective, and that makes it easy to get recognized and pulled into engagements that otherwise would not have been possible.

You can be a superstar at your previous firm, but at your new firm you are a newbie, an unproven commodity as far as anybody is concerned. You gain the respect of your peers or your clients by demonstrating your experience. By the same token, your ability to gain the trust of your customers, your peers, as well as people who work for you. That is the key.

If you cannot accomplish even one of them, then you will have a tough time to succeed. When you start a new project, you need to assemble teams that share the same core values for the better part. You do not want to carbon copy yourself across the board. Nobody will challenge you. But, if they share values, if they do not share your perspective, that is fine, as long as they share values, and a mission, and then you will succeed.

Q. What is your secret travel tip to help create a sense of work-life balance while you are on the road?

A. When you travel, you basically have a tendency to work long hours because you're bored. That is dangerous because it is very easy to get caught in that cycle, and you will be out of touch with reality.

Work on the road as you do at home; always set up hours and boundaries. I know it's difficult but take breaks, go to places like a museum, or go for a movie, or any important historical monument. Take your time and learn the place. That way your mind will keep fresh. Don't forget to call home at least once a day. When you go on international work trips, even if it is short, try to sleep on the plane to adjust to the time zone of where you are going to.

Q. Last remarks on becoming a great consultant?

A. When you are walking in the premises of a customer they always have a dollar sign on your head; they always expect you to bring value. Don't just think you have closed the deal, you are done. You constantly have to bring value to your client, otherwise your days will be numbered regardless of your level.

CONCLUSION:
MECE MUSE MANIFESTO OF
GREAT CONSULTANTS

The concepts highlighted in this book fall under a set of guiding principles that I use within my career called the MECE Muse Manifesto of Great Consultants. Live these principles every single day. I include a pdf version of the manifesto for download on my website, www.mecemuse.us. Memorize it, visualize it, live it. I wish you the best in your consulting career. Here's to your journey to greatness.

1. **It's always personal in business.** Common courtesy and etiquette alone will take you far. Become a manners expert and use them to your competitive advantage.

2. **Create good consulting karma every day.** Be an active mentor and sponsor to others. Pay it forward. Focus on helping others shine and succeed. Your own success will follow. Freely give people around you credit for their contribution, no matter how big or small.

3. **Get out of your own way.** Do not allow the stories you tell yourself (or others try to tell you) shape your career decisions, ability to deliver,

or create impact for your client. Your age, skin color, who you love, education, experience, religion, socioeconomic status, or upbringing does not matter. What matters in consulting is the value you bring each day to your clients, colleagues, and the marketplace.

4. **Create a fulfilling, rewarding, and sustainable consulting career.** Develop solid consulting habits that create a sense of physical, mental, and emotional well-being. The journey of a consultant is a marathon, not a sprint. Leverage career lily pads and ladders. Embrace the journey and trust the chaos.

5. **It's not about being right but about being effective.** Give up the need to always be right and instead become obsessed with value creation. Do not be afraid to say that you are wrong. When you focus on the right thing, everything will always fall into place. Good consultants are self-driven and make decisions so that they appear smart. Great consultants are team-driven and make decisions so that everyone appears smart.

6. **Take ownership and accountability of your career.** Stop letting life just happen to you; take control of the things that are within your control. Do not let a fear of missing out (FOMO) guide your career decisions. Actively manage career experiences like you do currency. Proactively seek out as many numerous coaches,

mentors, advisors, and sponsors that you can obtain. Create a personal board of directors.

7. **Step up to a higher standard.** Maintain standards of excellence without striving for perfection. The day you let your standards down is the day you've decided to become mediocre.

8. **Once you find a like tribe you love, stay put.** If you are the hardest working, most capable, or motivated consultant in the room, on your team, or in your practice, find another room, team, or practice. Surround yourself with colleagues that challenge you and help you strive for greatness. Once you find a tribe of kindred spirits, stay put. The grass is not always greener elsewhere.

9. **Develop and execute basic habits remarkably well.** Fiercely protect your reputation, integrity, and credibility. Consultants are paid to think. Actively listen to what is being said or not being said. Take calculated risks and add creativity to your recommendations, deliverables, and engagements. Seek to always ask better questions. Always seek out constructive feedback to catapult your performance to the next level. Never underestimate the power of intent. Do better every day. Look and feel your best. Create an environment of excellence for yourself and those around you. Expect nothing less.

10. **Be empathically inclusive and compassionate to others.** Embrace the differences of others.

Accept people for who they are, not who you want them to be. Be willing to learn from someone with a different mindset and world-view other than your own. You don't have to always agree, but you should be receptive to different ways of thinking.

11. **Embrace authenticity as a competitive advantage.** Be intentionally aware of how you think, learn, and work in order to maximize your strengths.

12. **Make a conscious choice to be great.** Consulting greatness isn't born. It's learned habits, conscious decisions, and a way of being. You get to decide what type of consultant you want to be every single day.

ACKNOWLEDGMENTS

To all of my guardian angels, both seen and unseen, that continue to protect, lift, and guide me toward fulfilling my life's purpose. Thank you.

❧

My husband Karel and stepson Khamani for giving up home-cooked meals and quality family time to create the space for me to write this book in a loving and supportive environment.

❧

To my siblings Richard Jean-Baptiste, and Ted Jean-Baptiste. To my sister Maxia Nicolas for always helping me design a beautiful life and being one of my biggest cheerleaders. You have all continued to make me such a proud big sister. Thank you to my in-laws, Dr. Georgette Jeanty and Joseph Petion Lindor, for all of your support.

❧

To the women of Delta Sigma Theta, Sorority Inc. Special shout out to my Xi Tau chapter sorority sisters, particularly Sorors Eva Mitchell, Nicci Page, Kishshana Palmer, Lexer Quamie-Myers, Natalie Gill-Mensah, and Liz Miranda for supporting me unconditionally during the journey of this book.

❧

To feedback beta readers Nina Yu Yang, Nitya Karki, David Ermen, and Sowm Bhardharj. A special shout out to feedback beta reader Matt Boyle, a future go-getter college student at University of Michigan who provided generous feedback without hesitation or expectations. I cannot wait to see how you contribute to the world.

∽

To all of the amazing consulting partners and leaders interviewed for this book: Greg, Michael, Paige Arnoff-Fenn, Karyn Twaronite, David Kaufman, Joe, Marcelo Fava, Randy Martin, Steve Thomas, Nalika Nanayakkara, Craig Berkowitch, Diane, Siva, Amy Munichiello, John Tigh, Monica, Udanda, Ellen Zimiles, Jennifer Maddox, Kris Pederson, and Kathy. Thank you for being living role models of great consultants on your account and leadership teams, clients, and in the broader marketplace.

∽

Thank you to all of the consulting partners and leaders across the industry that preferred to remain anonymous. You put aside competitive differences in the name of advancing the profession to empathetically contribute to the book. You each are a class act and in a leadership league of your own.

∽

To my Seth Godin altMBA11 peers and coaches who were generous in feedback by helping me dig deeper and level up for my book: Jonathan Godwin, Shannon Fitzgerald, Jason Perkins, Volker Lobmayr, Conor McCarthy, Felix Koehler, Lucia Parker, Andy Ewing, Mack Wallace, Craig Morantz, Isabel Brito, Monica Paez Kusinka, Tony Wong, Lee Kantor, Jaime Windon, and Fredrick Haugen.

∽

To my superfans Stephanie Cole, Debasree Saha, Soror Eva Mitchell, Nina Yu Yang, Ron Jordan, Michaela Tolman, Carrie Hui Mingalone, Tanya Stevensen, Angelic Hagan, and Xuan Li. Your energy and passionate support continued to give me the drive to push through the hardest moments of this journey.

❧

To all of my past, present, and future mentees. Thank you for being such remarkable people. Thank you for sharing your dreams, fears, successes, failures, challenges, and aspirations with me. Being a part of your journey has been the privilege of a lifetime.

❧

To all past, present, and future mentors that shape my career and life, sometimes just by being who they are: Elizabeth Vo, Barbara Lindquist, John Witten, Sabine Awad, Craig Berkowitch, Alex Keany Carlton, Steve Thomas, Kevin Salsberry, Mary Elizabeth Porray, Larry Decuir, Amy Munichiello, Trusha Mehta, Angie Cercone, Mike Dilecce, Pamela Scott, Laura Giovacco, and Jamila Abston. To my colleague and mentor, Mary Beth Fee. Rest in Peace. Thank you for shining your amazing light, you will be missed. Thank you, Stone Payton, for the MECE Mentoring idea that has carried through this book and my podcast show. Thank you, Lee Kantor, Ernest Barbaric, James Sasser, Jonathan Braille Strong, and Jaime Jay for answering the call for help without any expectations. To the phenomenal women of The Boston Club that continue to show me unwavering support.

❧

To all of the past, present, and future guests of the MECE Muse Unplugged podcast show. Thank you for hearing the call and stepping up to share your thoughts, advice, and stories.

∽

My book publishing team: Lisa Akoury-Ross, Kathleen Tracy, Soror Alicia N'Kai Ingram, Howard Johnson, and Karen Grennan. Your book publishing expertise and guidance was invaluable.

∽

To all of the strangers who helped shape the selection of this book cover and interior design.

∽

Last but certainly not least: to all past, present, and future consultants worldwide. Your manifested and deferred dreams, analysis paralysis, business cases and methodologies, strategies and tactics, laughter and tears, random encounters and missed connections, slide decks and Excel pivot tables, rejected expense reports, whitepapers and proposals, sweat equity, all-nighters and pre-dawn mornings, team room shenanigans, worn out luggage and redeye flights, billable and unbillable hours are not in vain. I see you. I hear you. As consultants we collectively carry the weight of the business world on our shoulders. You are a business badass. Do not ever let anyone ever make you forget how truly special you really are.

APPENDIX A
CONSULTING TOOLKIT STARTER PACK

The following is a collection of the vast selection of books, resources, and websites in my consulting toolkit, or recommendations from the consulting partners and leaders I spoke with for this book. I have now passed them along to you. Remember to pay it forward to others that may be in need of one of these knowledge gems.

Building Habits

Better Than Before: Mastering the Habits of Our Everyday Lives by Gretchen Rubin

Frames of Mind: The Theory of Multiple Intelligences by Howard Gardner

Sleeping with Your Smartphone: How to Break the 24/7 Habit and Change the Way You Work by Leslie A. Perlow

Talent Code by Daniel Boyle

The 7 Habits of Highly Effective People: Powerful Lessons in Personal Change by Stephen R. Covey

The 8th Habit: From Effectiveness to Greatness by Stephen R. Covey

The Coaching Habit. Say Less, Ask More & Change the Way You Lead Forever by Michael Bungay Stanier

Careers and Job-Hunting

Designing Your Life: How to Build a Well-Lived, Joyful Life by Bill Burnett

Finding Passion, A Self-Discovery Approach for Navigating Career Crossroads by Jessica Manca

I Could Do Anything If I Only Knew What It Was by Barbara Sher and Barbara Smith

Pivot: The Only Move That Matters Is Your Next One by Jenny Blake

The Crossroads of Should and Must: Find and Follow Your Passion by Elle Luna

What Color Is Your Parachute? 2017: A Practical Manual for Job-Hunters and Career-Changers by Richard N. Bolles

Who Sunk My Yacht?: Your Personal Compass to Navigating the High Seas of Business and Career Change by Tanya Stevensen

You Deserve to Love Your Job: 20 Big Ideas for Succeeding in the New World of Work by Alexis Grant

Core Consulting Skills

Consulting 101, 2nd Edition: 101 Tips for Success in Consulting by Lew Sauder

Consulting on the Inside: A Practical Guide for Internal Consultants by Beverly Scott and B. Kim Barnes

Consulting: A Practitioner's Perspective by Mohan Kancharla

How to Read a Financial Report: Wringing Vital Signs Out of the Numbers by John A. Tracy and Tage Tracy

Management Consulting: A Guide to the Profession by David A. Fields

Peter Drucker on Consulting. How to Apply Drucker's Principles for Business Success by William A. Cohen

Pyramid Principle, The: Logic in Writing and Thinking by Barbara Minto

Say It With Charts: The Executive's Guide to Visual Communication by Gene Zelazny

slide:ology: The Art and Science of Creating Great Presentations by Nancy Duarte

The Art of Learning: An Inner Journey to Optimal Performance by Josh Waitzkin

The Back of the Napkin: Solving Problems and Selling Ideas with Pictures by Dan Roam

The McKinsey Way by Ethan Rasiel

The Trusted Advisor by David Maister

Communication

How to Win Friends and Influence People by Dale Carnegie

Crucial Conversations: Tools for Talking When Stakes Are High by Kerry Patterson and Joseph Grenny

Quiet: The Power of Introverts in a World That Can't Stop Talking by Susan Cain

Quiet Power: The Secret Strength of Introverts by Susan Cain

Kiss, Bow, or Shake Hands by Terri Morrison and Wayne A. Conaway

The Power of Nice: How to Conquer the Business World with Kindness by Linda Kaplan Thaler and Robin Koval

Conflict Management/Navigating Politics

Conflict Survival Kit: Tools for Resolving Conflict at Work (2nd Edition) by Daniel B. Griffith and Cliff Goodwin

Dealing with Difficult People: How to Deal With Nasty Customers, Demanding Bosses and Uncooperative Colleagues by Roberta Cava

Making Conflict Work: Harnessing the Power of Disagreement by Peter T. Coleman and Robert Ferguson

Perfect Phrases for Conflict Resolution: Hundreds of Ready-to-Use Phrases for Encouraging a More Productive and Efficient Work Environment by Antoine Gerschel and Lawrence Polsky

We Can Work It Out: Resolving Conflicts Peacefully and Powerfully by Marshall Rosenberg

Resolving Conflicts at Work: Ten Strategies for Everyone on the Job by Kenneth Cloke and Joan Goldsmith

The Eight Essential Steps to Conflict Resolution: Preserving Relationships at Work, at Home, and in the Community by Dudley Weeks

The Secret Handshake: Mastering Politics of the Business Inner Circle by Kathleen Kelley Reardon

Creativity and Innovation

Business Model Generation by Alexander Osterwalder and Yves Pigneur

Steal like an Artist by Austin Kleon

The War of Art: Break Through the Blocks and Win Your Inner Creative Battles by Steven Pressfield and Shawn Coyne

Entrepreneurship/Freelance/Independent Consulting

Anything You Want: 40 Lessons for a New Kind of Entrepreneur by Derek Sivers

Book Yourself Solid. The Fastest, Easiest, and Most Reliable System for Getting More Clients Than You Can Handle by Michael Port

Flawless Consulting: A Guide to Getting Your Expertise Used by Peter Block

Jab, Jab, Jab, Right Hook: How to Tell Your Story in a Noisy Social World by Gary Vaynerchuk

The 10 percent Entreprenuer: Live your dream without quitting your day job by Patrick J. McGinnis

The Consultant's Toolkit: High-Impact Questionnaires, Activities and How-to Guides for Diagnosing and Solving by Mel Silberman

The Freelancer's Bible: Everything You Need to Know to Have the Career of Your Dreams—On Your Terms by Sara Horowitz

The Lean Startup: How Today's Entrepreneurs Use Continuous Innovation to Create Radically Successful Businesses by Eric Ries

Exceptional Client Service

Customer Satisfaction Is Worthless, Customer Loyalty Is Priceless: How to Make Customers Love You, Keep Them Coming Back and Tell Everyone They Know by Jeffrey Gitomer

Delivering Happiness: A Path to Profits, Passion, and Purpose by Tony Hsieh

Strategic Customer Service: Managing the Customer Experience to Increase Positive Word of Mouth, Build Loyalty, and Maximize Profits by John A. Goodman

The Amazement Revolution: Seven Customer Service Strategies to Create an Amazing Customer (and Employee) Experience by Shep Hyken

The Best Service Is No Service: How to Liberate Your Customers from Customer Service, Keep Them Happy, and Control Costs by Bill Price

The Nordstrom Way to Customer Service Excellence: The Handbook For Becoming the "Nordstrom" of Your Industry by Robert Spector and Patrick D. McCarthy

The Spirit to Serve Marriott's Way by J. W. Marriott and Kathy Ann Brown

Uncommon Service: How to Win by Putting Customers at the Core of Your Business by Frances Frei and Anne Morriss

History of the Consulting Profession/General History

Lords of Strategy: The Secret Intellectual History of the New Corporate World by Walter Kiechel

Outliers by Malcolm Gladwell

The Smartest Guys in the Room: The Amazing Rise and Scandalous Fall of Enron by Bethany McLean and Peter Elkind

The World Is Flat by Thomas Friedman

The World's Newest Profession: Management Consulting in the Twentieth Century by Christopher D. McKenna

Management/Leadership/Change Management

A Whole New Mind by Daniel H. Pink

Built to Last: Successful Habits of Visionary Companies by Jim Collins and Jerry I. Porras

Clear Leadership: Sustaining Real Collaboration and Partnership at Work by Gervase R. Bushe

Death by Meetings: A Leadership Fable … About Solving the Most Painful Problem in Business by Patrick Lencioni

Good to Great: Why Some Companies Make the Leap and Others Don't by Jim Collins

How to Be CEO by Jeffrey J. Fox

How to Change Things When Change Is Hard by Chip Heath, Dan Heath

Influence: The Psychology of Persuasion by Robert B. Cialdini

Leaders Eat Last: Why Some Teams Pull Together and Others Don't by Simon Sinek

Never Eat Alone by Keith Ferrazzi

The 20-Minute Networking Meeting—Executive Edition: Learn to Network. Get a Job by Marcia Ballinger and Nathan A. Perez

The 5 Levels of Leadership: Proven Steps to Maximize Your Potential by John C. Maxwell

The Art of War by Sun Zhu

The Culture Blueprint by Robert Richman

The Good Jobs Strategy: How the Smartest Companies Invest in Employees to Lower Costs and Boost Profits by Zeynep Ton

The Heart of Change: Real-Life Stories of How People Change Their Organizations by John Kotter

The Industries of the Future by Alec Ross

The Practice of Management by Peter F. Drucker

The Speed of Trust by Stephen R. Covey

Tribes: We Need You To Lead Us by Seth Godin

Turn the Ship Around!: A True Story of Turning Followers into Leaders by L. David Marquet and Stephen R. Covey

Work Rules!: Insights from Inside Google That Will Transform How You Live and Lead by Laszlo Bock

Marketing

All Marketers are Liars: The Underground Classic That Explains How Marketing Really Works—and Why Authenticity Is the Best Marketing of All by Seth Godin

Contagious: Why Things Catch On by Ryan Holiday

Growth Hacker Marketing: A Primer on the Future of PR, Marketing, and Advertising by Ryan Holiday

Purple Cow, New Edition: Transform Your Business by Being Remarkable by Seth Godin

Tipping Point. How Little Things Can Make a Big Difference by Malcolm Gladwell

Mentorship and Sponsorship

Be Your Own Mentor: Strategies from Top Women on the Secrets of Success by Sheila Wellington and Betty Spence

Forget a Mentor, Find a Sponsor by Sylvia Ann Hewett

Lean In: Women, Work, and the Will to Lead by Sheryl Sandberg

Motivation

How to Win Friends & Influence People by Dale Carnegie

Start with Why by Simon Sinek

The Art of Learning: An Inner Journey to Optimal Performance by Josh Waitzkin

The Last Lecture by Randy Pausch and Jeffrey Zaslow

Think and Grow Rich by Napoleon Hill

Negotiation

Getting More of What You Want by Margaret A. Neale and Thomas Z. Lys

Getting to Yes by Roger Fisher and William L. Ury

Getting to Yes: Negotiating Agreement Without Giving by Roger Fisher and William L. Ury

Pitch Anything. An Innovative Method for Presenting, Persuading, and Winning the Deal by Oren Klaff

Stop Complainers and Energy Drainers: How to Negotiate Work Drama to Get More Done by Linda Byars Swindling

Preparing for Consulting Interviews/Onboarding and Ramp Up

Case in Point by Marc Cosentino

How to Get Into the Top Consulting Firms: A Surefire Case Interview Method - 2nd Edition by Tim Darling

Interview Math: Over 50 Problems and Solutions for Quant Case Interview Questions by Lewis C. Lin

Secrets of Mental Math: The Mathematician's Guide to Lightning

Calculation and Amazing Math Tricks by Arthur Benjamin and Michael Shermer

The Case Interview: 20 Days to Ace the Case: Your Day-by-Day Prep Course to Land a Job in Management Consulting by Destin Whitehurst and Erin Robinson

The First 90 Days: Critical Success Strategies for New Leaders at All Levels by Michael Watkins

What to Do When You're New: How to Be Comfortable, Confident, and Successful in New Situations by Keith Rollag

Personal Branding

301 Smart Answers to Tough Business Etiquette Questions by Vicky Oliver

Becoming a Life Change Artist: 7 Creative Skills to Reinvent Yourself at Any Stage of Life by Fred Mandell Ph.D. and Kathleen Jordan Ph.D.

Brag! The Art of Tooting Your Own Horn Without Blowing It by Peggy Klaus

How Successful People Think: Change Your Thinking, Change Your Life by John C. Maxwell

How to Establish a Unique Brand in the Consulting Profession by Alan Weiss

Linchpin: Are You Indispensible? by Seth Godin

Mastery by John C. Maxwell

The Expert's Edge: Become the Go-To Authority People Turn to Every Time by Ken Lizotte

The Road to Character by Laszlo Bock

Preparing for the Consulting of the Future

Artificial Intelligence and Machine Learning for Business: A No-Nonsense Guide to Data Driven Technologies by Steven Finlay

Artificial Intelligence: A Modern Approach (3rd Edition) by Stuart Russell and Peter Norvig

On Intelligence: How a New Understanding of the Brain Will Lead

to the Creation of Truly Intelligent Machines by Jeff Hawkins and Sandra Blakeslee

Rise of the Robots by Martin Ford

Robot is the Boss: How to do Business with Artificial Intelligence by Artur Kiulian

Relationships/Networking/Team Building

Give and Take by Adam M. Grant Ph.D.

Managing up: How to Forge an Effective Relationship with Those Above You by Rosanne Badowski and Roger Gittines

Real Relationships: From Bad to Better and Good to Great by Les Parrott and Leslie Parrott

Team Building: Proven Strategies for Improving Team Performance by W. Gibb Dyer Jr. and Jeffrey H. Dyer

Teamwork and Teamplay by Gervase R. Bushe

The Five Dysfunctions of a Team: A Leadership Fable by Patrick Lencioni

The Networking Book. 50 Ways to Develop Strategic Relationships by Simone Andersen

X-Teams: How to Build Teams That Lead, Innovate and Succeed by Deborah Ancona and Henrik Bresman

Self-Growth/Improvement/Productivity/Life Hacks

4-Hour Work Week by Tim Ferriss

Big Magic: Creative Living Beyond Fear by Elizabeth Gilbert

Blink: The Power of Thinking Without Thinking by Malcolm Gladwell

Do a Day: How to Live a Better Life Every Day by Bryan Falchuk

How Successful People Grow by John C. Maxwell

Life Reimagined: Discovering Your New Life Possibilities by Richard J. Leider

Power of Positive Thinking by Dr. Norman Vincent Peale

Radical Candor by Kim Scott

Relentless: From Good to Great to Unstoppable by Tim S. Grover and Shari Wenk

Rich Dad Poor Dad: What The Rich Teach Their Kids About Money That the Poor and Middle Class Do Not! by Robert T. Kiyosaki

Richest Man in Babylon by George S. Clason

The ONE Thing: The Surprisingly Simple Truth Behind Extraordinary Results by Gary Keller and Jay Papasan

The Power of Myth by Joseph Campbell

Tools of Titans by Tim Ferriss

What Got You Here Won't Get You There: How Successful People Become Even More Successful by Marshall Goldsmith and Mark Reiter

Year of Yes: How to Dance It Out, Stand in the Sun and Be Your Own Person by Shonda Rhimes

You 2: A High Velocity Formula for Multiplying Your Personal Effectiveness in Quantum Leaps by Price Pritchett

Work Life Balance/Managing Energy

God Never Blinks: 50 Lessons for Life's Little Detours by Regina Brett

Quarter Life Breakthrough: Invent Your Own Path, Find Meaningful Work, and Build a Life That Matters by Adam Smiley Poswolsky

Refuse to Choose! Use All of Your Interests, Passions, and Hobbies to Create the Life and Career of Your Dreams by Barbara Sher

The Power of Full Engagement: Managing Energy, Not Time, Is the Key to High Performance and Personal Renewal by Jim Loehr and Tony Schwartz

Recommended Services for Consultants

- Destin Whitehurt, ConsultingInterviewCoach.com
- Kofi Kankam, College Undergraduate & Graduate Admissions Coach
- Luis Vasquez, Introverted Consultants & Freelancers
- ManagementConsulted.com—Consulting Resume & Career Development
- Michael Beddows, Innovation Consulting Coach

- Michelle Florendo, Career Coach for Type A Professionals
- Victor Cheng, LOMS program for Case Interview Prep

Recommended Websites

- Bloomberg News, www.bloomberg.com
- Consulting Magazine, www.consultingmag.com
- Feedly, www.feedly.com
- Forbes, www.forbes.com
- Harvard Business Review, www.hbr.org
- LinkedIn, www.linkedin.com
- McKinsey Quarterly, www.mckinseyquarterly.com
- MindTools, www.mindtools.com
- Project Management Institute, www.pmi.org
- Strategy + Business, www.strategy-business.com

Recommended Podcasts

- Freakonomics
- HBR Ideacast
- Masters of Scale
- MECE Muse Unplugged
- The GaryVee Audio Experience
- The Tim Ferriss Show

APPENDIX B

SUMMARY OF 100+ SELECTED PRACTICES, UNWRITTEN RULES, AND HABITS OF GREAT CONSULTANTS BY CHAPTER

Preface and Introduction

1. Develop the skill of constant adaptive execution.

2. Maximizing downtime in between projects is just as critical as project time.

3. Navigate the organizational politics of your firm and client environment.

4. Reflect on the lessons learned of project experiences with mentors, sponsors, and leaders.

5. Embrace good and bad moments of your journey in order to create grit.

6. Learn the historical background of the profession and your targeted firms.

7. Decide everyday whether you will be a POS, Role-Player, and Great Consultant.

Section I: The Mindset of Great Consultants

8. Great consultants operate like great athletes.

9. Mindset and your character will make or break your consulting career.

10. Practice basic skills and intangibles daily to make them an unconscious competence.

Chapter One: Make Manners Your Competitive Advantage

11. Practice correctly pronouncing someone's name.

12. Give someone a nickname as a result of an established relationship and with consent, not because you are too lazy to learn how to pronounce someone's name.

13. Ask people how they are doing and genuinely listen to their response.

14. Respect cultural nuances of both your firm and the client organization.

15. Learn about the native culture when working in a different country. Honor and respect local customs.

16. Choose your words and actions wisely. How you treat others is a true character test.

17. Hand out more compliments than insults. The classic saying: If you don't have something nice to say, don't say anything at all still rings true.

18. Write or email timely thank-you notes is appropriate and highly underutilized.

19. Practice shaking people's hands; it has to be firm, not limp or bone crushing.

20. Refrain from divisive behavior in an attempt to shame or discount the opinions of others that are different from yours.

21. Refrain from constantly monopolizing a conversation or cutting someone off in mid-sentence in an attempt to rush through a conversation.

22. Facilitate introductions between different groups of people that may not know each other.

23. Practice the order of how you make introductions to people such as introducing the most senior person first or a woman first.

24. Please and thank you are still powerful words. Use them genuinely daily.

25. Refrain from using your phone in meetings.

26. Do not hold phone conversations in public areas, particularly when discussing confidential personal or client matters.

27. Think before putting a caller on speakerphone without their consent or knowledge.

28. Obtain consent before using a camera phone to record a work conversation or meeting, particularly if confidential information is being shared.

29. Don't respond to any hostile emails sent to you in the same manner you received them.

30. Think twice about "friending or following" colleagues, leaders, and clients on social media sites such as Instagram and Facebook.

31. Be cautious on forwarding tasteless email jokes, chain letters, or inappropriate memes amongst colleagues or business contacts.

32. Refrain from sending real-time emails, tweets, or text messages when you are supposed to be listening or participating in practice or firm-wide town halls and meetings. It will be noticed and noted whether it is mentioned to you or not.

33. Ask the sender before you forward emails deemed confidential.

34. Refrain from replying to all on a broad email unless the response truly pertains to the entire distribution list.

Chapter Two: Boost Your Personal Brand as Low Hanging Fruit

35. Develop your personal brand as low-hanging fruit because it is the one area in your career that you have the most control over.

36. Identify the critical moments that matter in your day-to-day interactions, and take control of the narrative you create.

37. Never comprise integrity given the negative, irreparable impact it can have on a career or a business.

38. Focus on developing executive presence every single day regardless of level.

39. Blend in with your client's dress style and culture to better connect with individuals and acclimate in the culture.

40. Practice presentations and speeches in advance and out loud.

41. Learn to analyze stakeholder groups to determine what is important for them to be aware of. Obtain feedback from others to refine messaging.

42. Discover how you personally think and learn to unlock key methods to maximize your core consulting skills.

43. Being coachable and learning to aggregate different points of view is a critical skill.

44. Develop and hone in on interests or hobbies outisde of work that will help accelerate relationship building and your ability to influence.

45. Fiercely protect and manage your online and offline personal brand.

Chapter Three: Network To Unlock Any Door

46. Focus on building and maintaining their network before you need to leverage it.

47. Surround yourself with like-minded individuals.

48. Identify the different types of stakeholders you need in your consulting network and create a relationship management plan.

49. Network with a position of genuinely expecting nothing in return.

50. Seek out mentors and sponsors earlier on within your consulting career.

51. Pay it forward by becoming a mentor and/or over time, a sponsor to others.

52. State your intent of the relationship goals upfront.

53. Be present when conversing. Have a set of go-to, open-ended questions to start meaningful conversations.

54. Leverage memory techniques to internalize information to remember facts about people (birthdays, anniversaries) and practice these techniques until they become an unconscious competence.

55. End each conversation in a way that allows you to pick up on it in a future discussion; steer away from transactional discussions.

56. Respect and value every human interaction made.

57. When traveling, carve out networking time to connect with friends, coworkers, or former classmates.

58. Strategically join professional organizations, associations, internal firm networking meetups, etc., without wearing yourself too thin.

59. Be aware of body language, and respect people's boundaries.

60. Stay in touch. People move in and out of our lives. Do not just say you will keep in touch. Actually do it.

61. Focus on rekindling past relationships more than building new ones.

Chapter Four: Balance Life as a Consultant

62. Set aside time to reflect and rank what is important in your life.

63. Find a time management approach that works for your lifestyle such as Stephen Covey's First Things First framework.

64. Do not allow travel delays or hiccups to affect your well-being and/or attitude.

65. Design life plans and plan friends and family time in advance.

66. Sign up for major airline, hotel, and car rental loyalty programs then centrally manage accounts.

67. Strategically plan vacations and side trips as allowed with the loyalty programs.

68. Take advantage of the digital tools and hacks when available.

69. Create and honor boundaries.

70. Always have a suitcase packed and ready to go.

71. Leverage mindfulness or meditation techniques.

72. Always have a downtime plan while traveling. Travel with just-in-case work or reading that does not require internet connectivity.

73. Learn the difference between non-chargeable hours and value-added hours.

74. Develop self-care health and wellness rituals.

75. Food is the biggest lever you can pull to keep your body in tip-top shape.

76. Seek and schedule professional mental health support if you need it.

77. Try online exercise programs accessible via laptop or mobile phone you could use in your hotel room if you do not have access to a gym.

78. Take mandatory mental breaks throughout the work day, even if it is for five minutes. Try exercise techniques like Braingym.

79. Seek fun ways to train your brain with enrichment activities regularly such as chess, crossword puzzles, Sudoku, or using apps like Lumosity.

80. Drink tons of water, consume supplements/vitamins as prescribed, and eat whole foods. Regularly detox or fast to reset your system as prescribed.

81. Purchase ergonomic-friendly business and travel equipment.

82. Find ways to declutter and destress in all areas of your life.

83. Stop and listen to your body.

Chapter Five: Celebrate Moments with a Happy Hour

84. Regularly celebrate big and small wins on a weekly, sometimes daily basis.

85. Incorporate celebrations with grace while celebrating others.

Chapter Six: Commit to a Consulting Career

86. Make sure you know why you want to go into consulting or have a particular client.

87. Determine your desired consulting experiences, what type of firms to seek employment, which industries and preferred clients based on the marketplace trends.

88. Decide early on how to be positioned, both internally in a firm and externally out in the marketplace.

89. Explore formal and informal channels to conduct due diligence about targeted consulting firms or clients.

90. Articulate your value proposition regardless of level.

91. Understand the iceberg model of firm cultures and subcultures.

92. Recruit with a specific consulting practice or client environment based on both career and experience fit.

93. Seek credible sources to determine insights in your local market for your earnings potential.

94. Understand the fine print of the offer, particularly where there are variable pay bonuses, stock options, college tuition, and other discretionary benefits.

Section II: Performance and Conditioning of Great Consultants

95. Follow a nutrition and training regimen designed to create optimal conditioning environment for career success.

96. Learn to upskill, acquire clients, secure projects, manage relationships and expectations, complete deliverables, and close out projects in a cyclical fashion in alignment with the marketplace.

97. Become purposeful in every aspect of the profession through the conditioning found in daily habits and decisions.

Chapter Seven: Make the Most of Downtime

98. Treat bench with the same level of respect and rigor as a client engagement.

99. Go to your local office every day you're on the bench and connect.

100. Learn a new skill, refresh a certification, complete expense reports, write an article, or contribute to a proposal.

101. Don't underestimate the importance of mindfulness. Reflection can be powerful to help evaluate performance and identify career developmental needs.

102. Research and learn about the state of the business, practice leadership, and emerging trends.

103. Share information you learned with others.

104. Be prepared to travel at a moment's notice.

105. Meet or reconnect with key stakeholders you do not normally cross paths with.

106. Begin scheduling networking activities and meetups before downtime begins.

107. At each stage of your career, determine and seek out the experiences to accomplish career goals or meet firm or client requirements.

108. Seek to get staffed on the right projects with the right leadership culture based on your current experience and skills development needs.

Chapter Eight: Build a Consulting Career Toolkit That Lasts

109. Create an ever-evolving consulting toolkit, which is a collection of information, resources, and materials that can give you a competitive edge throughout your career.

110. Take inventory of the core skills and experiences you will need to gain competence in a specific area of technical, domain, or industry competence. Build out the resources around those skills to support your developmental goals.

111. Strawman of a consulting career toolkit includes, but not limited to: go-to industry or solution white papers and reports, template library of sample deliverables, project plans, reports, work products, analysis tools and templates, materials from previously attended courses and workshops, business books including audiobooks and book summaries, magazine or journal subscriptions, bookmarked websites, blogs, apps, and other sources.

112. Learn and understand the language of business and consulting.

Chapter Nine: Ramp Up on an Engagement

113. The first hours and days of your project determines your credibility and sets the tone of the brand you will build on that particular project.

114. Conduct extensive research before you begin any engagement.

115. Habits are usually established within the first seven days of a project and are difficult to break; purposefully create and maintain good habits during the first few weeks.

116. Understand the organizational dynamics of the project as a first priority.

117. Learn the unwritten rules of your team and the client site.

118. Harness the power of intention during project ramp up.

119. Develop a sense of comfort and confidence in your ability to deliver with clients, leadership, and colleagues alike.

120. Create a legacy and impact on every client, project, and team.

Chapter Ten: Make the Best of Life in the Team Room

121. Make the most of your project team experiences by learning from past team experiences, being a team player, and learning how to maximize relationships with different team member personalities.

122. Become a great team member by always giving; regularly show vulnerability, sharing, active listening, asking questions, and showing authentic curiosity about the interests of others.

123. Accept people for who they are, not who you want them to be. Celebrate and leverage people's strengths.

124. Learn how to effectively work and build relationships with the eight common personality types found on consulting projects: dominant, slacker, spotlight/credit stealer, complainer, team parent, drama queen/king, passive-aggressive, and the brain.

Chapter Eleven: Achieve Breakthroughs by Managing Relationships

125. Spend just as much time building and sustaining relationships as they do building expertise.

126. Your job as a consultant is to be able to manage expectations and promises.

127. Be mindful of not setting false expectations. As the saying goes, today's favor is tomorrow's job.

128. Address questions, issues, and action items as soon as possible; allowing open items to fester derails your best efforts to manage relationships effectively.

129. Take ownership of mistakes and course correct immediately. Do not throw your team under the bus.

130. Actively share the spotlight or taking credit for work you didn't do, especially when it was a team effort.

131. Be authentic when offering ideas, suggestions, and feedback. People sense disingenuous interactions a mile away.

132. Be empathetic to the needs of your teams and clients.

133. Identify your stakeholders, prioritize them, and then plot them on the matrix. Determine how to best manage relationships using an action plan.

134. Great consultants have a good grasp of core fundamentals of project management.

135. To manage client dynamics effectively, understand and embrace the concept of optics.

136. Great consultants become politically competent by embracing and accepting organizational politics for what it is, not what they want it to be.

Chapter Twelve: Nail Your Deliverables Each and Every Time

137. Put considerable thought and energy into storyboarding, research, insights, quality of content, and the look/feel of a deliverable for the clients.

138. Take time to storyboard a logical structure before getting started.

139. Once you have a storyboard, save time by building out the deliverable with an appropriate template.

140. Determine the insights and *So what?* early and often.

141. Have cited and accurate information, data, and verifiable resources. Your data must have journalistic integrity.

142. Do not ever plagiarize content.

Chapter Thirteen: Take Your Clients along for the Journey

143. Take time to understand the mindset of a client, establishing relationships to become a trusted advisor, taking clients along the project journey, while dealing with conflict head on.

144. Focus on partnering with a client by helping them identify key insights to solve extremely complex problems within their organization instead of talking at them.

145. Co-create the solution with your client, not for them.

146. Focus energies on giving your clients the best engagement experience as possible after the contract has been signed, not before.

147. Don't agree or commit to a deadline, scope, or budget decision you cannot realistically deliver.

148. Treat all employees at your client's organization with respect, regardless of role.

149. Seek to empathetically understand your client's worldview when dealing with difficult clients.

Chapter Fourteen: Manage Energy and Bandwidth Remarkably Well

150. Understand, identify, and assess your energy strategy within each dimension—body, emotions, mind, and spirit—to create shortcuts, life hacks, and mental breaks.

151. Evaluate habits and actions in order to structure time for deep work.

152. Schedule deep work time on your calendar like an important client meeting.

153. Commit to activities that you have a passion for.

Chapter Fifteen: Learn the Art of Influence, Pushback, and Negotiation

154. Pushback is a series of discussions unfolded, explored options, and most of all being transparent by socializing ideas with all invested parties.

155. Consistently outperform in your current role and stay patient while seeking new opportunities.

156. Knowing how to gracefully push back is critical.

Chapter Sixteen: Roll Off with Grace

157. End the project as strong as you began. Roll off with the same level of enthusiasm and professionalism as you had when you obtained the opportunity in the first place.

158. Think through the entire lifecycle of your time on an engagement then script out your desired outcome. Plan your roll off months ahead.

159. Structure project folders to easily transfer knowledge to someone taking over your role or shutting the project down.

160. Understand what is expected of you when rolling off of an engagement.

161. Keep relationships intact when rolling off a project.

Section III: Reflections of a Consulting Career

162. Have a method of pausing and reflecting to make critical career decisions.

163. Create a personal board of directors comprised of mentors, advisors, and sponsors to help you make career decisions.

164. Gather information, conduct analysis, and consult trusted sources to make informed career decisions.

165. Seek to have harmony in your career but also have contingency career plans.

Chapter Seventeen: Shape Your Consulting Experience

166. Great consultants have an open mind and stay receptive to a wide variety of experiences to develop and refine core consulting skills.

167. The best way to gain experience is to step up and ask.

168. Embrace the grunt work to build the skills, habits, and stamina of the business.

Chapter Eighteen: Follow the Traditional Consulting Path

169. Proactively plan your career trajectory on a traditional path as early on as possible.

170. Do not seek out promotions prematurely; you will set yourself up for failure.

171. Treat constructive feedback as a performance and career booster shot. Feedback gives you a glimpse of what you can do to take your performance to the next level.

172. Do not refuse a project because you don't think the client or work is not glamorous enough.

173. Stay clear of vindictive team cultures.

174. Do not limit yourself solely to tried and true career paths.

Chapter Nineteen: Explore Nontraditional Consulting Careers

175. Determine if a subject matter expert path in consulting is more suitable for you if you crave the ideation and service delivery side of the business.

176. Determine if an internal consultant path is more suitable if you want to gain experience in creating and actually owning the implementation and sustainment of your recommendations.

177. Explore if being an independent/freelance consultant is more suitable for you if you are a seasoned professional with significant experience and a strong network.

178. Gauge if starting your own consulting firm is a more suitable path for you if you are entrepreneurial with a solid network and willing to take risks.

Chapter Twenty: Make Consulting Career Decisions That Matter

179. Don't allow bad days to dictate key decisions in your consulting career

180. Determine key differences and nuances between consulting firms.

181. Leave a consulting firm for key reasons such as culture or experience fit, not short-term or emotional setbacks.

182. Individuals joining a consulting firm as an industry hire or from an acquisition bring a fresh perspective to consulting engagements.

Chapter Twenty-One: Prepare for Consulting of the Future

183. Consulting as a profession will not go away, but the operating models, business models, and organizational structures of firms will have to change.

184. Leverage practices and unwritten rules to unconsciously build habits of a great consultant.

185. Become a trusted advisor who seeks to maintain connectivity to all types of people.

186. Stay informed on the latest trends in the various industries.

187. Develop a niche or unique skillset within your profession.

BIBLIOGRAPHY

"Best Business Schools." *USNews.com*. Accessed September 1, 2017. https://www.usnews.com/best-graduate-schools/top-business-schools/mba-rankings.

"Best Companies to Work For." *Vault*. Accessed July 17, 2017. http://www.vault.com/company-rankings.

Casciaro, Tiziana, Francesca Gino, and Maryam Kouchaki. "Learn to Love Networking." *Harvard Business Review*. May 2016. https://hbr.org/2016/05/learn-to-love-networking.

Casciaro, Tiziana, Francesca Gino, and Maryam Kouchaki. "The Contaminating Effects of Building Instrumental Ties: How Networking Can Make Us Feel Dirty." *Harvard.edu*. April 28, 2014. doi:10.2139/ssrn.2430174.

Covey, Stephen R. *The 7 Habits of Highly Effective People: Powerful Lessons in Personal Change*. New York: Simon and Schuster, 2014.

Eckel, Sara. "Office Etiquette Essentials." *Forbes*. January 08, 2010. https://www.forbes.com/2010/01/08/business-etiquette-office-manners-forbes-woman-leadership-work.html.

Eyring, Pamela. "Modern Etiquette: Minding Your Manners in the Workplace." *Reuters*. September 16, 2013. http://www.reuters.com/article/us-etiquette-workplace/modern-etiquette-minding-your-manners-in-the-workplace-idUSBRE98F06920130916.

Ford, Martin. *Rise of the Robots: Technology and the Threat of a Jobless Future*. New York: Basic, 2016.

Gardner, Howard. *Frames of Mind: The Theory of Multiple Intelligences*. New York, NY: Basic Books, 2011.

Grant, Adam M. *Give and Take: Why Helping Others Drives Our Success*. New York: Penguin, 2014.

"IT Glossary: Small and Midsize Business (SMB)." Gartner. Accessed July 17, 2017. http://www.gartner.com/it-glossary/smbs-small-and-midsize-businesses.

Hewlett, Sylvia Ann. "The Real Benefit of Finding a Sponsor." *Harvard Business Review.* July 23, 2014. https://hbr.org/2011/01/the-real-benefit-of-finding-a.

Hewlett, Sylvia Ann. *Forget a Mentor, Find a Sponsor: The New Way to Fast-Track Your Career.* Boston, MA: Harvard Business Review Press, 2013.

Hutson, Matthew, and Tori Rodriguez. "Dress for Success: How Clothes Influence Our Performance." *Scientific American.* Jan 1, 2016. https://www.scientificamerican.com/article/dress-for-success-how-clothes-influence-our-performance.

Jackson, Amy Elisa. "8 Secrets Recruiters Won't Tell You (But Really Want To)." *Glassdoor* (blog). August 30, 2017. https://www.glassdoor.com/blog/8-secrets-recruiters-wont-tell-you.

Kaplan, Jerry. Humans Need Not Apply: *A Guide to Wealth and Work in the Age of Artificial Intelligence.* New Haven: Yale UP, 2015.

Kessler International. "Survey Shows Workplace Etiquette and Ethics Lacking in Workplace." Jan 9, 2015. https://www.prnewswire.com/news-releases/survey-shows-workplace-etiquette-and-ethics-lacking-in-workplace-300018254.html.

Korb, Alex. "The Grateful Brain." Psychology Today. November 20, 2012. https://www.psychologytoday.com/blog/prefrontal-nudity/201211/the-grateful-brain.

Kreider, Tim. "The 'Busy' Trap." *New York Times.* June 30, 2012. https://opinionator.blogs.nytimes.com/2012/06/30/the-busy-trap.

Lastoe, Stacey. "12 Little Milestones You Should Be Celebrating at Work." *TheMuse.com.* Accessed June 30, 2017. https://www.themuse.com/advice/12-little-milestones-you-should-be-celebrating-at-work.

Libert, Barry, and Megan Beck. "AI May Soon Replace Even the Most Elite Consultants." *Harvard Business Review.* July 24, 2017. https://hbr.org/2017/07/ai-may-soon-replace-even-the-most-elite-consultants.

Loehr, James E., and Tony Schwartz. *The Power of Full Engagement: Managing Energy, Not Time, Is the Key to High Performance and Personal Renewal.* New York: Free Press, 2003.

Maister, David H., Charles H. Green, and Robert M. Galford. *The Trusted Advisor.* New York: Free Press, 2001.

"Management Analysts." *bls.com.* Accessed January 17, 2017. https://www.bls.gov/ooh/business-and-financial/management-analysts.htm.

"Management Consulting Outlook." *Consultancy.uk.* Accessed January 17, 2017. http://www.consultancy.uk/consulting-industry/management-consulting.

"Managers: How Can You Improve Office Etiquette?" *RobertHalf.com.* July 3, 2017. https://www.roberthalf.com/blog/management-tips/managers-how-can-you-improve-office-etiquette.

"Moore's Law." *Investopedia.* Accessed July 17, 2017. http://www.investopedia.com/terms/m/mooreslaw.asp.

"The Multi-Generational Job Search Study 2014." *Millennia Branding.* Accessed July 13, 2017. http://millennialbranding.com/2014/multi-generational-job-search-study-2014/.

Newport, Cal. *Deep Work: Rules for Focused Success in a Distracted World.* New York: Grand Central, 2016.

O'Donnell, J.T. "Study Says, Stop Worrying about Robots Taking Your Job. Do This Instead ..." Inc., December 14, 2016. https://www.inc.com/jt-odonnell/study-says-stop-worrying-about-robots-taking-your-job-do-this-instead.html.

Poswolsky, Adam Smiley. *The Quarter-Life Breakthrough: Invent Your Own Path, Find Meaningful Work, and Build a Life That Matters.* New York, NY: Tarcher Perigee, 2016.

Schwartz, Tony, and Catherine McCarthy. "Manage Your Energy, Not Your Time." *Harvard Business Review.* October 2007. https://hbr.org/2007/10/manage-your-energy-not-your-time.

ABOUT THE AUTHOR

Christie Lindor is a management consultant, speaker, expert mentor, and career reinventionist focused on personal, team, and organization transformation. Christie has spent her entire sixteen-plus year career working for some of the top consulting firms in the world such as Deloitte Consulting LLP and IBM Business Consulting Services.

Christie is on a mission to be the mentor she wishes she had had earlier in her career and is host of the *MECE Muse Unplugged* podcast, where she focuses on giving consultants and others strategies for career success.

Christie is a passionate, coffee-drinking futurist who loves animals, is a political junkie, and a recovering workaholic. She regularly blogs on her website, www.christielindor.com. and currently resides in Boston, Massachusetts.

When Christie is not consulting, mentoring, speaking, or writing, you can find her reading business books, talking politics, or indulging in an unhealthy, addictive quest for the perfect pair of high heels and pearls.

CPSIA information can be obtained
at www.ICGtesting.com
Printed in the USA
BVHW040729100219
539880BV00024B/1233/P

"A generous primer, a useful toolbox for anyone seeking to become one of the rare and valuable cadre of great consultants."
Seth Godin, author of "Linchpin"

The
MECE
Muse

100+ *Selected* Practices,
Unwritten Rules,
and Habits of
Great Consultants

CHRISTIE LINDOR

The MECE Muse: *100+ Selected Practices,*
Unwritten Rules, and Habits of Great Consultants

Christie Lindor

www.mecemuse.us

Publisher: SDP Publishing
Also available in ebook format

Available at all major bookstores

SDP Publishing

www.SDPPublishing.com
Contact us at: info@SDPPublishing.com

CONSULTANTS

Ma
cho

It's always personal in business.

Create good consulting karma every day.

Get out of your own way.

a fu

It's not about being right

rewa

but about being effective.

sus

Take ownership

Step up to a

co

and

accountability

higher standard.

ca

of your

De

career

 and

find a like tribe

basi

you love

remark

and stay

put; the grass is not alwa

Be empathically inclusive

En

and compassionate to others.

auth

a competi